BACK IN THE FIGHT

ALSO BY CHARLES W. SASSER

Fiction

Sanctuary

A Thousand Years of Darkness

The 100th Kill

Liberty City

The Return

Operation No Man's Land (as Mike Martell)

Detachment Delta: Punitive Strike

Detachment Delta: Operation Iron Weed

Detachment Delta: Operation Deep Steel

Detachment Delta: Operation Aces Wild

Detachment Delta: Operation Cold Dawn

OSS Commando: Final Options

OSS Commando: Hitler's A-Bomb

"No Longer Lost" (novella)

No Gentle Streets

Dark Planet

The War Chaser

Nonfiction

Back in the Fight (w/Joseph Kapacziewski)

None Left Behind

Homicide!

Always A Warrior

Raider

Patton's Panthers

Warriors

First SEAL (w/Roy Boehm)

Fire Cops (w/Michael Sasser)

Magic Steps to Writing Success

Taking Fire (w/Ron Alexander)

The Soldier of Fortune

The Walking Dead (w/Craig Roberts)

One Shot-One Kill (w/Craig Roberts)

In Cold Blood: Oklahoma's Most Notorious
Murders

Last American Heroes (w/Michael Sasser)

Doc: Platoon Medic (w/Daniel E. Evans)

Arctic Homestead (w/Norma Cobb)

Crosshairs on the Kill Zone (w/Craig
Roberts)

Going Bonkers: The Wacky World of
Cultural Madness

The Shoebox: Letters for the Seasons
(w/Nancy Shoemaker)

Devoted to Fishing: Devotionals for
Fishermen

Predator: The Remote-Control Air War over
Iraq and Afghanistan (w/Matt J. Martin)

The New Face of War (Time/Life series
contributor)

True Detective (Pinnacle true-crime series
contributor)

God in the Foxhole

Shoot to Kill

Smoke Jumpers

Sniper Anthology (contributor)

At Large

My Mom Is My Hero (contributor)

Hill 488 (w/Ray Hildreth)

Encyclopedia of Navy SEALs

BACK IN THE FIGHT

The Explosive Memoir of a Special Operator Who Never Gave Up

SERGEANT JOSEPH KAPACZIEWSKI

AND CHARLES W. SASSER

ST. MARTIN'S PRESS ✹ NEW YORK

BACK IN THE FIGHT. Copyright © 2013 by Sergeant Joseph Kapacziewski and Charles W. Sasser. All rights reserved. Printed in the United States of America. For information, address St. Martin's Press, 175 Fifth Avenue, New York, N.Y. 10010.

www.stmartins.com

Library of Congress Cataloging-in-Publication Data

Kapacziewski, Joseph.
    Back in the fight : the explosive memoir of a special operator who never gave up / Sergeant First Class Joseph Kapacziewski and Charles W. Sasser.—First edition.
       p. cm.
    ISBN 978-1-250-01061-2 (hardcover)
    ISBN 978-1-250-02128-1 (e-book)
    1. Afghan War, 2001—Personal narratives, American.   2. United States. Army. Ranger Regiment, 75th. Battalion, 3rd. Alpha Company—Biography.
3. United States. Army—Officers—Biography.   4. Amputees—United States—Biography.   5. Iraq War, 2003–2011—Personal narratives, American.   I. Sasser, Charles W.   II. Title.   III. Title: Explosive memoir of a special operator who never gave up.
  DS371.413.K37 2013
  958.104'742092—dc23
  [B]

                        2013004032

First Edition: May 2013

10 9 8 7 6 5 4 3 2 1

For my wife, Kim, and my sons, Wyatt and Cody.

Dedicated to the modern-day Spartans
who have worn the scroll.

AUTHOR'S NOTE

This is a personal narrative of the making of a U.S. Army Ranger and of Ranger combat in Iraq and Afghanistan. While it is my story, it is also the story of others who played major or minor roles in the events narrated. Actual names are used throughout except in those instances where names could not be recalled due to the passage of time, where public identification would serve no useful purpose, or for reasons of operational security.

I have strived to render the truth as accurately and vividly as possible. Some dialogue and scenes have by necessity been re-created. Where these occur, I tried to match personalities with the situation and action and maintain factual content at the same time. I therefore cannot be certain every quote is entirely accurate word for word or that my interpretation of events will be exactly the same as someone else's. Time has a tendency to erode memory in some areas and selectively enhance it in others. Where errors in recollection occur, the author accepts full responsibility and asks to be forgiven.

I should like to acknowledge the following people, without whose cooperation and assistance this personal history would not have been possible: my wife, Kimberly, first of all, who has the mettle of a Ranger herself and whose devotion to family provided me an island from a decade of warfare, and who stuck with me through trying times; the rest of my family members and friends, most of whom are noted in this book; all the brave Rangers of the U.S. Army 75th Ranger Regiment, a number of whom made the ultimate sacrifice for country; wounded warriors who, in spite of devastating injuries, continue to live productive and useful lives; Major Brian DeSantis (75 RGR) and Ms. Tracy Bailey (75 RHQ), who encouraged and assisted in this work; my editor, Mark Resnick, who recognized the value of this story; literary agent Ethan Ellenberg; and, finally, American Rangers throughout history who have always "led the way."

I must emphasize that the account in this book and the opinions I express are from my personal viewpoint and do not necessarily represent the views of the U.S. Army, the Department of Defense, or the United States government.

Lastly, I should like to apologize to anyone omitted, neglected, or slighted in the preparation of this book. While some interpretational mistakes are bound to occur in a work of this scope, I am certain that the content of this book is true to the spirit and reality of U.S. Army Rangers who have served—and continue to serve—the greatest country on earth: the United States of America. To that end, I am confident I have neglected no one.

—SERGEANT FIRST CLASS JOSEPH KAPACZIEWSKI

BACK IN THE FIGHT

1

AFGHANISTAN 2009

If there was one thing U.S. Army Rangers were good at—other than killing terrorists who needed killing—it was walking long distances with obscene weight on our backs. Busting balls, in soldier jargon. At altitudes of 10,000 feet, 65 pounds of kit was murder, but necessary gear for modern, *safe* warfare—Kevlar helmet, "bulletproof" jacket with Kevlar plates, weapons, desert boots, ammo, radio, NODs (night optical devices), MREs (Meals, Ready to Eat; chow)—and you were toting some real weight.

Nothing could bust balls like the Hindu Kush Mountains along the border between Afghanistan and Pakistan. Just ask the Russians who had been here. It was Taliban country. A hardy breed, the Taliban were, just as cunning at fighting in the mountains as the Apaches had been in the deserts of Arizona and Mexico. They fought lightweight, too. Give a Taliban a rifle, a baggy pair of shepherd's trousers, a handful of dried mutton and another of cartridges, and he was ready to run through these mountains like a goat. Up here, the Taliban claimed the advantage. After all, Afghans had been defending this land for generations. In these mountains, you were always behind enemy lines.

For the past two months, Alpha Company, 3rd Battalion, 75th U.S. Army Ranger Regiment had been beating these mountains for enemy training camps and HVTs. An HVT was a "high-value target," usually someone in a leadership position with the Taliban or al Qaeda whose only purpose in life was to kill Americans. By that definition, every mother's son south and east of FOB (forward operating base) Salerno was an HVT. Our job was to kill them first. When we could find them.

Intel advised of an enemy training camp up here, protected in some almost-inaccessible nook or cranny. Alpha Company had two platoons out looking for it in movement to contact. My platoon, the 1st, had been humping hard in the dark for the past four hours, wending our way upward toward the summit of the Khost-Gardez Pass, better known from ancient times as "the Death Pass" for reasons best left unconsidered.

It was cool at this altitude, but I was damp from the skin out from sweating as the platoon gained elevation, climbing immense verticals, banging against boulders, squeezing through holes barely big enough for a rabbit, and worming through spine-twisting avalanche slag as we sucked for oxygen in the thin air.

"How does he do it?" I overheard one of the new privates whisper wearily during a take-five. "My ass is dragging and he just keeps going and going like the Energizer Bunny. Well, you know, what with everything . . ."

"Sergeant Kap is hardcore," came the response. "Don't let him hear you talking about it."

As far as I was concerned, I, Staff Sergeant Joe Kapacziewski, Third Squad Leader, 1st Platoon, was an Army Ranger like any other ball-busting grunt in this man's outfit.

A fogbank silver in the wan moonlight slithered through the valley below K-G Pass as 1st Platoon approached the top. I thought it a spectacular sight. Moonlight glinted off mountain peaks while sheening opaque off the fog in the valley. Then the moon ducked back out of sight in the higher clouds, and it was as dark again as your crotch at midnight. We would have been blind in the dark save for NODs providing a liquid, greenish view.

In the valley below, beneath the fog, Alpha Two maintained radio contact in order to parallel Alpha One on the high ground. In this ter-

Sgt. Joseph Kapacziewski and Charles W. Sasser

rain, there was no way we could support each other if one of the platoons ran into a shit storm.

My 1st Platoon moved in two elements, the rearmost overwatching the point element ahead as we cautiously approached a ridgeline that dropped steeply off on the other side from Gardez Province into Khost Province. First Squad leader Joe Edwards, a country boy from Georgia and an implant from the regular army, led the first element. He was one of my best team leaders at one point, now he was one of the best Squad Leaders in A Company. Second Squad trailed behind him with the CP (command post) element and attachments. I and my boys in Third Squad brought up the tail of the formation.

Infantry tactics had changed little in more than a century. Even in an age of unmanned drones in the sky and robots in the field, what war came down to was still opposing bands of soldiers on the ground shooting at each other. Only the geography changed. Sergeant First Class Soroken insisted that wars starting from World War II were actually one continuous war with occasional breaks to rearm and bury the dead.

This was prime geography for an ambush.

That thought passed through my mind like some kind of primal instinct. Like you had this feeling something was about to happen—and then it did.

The ridgeline directly ahead suddenly lit up with a twinkling of muzzle flashes and the fierce crackle of rifle fire as Edwards's lead element triggered the ambush waiting for us. Green tracer rounds streaked into our front like supersonic fireflies. Edwards and his boys immediately opened up to establish fire superiority, the protocol for a near ambush. The deep-throated cracking of enemy AK-47s counterpointed the thinner, more spiteful popping of M-4s and grenades exploding. PL (platoon leader) Captain Charlie Felker, a huge officer from St. Louis, got on the radio and started calling for fire.

The ambushers were dug in at the ridge, looking right down our throats. My squad hit the dirt with the first sound of guns. In a situation like this, the lead element kept the bad guys busy while the trail element maneuvered. Unfortunately, we had little maneuver room. The terrain was nasty: rock ledges, loose shale, and stunted brush.

Sergeant Soroken moved forward and offset to get a clear shot at the ambush past the PL and his element. I yelled at my squad. We scrambled even farther to the right flank and took cover behind a low ledge. Damn! All that *safe* soldier gear exhausted your ass with its weight when you had to rush around to get to higher ground.

We possessed NODs. The Taliban didn't. Their night vision might have been better than ours, but no naked eyes were keen enough to hold a good, accurate firefight in the dark. We held the advantage there. Although bright muzzle flashes flared through the devices, almost blindingly so, the goggles still provided greenish shadows of movement on the ridge less than 200 meters away. We tapped off a few rounds every time we spotted movement. Slinging lead.

I heard Sergeant Soroken on the radio with PacMan One-Three, the call sign for either a patroling aircraft or a Predator drone appointed as an angel in the sky to overlook ground pounders. Wes was trying to get the aircraft to "sparkle" targets with his infrared (IR) marking laser, lighting them up for the IR sensors in our NODs to detect. PacMan kept sparkling us instead. A sharp exchange ensued.

"*PacMan, you're getting us . . .*"

"*That's negative, Alpha One . . .*"

"*It's on us again . . .*"

"*You're moving, Alpha One . . .*"

Other things were starting to happen.

"*We got a couple of squirters headed down back of the ridge,*" the platoon sergeant radioed, as calm as if he were back at Fort Benning buying a round of beers for the boys at Coach's Corner. One cool dude under pressure. "*They might be trying to flank us.*"

I volunteered to take care of them. I tapped Smith, Housner, Timmy Bowman, and a new private from my squad. All hard chargers.

"Follow me."

The incline was about 45 degrees. NODs helped us avoid most of the bad shit as we scrambled down the other side of the ridge. Firing ceased at the ambush site. It would pick up again if the other side got a machine gun placed farther down the ridge with which to rake our flank.

I dropped on my belly at the military crest and crawled up to look over the top, my Rangers with me. It was pitch black looking down the other side. Even with NODs, I barely made out more rock ledges and some stunted brush. I heard movement down there somewhere in the dark, scuffing sounds of soft-soled shoes or sandals on shale and rock. Even Apaches made *some* noise in this kind of country.

Sergeant Soroken was still on the radio with PacMan, who insisted he had his sparkle on the bad guys and not on us. I realized he was right. He *was* on the bad guys, but they were so near that *we* were part of his target.

I spotted shadows flitting fast through the brush and rocks, climbing in an oblique run toward the crest farther down. I jumped up and led the way paralleling the squirters, hoping to cut them off and get a shot.

Loose shale unexpectedly gave way beneath my boots. My feet flew out from under me, and my ass hit the ground hard. Next thing I knew I was the centerpiece of a miniavalanche blasting downhill at about Mach 1. Everything I grabbed at to stop my rapid descent ripped free and became part of the slide. I pictured myself hurtling over a precipice into the fog of the valley a few thousand feet down.

I spotted a small tree clinging to the side of the mountain about 25 feet ahead. I tried to wrench myself toward it, clutching my rifle in one hand and reaching for the tree with the other. Loose rock pelted the tree like a hailstorm.

Next to the tree crouched one of the Talibs. All I could tell about him through NODs was that he was garbed in black and was armed with an assault rifle. I doubted he had seen me yet; he was too busy ducking and dodging the shower of rock and shale I had loosed on him. We were going to get real close, real soon.

I caught the tree with my extended left foot and checked my momentum. I could have reached out with the muzzle of my M-4 and shoved it down the Talib's throat. Imagine his surprise when he realized that I wasn't a boulder. Talk about shock and awe.

I recovered first and tapped off a couple of 5.56 rounds into the guy at point-blank range. His body masked my muzzle flash. I smelled singed cloth and the sudden effusion of pink blood cloud in the air. The guy screamed, muffled-like, before he dropped facedown at my feet next to the tree. The avalanche rumbled over him, piled up around his body, and stopped. I knew he was dead, taking a dirt nap.

From somewhere farther down, but very near, a second squirter began yelling the war cry made notorious by a generation of global terrorists.

"*Allahu Akbar! Allahu Akbar!*"

I hustled frantically back uphill on my boot toes and one free hand, my rifle in the other. I was done for if he got my range. From the ridge crest, Timmy Bowman, Smitty, Housner, and the new private laid down a base of cover fire. The exchange between them was one-sided; my guys knew how to turn on the lead faucet. I was panting like a steam engine trying to reach the safety of the ridge before the Talib nailed me.

Things went from bad to worse. The stump of my right leg where it had been amputated below the knee slipped out of its prosthesis cuff and dumped me on the ground. My heart almost stopped beating when I heard my artificial leg bouncing off rock and sliding back downhill toward the enemy. This guy was in for some shock and awe of his own when my steel-and-carbon-fiber leg with the boot still attached landed in his lap.

The only one-legged Ranger in combat with the U.S. Army wasn't going to be walking, running, or fighting without that hunk of metal, carbon fiber, and gears strapped to his stump. Maybe Ranger Regiment had been right all along: War was no place for an amputee.

2

DURHAM, CONNECTICUT, 2001

At 8:46 A.M. on September 11, 2001, five Islamic terrorists crashed American Airlines Flight 11 into New York's World Trade Center, North Tower. Seventeen minutes later, five additional hijackers flew United 175 into the South Tower. American 77 exploded into the Pentagon at 9:37. United 93 plowed into a field in Pennsylvania at 10:03 after passengers fought back and forced hijackers to scuttle the flight before it reached its target, the White House.

Grandma Alice Churchill shook me awake. She looked pale, startled. I sprang upright. My first thought was that something had happened to little brother Randy or to our older sister, Erin.

"Something terrible..." Grandma stammered. "It's on TV. We've been attacked. Like... like at Pearl Harbor."

Millions of Americans glued themselves to their television sets that morning to watch the tragic story unfold. The United States went on a war footing within hours of the attack. The military was put on the highest state of alert, National Guard units were called to Washington and New York, and two aircraft carriers were dispatched to New York harbor. President George W. Bush came on TV to vow that the United States would hunt down and punish those responsible for the "evil, despicable acts of terror" that had taken thousands of American lives.

Normally, I was an early riser and Grandma Churchill would not have had to shake me awake. However, I had enlisted in the U.S. Army on the delayed entry program immediately after graduating from Eastern High School in May, which gave me until September 18 to report to Fort Benning, Georgia, for basic training. After working all summer, I was taking the last two weeks off to hang out with my buddies. Go swimming, play a little touch football, run out to Lake Compounce, the oldest amusement park in the United States, go to the movies with my girlfriend Kristin, drag main street, and sneak into a bar for a cold beer with the guys. Like small-town kids all over America had been doing since ol' Henry Ford invented the horseless carriage and transformed the way boys and girls did things in America. I was fast burning up the days and nights getting in a last kid's summer before "real life" started.

September 18 was only one week away. Today would become forever known simply as 9/11, my generation's equivalent to Pearl Harbor. Like other horrified Americans, Grandma, Erin, Randy, and I watched smoke boiling from the Twin Towers on TV as terrified people leaped from windows to their deaths rather than be burned alive. I had an odd feeling, call it precognition, that my life was about to change forever, that the world had suddenly become a much more dangerous place.

Life before 9/11, before my parents divorced and Dad got killed, was simple, idyllic, and small-town on the outskirts of Durham, Connecticut, population about five thousand or so flint-hard, hardworking Yankees. Uncles and aunts living up and down our stretch of road all had farms of one sort of another. One operated a dairy of Holstein cows; another grew corn. Everybody gathered every season to harvest, husk, and freeze bags of roastin' ears. We got together again to attend the Durham Fair, the largest volunteer agricultural fair in New England.

Dad—Bill Kapacziewski—owned a construction company that built private homes. Our farm wasn't all that big, just a few acres across from my uncle's cornfield. Dad thought it a good idea to have horses, chickens, rabbits, a goat, and a vegetable garden to teach us kids responsibility. After school, Erin, Randy, and I rushed home to milk the goat, gather eggs, feed the rabbits and chickens, and weed the garden. Erin was fifteen months older than me, Randy two years younger.

It was a pleasant way of life for a tough little kid like me who had always been kind of shy around people. I felt more at home out riding a horse or alone hunting squirrels. Sometimes I hopped a truck ride out to a construction site with Dad or my great-uncle down the road, who also worked construction. I picked up old shingles and pulled nails for a little spending money.

"A good worker," Dad said approvingly—and I beamed.

Everything changed the year I turned eleven. Dad and Mom divorced. They had started quarreling and picking at each other. They announced their decision to the family one afternoon when I came in from gathering eggs. Erin started bleating like the goat. Randy ran outside to hide. They always took things harder than I, or maybe it was just that I hid my feelings. I was like my dad that way. Taciturn.

I stood there and stared at my parents, and they didn't know what else to say. Dad's jaw tightened into knots. Tears ran down Mom's cheeks. I just stared. At first I was shocked. Then I got mad and walked away. What else could I do? Their minds were made up.

Mom left a few days later. I heard she went to Florida or somewhere south. I didn't see or talk to her other than in courtrooms for the next five years. I overheard relatives whispering how they thought she had met another man. That made me mad, too.

Dad and us kids stayed in Durham for a while, then moved to nearby Bristol for a year to be near Dad's mother, who had remarried a good man named Bob Churchill. They offered to help with the kids. Dad finally got an urge to move to Texas. He packed us all up and we moved to Fredericksburg. He died in a car accident there in 1995 when I was twelve years old, Erin was fourteen, and Randy ten.

Grandma and Grandpa Churchill took us in and moved us back to

Connecticut, where we had enough relatives that people would at least pronounce our last name correctly. Grandpa Churchill accepted three rowdy kids into his family as warmly as though we were real blood.

"You children always have a home with us, no matter what," Grandma reassured us.

She hugged us all, but by this time I was grown up enough that I wasn't much for hugging. You had to be careful. You let someone hug you, next thing you knew that someone was gone and all you had left was mad. Like with Kristin, my high school sweetheart. I knew it was over between us when I enlisted in the army right out of high school. I knew how to do "it's over."

I grew into an athletic kid, a little under six feet tall with broad shoulders and long, strong legs. I played football and other team sports but gravitated toward one-on-one sports like varsity wrestling. Somehow along the way I became intrigued with the military. Grandfather Churchill and some of my great uncles had been in the military. Some had gone to combat, but the military sounded more adventurous than working construction or sitting behind a desk. I thought about applying for one of the military academies, either West Point or the Coast Guard. That made me focus on getting a good GPA through my junior and senior years in high school.

Bristol police officer Mark Bernier, a family friend who was my father's age, had sort of taken me under his wing like a second father after Dad died. He was tall, balding on top with a mustache, built like a heavyweight fighter. We could be together all day fishing or something and I'd barely get in a half-dozen words. Officer Bernier was a talker. He was helping me with applications to West Point when I changed my mind.

"Mark, I don't want to spend the next years of my life sitting at a desk in some stuffy classroom. I want to *do* something."

He nodded sagely. "What's on your mind, son?"

"I'm still going in the army, only I want to go in as soon as I get out of high school."

Desert Storm, the first Iraq war, had been over and won since 1991, if you wanted to call it a win. There hadn't been a lot going on military-wise since then. The UN still had sanctions against Iraq. Every now and again, Saddam Hussein launched a missile at one of our planes or we shot down one of his MiGs in the no-fly zone. Terrorists almost sank the USS *Cole* in Yemen, blew up American embassies in Africa, kidnapped some cruise-boat tourists in the Mediterranean, hijacked a few airplanes, shot up Mogadishu, and bombed the World Trade Center the first time in 1993. Other than incidents like these, you might say we enjoyed relative peace in the world.

Even so, you could feel the potential. Mark said things were going to bust open sooner or later. I actually hoped it would be sooner. I wanted to do something important with my life.

Mark never tried to talk me out of it. He drove me to the Army Recruiting Station in Bristol. From there, I went alone to the induction center in Springfield, Massachusetts, where I met an old Ranger Battalion guy with shoulders so wide he almost had to turn sideways to get through a door. He had that special look. Confident. Like he *knew* he was the baddest dude in the room. Like he could take on a lion mano a mano—and *win*.

He put on a Ranger video for me to watch.

"If you got what it takes . . ." he said in a tone that suggested you either had it or you were a hairdresser.

The video started with the creed: *Rangers Lead the Way*. It showed all these fit, young, tough guys wearing black berets parachuting out of airplanes, fast-roping from helicopters, firing weapons, running PT . . . This was before General Eric Shinseki awarded *all* soldiers the black beret and Rangers had to switch to tan.

> *I wanna be an Airborne Ranger,*
> *I wanna live a life of danger . . .*

I was hooked. I left with an Airborne Ranger contract. It worked like this: I went on to Airborne parachute school if I completed basic training and MOS (military occupational specialty) training. Successful graduation from Airborne gave me a shot at the Ranger program. There were no guarantees that I would make it, but a shot was all I needed, all I had ever asked of anything in life.

Now, one week before I left for Fort Benning, America had been attacked and was on a war footing. I was shocked at first. When that wore off, I got mad that these guys could come over and do bad things to innocent people. In my eighteen-year-old mind, I had no idea where the War on Terror would lead nor what pieces of my life it would eventually claim.

3

It might be said that I had a predisposition to jump into the bog without looking for alligators first. A majority of rough eighteen-year-old boys are likely prone in that direction as we leave home to seek fame and fortune, slay dragons, and rescue damsels in distress. What I knew was that I was ready to catch the bus, the plane, the train, the thumb, or whatever in order to get it on, to start my *real* life as a bona fide adult.

Fort Benning was a wake-up call, as people like to say. Not good, not bad, just . . . army. The post stretches across Georgia southeast of Columbus and into Alabama, 182,000 acres of meadows, hills, piney woods, swamps and, for some, pure-dee hell. Like most other stateside military installations, the structure was a mixture of World War II anachronism and Burger King. The PX (post exchange) sold video games next to olive drab wool socks and skivvies that could have been worn by General Patton.

Located here were the army infantry schools. It was one of five locations for Basic Combat Training (BCT), where every army recruit got introduced to uniform life. Next, new soldiers attended AIT (Advanced Infantry Training) in their assigned MOS, such as communications, intelligence, and 11B: One-One-Bravo—*infantryman*. Every Ranger was, first of all, an infantryman.

After BCT and AIT, the average soldier was through with his initial training. He shipped out to the 3rd Infantry Division or the 25th Infantry Division and, well, *soldiered*. Not so for Ranger candidates. We had barely begun. Ahead lay some of the roughest, toughest training in the military world, enough to make a French Foreign Legionnaire take a second look. I'm talking about the legionnaires of legend, not the sissified new model. Would-be Rangers had to go on to complete the Basic Airborne Parachute Course and RIP (Ranger Indoctrination Program) before they could be assigned to one of three battalions that made up the 75th Ranger Regiment.

Regimental Headquarters and the three companies of 3rd Battalion were stationed at Fort Benning. The other two battalions, the 1/75 (1st Battalion, 75th Regiment) and 2/75 (2nd Battalion, 75th Regiment), were headquartered respectively at Hunter Army Airfield, Georgia, and Fort Lewis, Washington.

The weather in Connecticut when I left was getting cool, even frosty at night. Georgia was still in Indian summer. It was balmy and a lot warmer than we Yankees were accustomed to. I sweated through skinhead haircuts, assembly-line inoculations, the issuance of uniforms, and being yelled at by sergeants. Awkward in crowds, I found myself herded around with a bunch of strangers from all around the nation, from different walks of life, different backgrounds... What had I done, what had I gotten myself into?

"You'll be sor-r-rry!" upperclassmen in BCT shouted out windows of their barracks at the newly arrived unwashed.

Before I left home, my friends who had army experience advised that the best way to get through training was not to step on anybody's toes, not to stand out in any way or be noticed. If the drill sergeants didn't get to know you, they weren't as apt to screw with you. So I hunkered down, kept my mouth shut, and tried to be the gray man.

"Kain?"

"Here, Sergeant!"

"Kalm?"

"Sergeant!"

It was morning muster, the first in our new uniforms. We smelled new and green.

"Kapa...uh...Kapa...What kind of fucking Polack name is that?"

"Kapa-*chess*-ski, Sergeant!"

"Are you making fun of me, boy?"

"No, Sergeant!"

"From now on, you're Kap, boy. Or Private Krap."

So much for not being noticed.

My training platoon consisted of about forty guys, all with the Ranger option in their recruiting contracts. We got to know each other pretty well during the next twenty weeks of BCT, AIT, jump school, and RIP. Fewer than half of us survived to be assigned to a Ranger Battalion. The rest of us were weeded out and sent worldwide as common, ordinary, non-Ranger grunts.

As I was athletic with a good attitude and enough sense to strive for the gray-man profile, I breezed through BCT and AIT, no sweat. I came out the other end mean, lean, and green with the 11B MOS and a pretty cocky feeling that I could handle anything thrown at me. Most of the survivors had that mindset.

We had to wait about a week in layover for the next Airborne class. Walk out the door of the transient barracks and the first thing you saw was the three 249-foot jump towers; in fact, they were visible from pretty much anywhere on the main post. They reminded me of the monster-machines out of *War of the Worlds*. After you got hoisted to the top of a tower and dropped, the next step was out the open door of a C-130 Hercules 1,200 feet over Fryar Drop Zone. I could hardly wait to catch the wind.

I almost didn't make it that far.

The night before jump school started, Ken Roundy, Kain, Scott Lockhart, and a couple of other guys and I engaged in a bit too much youthful revelry in a little soldier bar within walking distance of the main post gate. Only one of us was legal drinking-wise, but that was enough to get us all inside. We staggered out of the bar about midnight.

Kain was shit-faced, wiped out, stinko. Roundy and I half carried, half dragged him back to the barracks. He was loud, chanting old Airborne Jody calls and generally making a southern-fried ass of himself.

"Hold it down, you fuckers!" rose a cacophony of complaints.

I tossed Kain onto his bunk. "Shut up and get to sleep."

A few minutes later, I heard Kain stumble out of bed, muttering to himself. Then I heard him pissing in the center aisle. I jumped up and hustled him off to the latrine in a stream of piss. Too late. A buck sergeant escorted him to the charge of quarters watch. MPs took over from there.

I knew the asses of all the barroom revelers were in a crack the next morning at PT (physical training) formation when one of the Black Hat instructors from Airborne training stood out front of us on the PT strip and glared at us for a solid minute. Like a cat eyeballing a mouse before pouncing on it. I started to sweat.

"Kain is gone," the Black Hat announced. "Which of you shitbirds was with him getting drunk last night?"

The little Airborne Ranger image of myself I carried around inside my head went up in smoke. It seemed no one breathed. It occurred to me that the Black Hat likely knew the names of those who had been with Kain last night. Maybe he was testing us to see who had the balls to stand up.

I could almost have wept. I didn't want to step out. I would rather have been shot. I saw myself packing my duffel bag to get transferred off to some "leg" non-Airborne, non-Ranger outfit. I drew in a deep, painful breath of resignation. Dad had always told Erin, Randy, and me that you always had to do the right thing, no matter the cost.

I took a step forward out of ranks and froze at rigid attention. From the corner of my eye, I glimpsed Roundy doing the same thing. None of the others budged. The Black Hat sergeant stalked over and got in my face. I thought he was going to punch me out.

"You shitbirds!" he raged. "Kain was your buddy. Why didn't you take care of him? My sole mission in life from this moment on is to make sure you two don't graduate from Airborne. I'm going to blow so much smoke up your asses that you'll beg to quit."

No, sir. I ain't never quitting.

"Get back in formation, shitbirds."

Whew! Dodged that bullet.

The Black Hats ragged on Roundy and me, but I had a feeling that it was only halfhearted and that they secretly respected us for having the guts to stand up. I kept a low profile nonetheless and played the gray man. Three weeks later it all started to become real when I realized I was actually going to parachute out of a perfectly good airplane.

All 'chuted with my helmet pulled down tight, I found myself jammed into the wide belly of a C-130 with the rest of my training company. Engines revved and we took to the sky. In the canvas seating across from me, our knees touching, sat the Airborne School commander getting in his "pay jump" for the period. He appeared as cool and relaxed as if he were sitting down to dinner. He must have noticed I was nervous.

"Hey, boy," he advised. "Keep your feet and knees together and everything will be all right."

We were jumping out the right door. It slid up and open, and bright sunlight splashed in. Wind from the slipstream howled past. The jumpmaster leaned way out, holding to the sides of the door, and checked the drop zone markers. Then he snapped back inside, stamped his feet to get attention, and started through the five jump commands.

Stand up!

Hook up!

Sound off equipment check!

Stand by!

Go!

I was second man out the door in my stick of jumpers. God, it was exhilarating. I knew I had found my calling.

Jump week ended with four more jumps: night, individual, equipment, and, at the end, a mass tactical jump with equipment at the combat altitude of 1,000 feet. My 'chute popped open, I swung out once, and the next thing I was doing a parachute landing fall on the drop zone. We were that close to the ground.

Scott Lockhart's dad was an old marine. He came out for the graduation and pounded the sharp little prongs of my "blood wings" into my chest. I refused to flinch. *Airborne! All the way!*

Next step—RIP. The final stage before Ranger Battalion. Nothing could stop me now.

Come Monday morning, Black Hats assembled the platoon on the bottom floor of the barracks, in a big open bay with chairs. We realized we were entering a different, more challenging phase of training when the Ranger cadre stormed in wearing their tan berets to take us over. They looked like GI Joes on steroids, like if they grinned their faces would crack.

"Shut up!"

"Sit down!"

"Be quiet!"

"Fill out these papers!"

"Fuck up and your ass is outa here!"

These guys meant business.

Our duffels were already packed for the transfer across post to RIP. A deuce-and-a-half truck drove up outside and parked to wait until the paperwork was completed. We tossed our stuff in the back. The instructor cadre promptly disabused us of the notion that anybody was going to ride. They ran us in formation the mile and a half from the Airborne barracks to the RIP barracks. No pussy airborne shuffle, either. We *ran*.

The truck was waiting on us when we got there.

"Ladies, you got five minutes to get your shit sorted out of the truck and get in alphabetical formation. Go!"

It was a goat rope. We didn't make it.

"You're slow, your breath stinks, and you don't love Jesus. Get down! Get down!"

Get down! That automatically meant in the push-up position. The platoon knocked out twenty or thirty, although we were already smoked and sweating and stinking like a bunch of hogs.

"You aren't going to make it. Quit now and save us all a bunch of trouble. On your feet!"

This time we had *two* minutes to sort things out and muster. Again we didn't make it. Another goat rope.

"Get down!"

This went on for two or three hours. Several guys were ready to quit by the time everyone claimed his own gear and the platoon made correct formation. My ass was dragging. It was only the beginning.

During holdover waiting for RIP to begin, I got put on a detail with about twenty other guys to pull targets for the Army Marksmanship Unit. Staff Sergeant Jared Van Aalst was in charge of the range. He was a tall, well-built guy with dark hair and broad shoulders. Only a few years older than me, he had already been in the Rangers a half-dozen years. When he talked, people listened. He took the detail aside on the day before RIP started to offer a few do's and don'ts for getting through it.

"The main thing," he counseled, "is not to quit, no matter how tough it gets. Remember, people have done this before. Keep your eye on the prize and live by the Ranger Creed."

4

THE RANGER CREED

Recognizing that I volunteered as a Ranger, fully knowing the hazards of my chosen profession, I will always endeavor to uphold the prestige, honor, and high esprit de corps of my Ranger Regiment.

Acknowledging the fact that a Ranger is a more elite soldier who arrives at the cutting edge of battle by land, sea, or air, I accept the fact that as a Ranger my country expects me to move further, faster, and fight harder than any other soldier.

Never shall I fail my comrades. I will always keep myself mentally alert, physically strong, and morally straight, and I will shoulder more than my share of the task whatever it may be, 100 percent and then some.

Gallantly will I show the world that I am a specially selected and well-trained soldier. My courtesy to superior officers, neatness of dress, and care of equipment shall set the example for others to follow.

Energetically will I meet the enemies of my country. I shall defeat them on the field of battle, for I am better trained and will fight with all my might. Surrender is not a Ranger word. I will never leave a fallen comrade to fall into the hands of the enemy, and under no circumstances will I ever embarrass my country.

Readily will I display the intestinal fortitude required to fight on to the Ranger objective and complete the mission, though I be the lone survivor.

5

At the beginning of World War II, U.S. Army Chief of Staff George C. Marshall trained special units of troops in commando methods. He, along with Generals Lucian Truscott Jr. and Dwight D. Eisenhower, dubbed the new units "Rangers." The exploits of "Darby's Rangers" and "Merrill's Marauders" during the war introduced U.S. Army Rangers as the finest light infantry in the world. Previous American units bearing the "Ranger" designation had set the standard for, as historian Michael King put it, "individual courage, determination, ruggedness, fighting ability, and achievement."

The American Colonial period brought "Ranger" into general usage to describe fast, light, often clandestine units engaging in strike operations, deep-penetration raids, interdiction, recovery, and reconnaissance missions. Often threatened by hostile Indians, New World colonists built a defensive screen of forts and blockhouses along the frontier. At the first sign of trouble, settlers grabbed their weapons and what possessions they could carry and rushed to hole up in and defend the nearest stronghold. Small mobile forces "ranged," or patrolled, between the fortresses to disrupt and harass marauding Indians.

The most famous of these outfits was "Rogers's Rangers." In 1756, a New Hampshire backwoodsman named Robert Rogers recruited four companies of irregulars to operate in the Lake Champlain–Hudson River Valley to block the Indians and their French allies from New York. He created so much havoc during the Seven Years' War that British General George Howe changed the tactics of his military in the wilderness by ordering tails cut off red coats and queues off hats. "Redcoat Rangers" began using leggings in the bush and staining their muskets to reduce reflection.

Rogers and his Rangers took to the woods mean and lean, a tradition that has carried over into the modern 75th Regiment. In the field, each man packed only enough supplies to do him until he could resupply either by hunting and fishing or arriving at another settlement. He carried dried food in a haversack and for comfort a blanket roll draped around one shoulder and his waist and a wooden or metal canteen containing a mixture of rum and water. Weapons included a skinning knife, a tomahawk, sometimes a cap and ball pistol or bayonet, a musket sawed down for the woods, and 60 rounds of ball and powder. The "Standing Orders" Rogers issued to his Rangers still stand as the core of modern special operations forces.*

STANDING ORDERS FOR ROGERS'S RANGERS

1. Don't forget nothing.
2. Have your musket clean as a whistle, hatchet scoured, sixty rounds powder and ball, and be ready to march at a minute's warning.
3. When you're on the march, act the way you would if you was sneaking up on a deer. You'll feel better afterwards if you see them first.

---

* This is how Sergeant McNott explains the rules to new recruits in the novel *Northwest Passage,* by Kenneth Roberts (New York: Doubleday, Doran, 1937). For readability, I put them into a numbered list and edited them for length. At http://www.rogersrangers.org/rules/index.html you can read them as they appeared in Rogers's journal for 1765.

4. Tell the truth about what you see and what you do. You can lie all you please when you tell other folks about the Rangers, but don't never lie to a Ranger or an officer. There's an army depending on us for correct information.

5. Don't never take a chance you don't have to.

6. When we're on the march we march single file, far enough apart so one shot can't go through two men.

7. If we strike swamps, or soft ground, we spread out abreast, so it's hard to track us.

8. When we march, we keep moving till dark, so to give the enemy the least possible chance at us.

9. When we camp, half the party stays awake while the other half sleeps.

10. If we take prisoners, we keep 'em separate till we've had time to examine 'em, so they can't cook up a story between 'em.

11. Don't never march home the same way. Take a different route, so you won't be ambushed.

12. No matter whether we travel in big parties or little ones, each party has to keep a scout 20 yards ahead, 20 yards on each flank, and 20 yards in the rear, so the main body can't be surprised and wiped out.

13. Every night you'll be told where to meet if surrounded by a superior force.

14. Don't sit down to eat without posting sentries.

15. Don't sleep beyond dawn. Dawn's when French and Indians attack.

16. Don't cross a river by a regular ford.

17. If somebody's trailing you, make a circle, come back onto your own tracks, and ambush the folks that aim to ambush you.

18. Don't stand up when the enemy's coming against you. Kneel down. Lie down. Hide behind a tree. Let him come till he's almost close enough to touch. Then let him have it, and jump out and finish him up with your hatchet.

•   •   •

The American Revolution produced another flurry of "Ranger" activity, including the so-called Leather Shirts who employed Indian-like tactics in battle, and an official Ranger unit of 120 men raised by Lieutenant Colonel Thomas Knowlton under General George Washington. Knowlton was slain and his men captured by the British at Harlem Heights on September 16, 1776.

Colonel Francis Marion, dubbed "the Swamp Fox" by British Lieutenant Colonel Banastre Tarleton, was the most effective and famous of the "Rangers." From 1780 until the war ended, he harassed the British and their Tory allies with hit-and-run raids on supply lines, warehouses, and other strategic installations, forcing the British to withdraw regular troops to protect against Marion and his men. Sent to run down Marion, Colonel Tarleton finally gave up in exasperation.

"Come on, boys, let's go back," he exclaimed. "As for this damned old fox, the devil himself could not catch him."

Threatened by Indian raids along the early American frontier, settlers demanded government protection. The U.S. Congress responded by authorizing the formation of Ranger units. By 1814, 1,070 Rangers in ten independent companies patrolled from Michigan to Louisiana. General Andrew Jackson commanded Rangers in the Florida Panhandle. After his election to president of the United States, he deployed mounted Rangers out west as part of his Indian policy to show force and protect commercial routes.

The Great Plains Indian tribes were technically Rangers in the fullest sense of the word. They were regarded as "the finest light cavalry in the world." Beginning in the 1830s, Texas Rangers in twenty or more companies patrolled against Indian raids and helped maintain law and order. Although Texas Rangers were not part of the military, General Zachary Taylor used them extensively during the Mexican War.

· · ·

Either officially or unofficially, more than four hundred separate units known as Rangers served during the Civil War with both Union and Confederate forces. They proved controversial from the beginning since they were allowed to profit in confiscated goods and the spoils of war. Some of the outfits, such as Mosby's Rangers, enjoyed good reputations. Others, as General Robert E. Lee was informed, "have engaged in this business for the sake of gain."

The northern states raised Rangers to counterbalance Confederate Rangers. In April and May 1863, Colonel Benjamin Grierson led a Ranger excursion into Mississippi, where, eluding pursuers, his troops wrecked more than 50 miles of railroad and destroyed several supply bases.

Later, in the winter of that same year, his mounted troops raced across Tennessee, where, much like Merrill's Marauders of World War II, they cut enemy supply lines, took hundreds of Confederate prisoners, captured herds of cattle and horses, destroyed railroad tracks and rolling stock, seized a total of five thousand weapons, and set flame to mountains of baled cotton. Only General Sherman's march through Georgia created more havoc and destruction.

Disbanded following the end of the Civil War, Rangers did not reappear until the beginning of World War II.

General George C. Marshall commissioned a total of six Ranger battalions for use in World War II, beginning with the 1st Ranger Battalion under the command of Lieutenant Colonel William O. Darby, "Darby's Rangers." Darby's men began training in Northern Ireland in June 1942 under British instructors. It seemed the Brits might have learned something from the American Revolution about commandos. British special operations forces of the time were considered the best in the world in such commonsense skills as self-defense, weapons, scouting, mountaineering, seamanship, demolitions, small-boat handling, and anything else that extremely flexible troops working unconventionally and often behind enemy lines might require.

Darby's Rangers, the 1st Battalion, first saw action in November 1942 when they captured and secured a beachhead for Operation Torch, the invasion of North Africa. From there, the 1st linked with the 3rd and 4th Ranger battalions to spearhead beach invasions at Sicily (July 1943), Salerno (September 1943), and Anzio (January 1944).

Following the landing at Anzio, the three Ranger battalions were tasked with fighting their way to the heavily garrisoned city of Cisterna. Of the 767 men who finally reached the objective through bitter conventional fighting, only 6 survived to make their way back to American lines. The rest were either killed or captured. Despite their failure, Rangers inflicted some 5,500 casualties on the Germans.

While the 1st, 3rd, and 4th Battalions were busy in the Mediterranean theater, the 2nd and 5th were fighting in France. The 2nd landed in Normandy with D-day assault troops west of Omaha Beach, their mission to scale a 100-foot cliff to take out emplaced heavy guns that had the beachhead covered. Fifteen Rangers lost their lives, but they accomplished their mission.

Not far away, the 5th Rangers landed in the Vierville sector of Normandy behind the 116th Infantry Regiment. Both the 2nd and 5th moved inland and saw action across France, Belgium, and Germany. Toward the end of the war, the 5th Rangers were employed in long-range penetration missions against the enemy in Germany.

The 6th Ranger Battalion saw action in the Pacific. Along with the 6th Army's Alamo Scouts, it went ashore in the Philippines three days ahead of the landing at Leyte Gulf to scout the region, guard the entrance to the gulf, destroy Japanese radio facilities and targets of opportunity, and prepare for General Douglas MacArthur's "return." MacArthur kept his promise and returned to the Philippines on October 20, 1944.

Alamo Scouts linked up with the 6th Rangers in January 1945 to conduct perhaps the most famous behind-enemy-lines raid in U.S. history.

The dramatic raid took them 65 miles behind Japanese lines to rescue 531 American prisoners from the POW camp at Cabanatuan, survivors of the Bataan Death March. All 225 Japanese soldiers in the camp garrison were killed. Only two Rangers lost their lives.

Elsewhere in the Pacific theater, Merrill's Marauders under the command of General Frank D. Merrill operated in Burma under General Joseph Stillwell. Although not specifically a Ranger outfit, the 5307 Composite Unit (Provisional) nonetheless functioned as Rangers. In January and February 1944, while suffering from hunger, exposure, and deprivation, Merrill's men engaged in a series of operations with Chinese troops to block trails, cut Japanese supply lines, and capture Myitkyina airfield and town.

World War II ended with Korea partitioned between the Communist North under the influence of China and Russia and the South under the patronage of the United States. On June 25, 1950, the North Korean Army attacked South Korea across the 38th Parallel. Six Ranger companies, including the all-black 4th (later designated the 2nd) Ranger Company, were utilized early in the fighting for reconnaissance, sabotage behind enemy lines, and blocking enemy movements.

After the front lines hardened in 1951 and the fighting turned static, the Ranger units were deactivated and their personnel reassigned to the 187th Airborne Regimental Combat Team. However, the Ranger command was reconstituted almost immediately as the Ranger Department of the Infantry School at Fort Benning, where individuals received instruction in Ranger tactics and then returned to their parent organizations. No Ranger units existed at the end of the Korean War, a hiatus that continued until the Vietnam War.

In 1969, Army Long Range Reconnaissance Patrols (LRRPs) were designated as Rangers since their missions in Vietnam were similar. On January 16, 1969, the army authorized the creation of two new Ranger companies:

Alpha Company at Fort Benning and Bravo Company at Fort Carson, Colorado. Five years later, in January 1974, after America's active combat participation in the war had ended, the Pentagon became concerned with the army infantry's lack of mobility and authorized the resurrection of Ranger battalions. The 75th Ranger Regiment emerged with the 1st Battalion at Fort Stewart, Georgia, and the 2nd Battalion stationed at Fort Lewis, Washington. The 3rd Battalion would not be activated at Fort Benning until October 1984 following the short operation at Grenada.

Throughout most of the rest of the twentieth century, United States Rangers were utilized in a series of "brush fire" actions that spanned the globe. Most of these were short, sometimes only a day or two, and consisted of specific missions to accomplish a designated task. One of the first of these began in 1980 after radical Iranian Islamicists in Tehran seized the American embassy and held its personnel hostage.

The military rescue plan was code-named Operation Eagle Claw. Army Rangers of Charlie Company 1/75 were assigned two missions in the operation. They would provide security for men and equipment at a secret rescue launch site inside Iran, code-named Desert One, and then secure either by parachute or by helicopter a landing zone near Tehran from which to air evac the rescued hostages.

Things turned bad at the launch point, however, when a helicopter crashed into another aircraft in a sandstorm. The mission was scrubbed at the last minute. The embassy people were subsequently and promptly released after Ronald Reagan became president.

Less than three years after the Desert One debacle, a military coup took place on the tiny island republic of Grenada, trapping and endangering American medical students at the True Blue campus near the Point Salines Airport. President Ronald Reagan launched Operation Urgent Fury on October 25, 1983. Rangers from the 1/75 and the 2/75 parachuted onto the Point Salines airfield to secure it for troop landings. The mission ended after four days with the rescue of the students and Castro's withdrawal from the island. (Cuban troops had been stationed on Grenada with the consent of its government.) Five Rangers lost their lives, and six were wounded.

Partly as a result of confusion during Eagle Claw and Urgent Fury, the United States established the Special Operations Command (SOCOM) in 1984 to coordinate special operations and special operations forces. Air assault missions were planned and practiced for several years before SOCOM received the opportunity to prove itself with the invasion of Panama. Strongman Manuel Noriega had been charged in the United States with international drug smuggling. The mission of the invasion was to oust Noriega from office and bring him back for trial.

The operation kicked off on December 17, 1989, when Rangers made two separate combat jumps, one to secure Torillos International Airport at Panama City and the other Rio Hata military airfield farther west. Heavy antiaircraft fire filled the darkened sky over Rio Hata as C-130s flew in at 500 feet to drop Ranger paratroopers. A bullet struck one Ranger in the back of the head while he was still in the aircraft. He survived. Four other Rangers who jumped were killed on the ground by hostile fire.

After taking the airfield, Rangers moved into Panama City to seize the military headquarters of the Panamanian Defense Forces and other key installations held by "Dignity Battalions." SEALs and other military units fought several fierce battles before the fighting ended. Noriega was eventually captured, extradited to the United States, tried on various drug charges, and sentenced to a long prison term.

Army Rangers with their three combat battalions, which now included 3/75 at Fort Benning, were back to stay by the time Operation Desert Storm, the first war in the Gulf, began in early 1991. They were particularly suited for the fast and furious special operations pace of the twentieth century. Because of the war's short duration—"the One-Hundred-Hour

War"—most of the 75th Ranger Regiment remained in reserve for contingency operations. Only a few Ranger platoons took part in several quick ops in the desert against radar, communications, and Scud missile sites. The war, such as it was, ended with a ceasefire that allowed Saddom Hussein to consolidate his rule after his troops had been driven off with heavy losses from Kuwait.

The Battle of Mogadishu that occurred on October 3–4, 1993, is still known to Somalis as "Day of the Rangers" in grudging respect to Rangers of the 3/75 who carried much of the fight into the heart of the armed and hostile city to rescue the pilots and crew of two U.S. Black Hawk helicopters shot down by RPGs. It might be considered the first skirmish of what, less than a decade later, would become known as the War on Terror.

The fight started when a task force made up of nineteen helicopters, twelve vehicles, and a total of 160 men from Delta Force, SEALs, 16th Special Operations Aviation Regiment, and Rangers of the 75th Regiment entered the heart of the city to capture aides and advisers of terrorist warlord leader Mohamed Farrah Aidid.

During the previous two years following the overthrow of Somalian president Mohamed Siad Barre, Aidid and opposing warlord leaders had turned the East African nation into a killing ground. More than a half-million people had been killed, while one and a half million had been displaced. In an attempt to bring order to the land, the United Nations, led by the United States under the banner of Operation Restore Hope, moved in to protect the city and its people and put an end to the brutal warlords.

Thousands of Somalis loyal to Aidid ambushed the U.S. convoy with automatic weapons, Molotov cocktails, and RPGs as it moved in on Aidid's people. During the ensuing two-day battle, eighteen Americans died and seventy-three were wounded. Among the dead were six Rangers of 3rd Battalion from Fort Benning.

Estimates of enemy casualties range as high as three thousand with perhaps half that number dead. Rather than continue the effort to free Somalia from the grip of corrupt and violent leaders per UN mandate, President Bill Clinton ordered all U.S. troops to withdraw.

U.S. Army Green Berets, Navy SEALs, and Rangers were particularly suited for the quick-paced, often clandestine War on Terror that followed the attacks against America on 9/11. By the time President George W. Bush announced air strikes against al Qaeda and Taliban military camps in Afghanistan on October 7, 2001, the 75th Rangers were already in training to play a major role in the war against international terrorism. Rangers would be deployed to combat zones almost constantly for the next ten years.

This was the best time in all history to be a Ranger. Some guys did twenty or thirty years in the army without seeing combat. At Fort Benning, Georgia, I had successfully completed the first three phases of my enlistment contract. BCT, AIT, and Airborne School were behind me. All that remained was to make it through the Ranger Indoctrination Program. I was apt to go to war as soon as I completed training. I looked forward to becoming a part of it.

6

"Surrender is not a Ranger word."

It was primal. I understood it completely. One of the ironies of modern society is that men are being conditioned to apologize for male aggressiveness, for being men, to be replaced by all that sensitive, touchy-feely, "inner child" and "get in touch with your feminine side" bullshit. The infantry, especially special ops forces like the Rangers, is one of the last surviving bastions of the alpha male, that most endangered of endangered species. I ate it up. I wouldn't have been anywhere else or doing anything else. I wanted that Ranger scroll on my sleeve more than I had ever wanted anything.

You didn't have to go to Ranger School in order to be assigned to the Rangers, although you had to complete it sooner or later if you wanted to advance in rank and stay in the battalion. You did have to finish RIP, however, the Ranger Indoctrination Program. My main beef with army training so far was that it had been *too easy*. That was about to change.

First day out of the gate, instructors in black sweat gear were all over us like flies on a goat's butt in summer, all of them yelling and countermanding orders so you didn't know which way to go or what the hell to do. I soon figured it out as calculated confusion. They didn't want you to get comfortable; they wanted to keep you on edge, they wanted you nervous in the service, they wanted to see if you could stand up under stress and still think. Okay, I understood that. Now what?

The first order of business was the Ranger PT test—a 5-mile run in less than forty minutes. The cadre made it clear that if you fucked up on it, you fucked up on *anything,* you were out of here. No argument, no appeal. Just out of here.

One of the instructors, who looked wiry enough to run to Atlanta and back and mean enough to munch railroad spikes as he ran, stood in front of the formation and froze us in place with his icy glare.

"Look at your buddy," he growled. "Don't get too cozy with him. Three weeks from now, one of the two of you won't be here."

Because formations were arranged alphabetically, the "buddy" on my left was a man named Ben Hunter. I hadn't known him before now. He was over six feet tall, thicker than me, and a few years older, with dirty blond hair, if you could tell the color of hair shorn so close to the scalp. When I glanced over at him, he wore an impish half-smile. The guy *winked* at me, as though to say, *Hey, buddy, we got this stuff whipped.* I didn't dare say anything, so I winked back.

Dark still lay over Benning when the platoon launched off the starting line, but the sun would be coming up by the time most of us finished the 5 miles. Since it was a test, everyone ran at his own pace. I quickly pulled out among the front-runners and worked up a fast patina of sweat in Georgia's summer air. I looked over and there was Hunter pounding alongside. He might be taking this "buddy" stuff a bit too far. I turned on the coal and pulled out ahead. He caught up.

That was how we finished. Challenging each other. It was the best PT score I had ever made.

"Winning ain't everything," I murmured between breaths.

Hunter chopped me a quizzical look.

I grinned. "It ain't *everything,*" I said. "It's the *only* thing."

"Yeah!" he rasped.

Some of the guys vanished after that first day, those who failed the PT test. We never saw them again. More and more of us disappeared like that all through the various phases. Many simply flunked out, couldn't make the grade. Others were injured and got the opportunity to heal up and catch the next class. A sizable minority did neither but still turned up missing from formation, fading into the ether for reassignment somewhere less challenging where they could connect with their "inner child."

Navy SEALs in their BUD/S (Basic Underwater Demolition/SEAL) course had this brass bell on the grinder. If anyone wanted to quit for any reason, no matter what, all he had to do was walk up and ring the bell and he was out of there. Catch was, he had to ring the bell in front of formation so everybody could see what a puss he was. Rangers didn't have a bell, but maybe we should have.

You could tell those who didn't have the motivation to see it through. They were the ones who shammed, tried to get through with minimum effort. Like cheating on push-ups, not going all the way down, or dropping on one knee when the instructors weren't looking. Others pretended they were hurt or sick, exaggerating their symptoms in order to save face when they quit. You could see through them. I didn't want them in *my* Rangers. They'd fade on you when you needed them most.

Like predators, the cadre sought out the weak and unmotivated and eliminated them from the herd, weeding us down. The game was constantly on. Most of the time I had no idea what the hell was about to happen, which way to go. Neither did Hunter or anyone else. Unlike other military training programs where daily training schedules were posted, nothing was ever spelled out all the way through RIP. Each day was a surprise, or a shock, according to your point of view and attitude. Maybe today it was airborne operations, map reading, and land navigation, battle drills . . . Tomorrow it was NBC (nuclear, biological, and chemical) warfare trials, fast-roping from the tower, water survival . . . In between, RIP instructors smoked us with push-ups, flutter kicks, and assorted other tortures disguised as calesthenic exercise, working us until our muscles knotted into kinks.

"You're slow, you're lazy!"

"You are one worthless, pathetic bunch of losers!"

Everything was designed, it seemed, to wash you out of the course. It was almost impossible to determine from day to day if you were doing well. Instructors could drop you out almost on a whim. Looking back, I could see a point to the apparent madness. It encouraged flexibility of thinking in order to effectively and efficiently confront unexpected situations. You could always depend on the instructors to put a little fuckup in your life.

"You got to think on your feet, numbnuts."

While some of the guys had been out drinking beer and getting soft during the holdover period waiting for RIP to begin, I was busy pounding the road every day, building up muscle and endurance. Apparently, Hunter had done the same. We goaded each other all through RIP, challenged, dared, and provoked. We could have become enemies. Instead, we got as close as brothers as the class continued to dwindle through more or less natural attrition.

Out on the range while the platoon low-crawled through muddy water and sand and while grenade and artillery simulators exploded mud all over us and machine-gun fire (blanks) raked the air above our heads, Jackson from New York got rattled and jumped to his feet and started flapping his arms and raving hysterically. Hunter and I looked at each other. Mud smeared our faces, and our eyes were red-rimmed from exhaustion and lack of sleep. Incomprehensibly, we began laughing.

"Another one bites the dust," Hunter sniped. "Just like *Full Metal Jacket.*"

He was a big movie fan. He claimed the only thing better than watching film was drinking beer.

An instructor ran out on the field and dragged Jackson away. That was the last we saw of him.

Next went Diebel. We were on a midnight 12-mile forced march with full combat load through the piney woods when Diebel began stumbling and muttering to himself. Ken Roundy tried to keep him going, but Diebel was looking for the bell to ring if we had had one.

He staggered to the side of the road and sat down.

"Whatta ya think?" Hunter asked. "Should we try to change his mind?"

We looked at each other and decided in unison, "Nah!"

Diebel was a quitter. We never saw him again, either.

Johnson fainted during First Response IV practice; Morris broke his leg on an obstacle course; Osgood caught a bug and vomited all night and ended up recycled through the aid station; Collins almost drowned during the Combat Water Survival Test—a 15-meter swim complicated by wearing BDUs (battle dress uniform), boots, and load-carrying equipment. That washed him out. Even Scott Lockhart vanished from ranks.

"This keeps up," Hunter remarked, "won't be anybody left except you and me."

"And sometimes I don't know about you," I quipped back.

He kept a calendar in his locker. Every night when we got in—*if* we got in that night—he took it out and marked off the day. He had our graduation date circled in red ink.

"I'll be there at the end," he said.

So would I. I kept my eye on the prize. Just like Staff Sergeant Van Aalst advised when we were on detail at the Marksmanship Unit.

I got to yelling back at the cadre in the middle of obstacle courses or on long runs or forced marches. Nothing intelligible. Just yelling in some wild, primitive response to the situation.

"Christ Almighty, Kap. I think you eat this shit up."

"Roger that, Sergeant!"

Some in the platoon, for whatever reasons, couldn't seem to do the right thing. They kept the rest of the class in constant trouble. Minor transgressions, not enough to get them kicked out but sufficient to bring down the wrath of God. It might not be fair to punish all for the sins of a few, but, hey, life sometimes sucks. An outfit is only as strong as its weakest link.

A couple of these shitbirds were late for formation one night. The cadre chased the platoon inside the barracks to grab the left boot of the pair we had worn in the mud that day.

"Get to work, girls. You can thank Blevins and Hardin for it. I want to see my face in the shine of your boots."

The platoon sat out on the tarmac, in the middle-of-the-night, shining left boots. We were all dirt-eating tired. Every time someone thought his boot good enough to pass inspection, an instructor wearing an expression like he hadn't had a good shit in a week looked it over and snapped, "Boy, you call that a shine. Drop down and grab a handful."

That was the way it went—shining left boots and doing push-ups in between for three hours.

Finally, the instructors got tired. It was after midnight.

"Listen up carefully. You got a right boot like your left. They both better look the same by morning formation or you ain't seen smoking yet. Got it?"

The platoon rushed inside and starting shining right boots. Hadn't anyone *listened*? Hunter, Jeremy Keller, a couple of other guys, and I laughed at them and racked out to snatch some much-needed sleep.

Come 0400, we jumped up, scuffed and muddied up our shined left boots so they matched our much-beat-up right boots, and reported to formation. A cadre instructor stiff-backed through the formation until he came to Hunter and me standing side by side at rigid attention. He looked at us, he looked at our sorry-looking boots. A ghost of a smile touched his mouth before he passed on without saying a word.

Both boots looked the same, right? Weren't we supposed to be flexible in our thinking?

About 120 of the original 300 or so who started RIP made it through to graduation. We were farmed out afterward all over the Regiment. Hunter and I, along with Jeremy Keller and a number of others, were assigned together to Alpha Company, 3rd Ranger Battalion at Benning. It was the proudest day of my life up to this point when I pinned the 3rd Ranger

Battalion scroll on the left shoulder of my uniform to match the silver jump wings on my chest. I was a U.S. Army Airborne Ranger.

Next stop? Most of us already suspected where that would be. I had still been in Basic Combat Training on October 7, not quite a month after 9/11, when the armed forces of the United States, Britain, Australia, and the Afghan Northern Alliance launched Operation Enduring Freedom against the Taliban and al Qaeda in Afghanistan. Teams from the CIA's Special Activities Division and from Army Special Forces began combat operations on the ground.

It was a war custom-made for special operations forces like the Rangers. I couldn't imagine missing out on it and having to sit at home guzzling beer and watching the Patriots on TV.

7

AFGHANISTAN 2002

The 3rd Ranger Battalion arrived at Bagram Airfield in the middle of the night like a dirty secret smuggled into the country. The C-17 Globemaster stuffed with Rangers and gear approached high before it dropped in quick to avoid ground fire. My stomach churning into my throat, where it shouldn't be, awoke me with a start. Next to me, dozing off with his head lolled over onto my shoulder, Ben Hunter came alert and looked around, gripping the seat rail between his legs as though to keep from flying up and banging his head. Packed like proverbial sardines into the airplane since Ramstein Air Base in Germany had left everyone stiff and a little grumpy.

"Holy—!" Hunter began. He rubbed his eyes with both hands.

"We're there, Ben."

"We at the war?"

"Looks like it."

Interior lights were all off, and we rode in darkness except for red dots marking the piss tubes. Hunter stared back at the red lights.

"They remind me of the little red pig eyes in *Amityville Horror*," he said.

Near-surface air turned the ride bumpy. Hunter held on. He didn't mind jumping out of airplanes, he just didn't like flying in them.

"Kap, I been thinking," he said. "What if somebody gave a war and nobody showed up?"

"Rangers always show up."

The Globemaster touched down, braked, rolled out, and dropped its ramp for off-loading. The reality of where I was and *why* rushed in with a lungful of hot dust and a distant smell I couldn't quite place. It was a mixture of sand and hot tarmac, of wind off the mountains, and maybe the fragrance of a distant barnyard. Whatever it was, it was *distinctive*. I forever afterward associated it with Afghanistan. Hunter took a deep breath as troops stacked up eager to unass the plane.

"God, I love the smell of napalm in the morning," Hunter cracked. *Apocalypse Now* was one of his favorite movies.

"You think we use napalm here?"

"How you going to make crispy critters without napalm?"

Out on the tarmac, I looked around before officers and NCOs started herding us around. You were always being herded when you were a lowly private. Most of the time you had no idea of what was going on. Guys training for the raid on the Son Tay POW camp during the Vietnam War created a special patch for themselves that showed a mushroom with a pair of eyes underneath and the lettering KITD/FOHS around the outside border. *Kept in the Dark, Fed Only Horse Shit.* Privates were mushrooms.

It was mostly dark, but enough dim lights scattered about indicated that we had landed at a major military airfield. Otherwise, there was nothing but quiet and darkness and the low, sad moan of wind blowing sand into our eyes and down our throats. Hunter gripped his M-4 rifle nervously. So far, there were no screaming, half-crazed, religious-fanatic, Arab-type bad guys exploding out of the night to slit our throats. Instead, a number of trucks and military buses were parked off the side of the ramp with yellow parking lights burning as they waited to deliver us to wherever we were going. Ours had been a rather inglorious arrival. We could have been on a routine field training exercise for all the fanfare.

The rest of the battalion and gear would be arriving via other aircraft. Alpha Company began assembling, rather noisily, I thought, considering I expected most of the petty shit to have been left back in the States, what with our being in a combat zone and all. A goat rope, it was, with leaders trying to get everything sorted out in the dark.

Get a move on!

Get your ass over here!

Get your ass over there!

Where's your gear, numbnuts?

You left your what where?

First Platoon's PL, Lieutenant Wence, short and stocky with blond hair, and Platoon Sergeant E-7 Ray Reid, a refrigerator who towered over Wence, soon had the platoon lined out.

"First Squad, you up?"

"Good, Sergeant."

"Second Squad?"

"Okay . . ."

"Third . . . ? Weapons Squad . . . ? Grab your gear and get on the first bus so we can go somewhere to get some sleep."

Staff Sergeant Smith's 1st Squad and about six other guys made a run for the bus. Hunter and I were the only ones in the squad still together out of RIP. We were cherries still and had little idea of what the hell was going on.

"You scared?" I overheard one Ranger ask another in a low voice.

His buddy scoffed. "What? Of ragheads who ride mules and camels and think they're Genghis Khan?"

"Let's get this shit started," cheered a third voice in the dark.

Everyone had been preparing for deployment for so long at Fort Benning that we were weary of it and ready to get it on. Moving a modern army wasn't like you could get up one morning, muster the outfit, get on an airplane, and go. Nothing moved in the army until the paperwork was done. Soldiers had stood in lines to update service records, get immunizations, verify pay records and next-of-kin information, update powers of attorney and wills . . .

"Why do I need a will? I'm nineteen years old. I don't own nothing."

"Son, your next of kin gets GI death benefits if you don't come back."

"But I'm coming back."

"Sign by the *X*."

Rangers were considered *light* infantry. If we were light, I could only imagine the gear a cav or armored outfit had to catalog, bundle, and load for deployment. Some of our guys went out and bought all kinds of "queer gear," like Hollywood sunshades, briefcases, high-speed flashlights with infrared, and personal GPSs.

"I want to know where I am and how to get out if I have to," explained Wright, who came back from town with a GPS and a sack of junk-food "pogue bait" candy bars. "For energy while I'm getting out," he added with a sheepish grin.

The atmosphere around the barracks in Georgia the night before we emplaned had been both somber and excited in turn as guys came in from saying good-bye to girlfriends, parents, wives, and children. Smokers chain-smoked. Hunter stepped outside and stared up at the sky after his girlfriend left. I didn't know if he was praying or what. Chaplains came among us to talk and hand out pocket New Testaments. Erin and Randy telephoned me from Connecticut. It was good to talk to them and my grandparents, but I was secretly relieved they hadn't come down to see me off. I was never much for good-byes.

Besides, I was still trying to wrap my mind around the enormity of it all. This was a historic occasion that seemed wasted on most of us. Until the War on Terror, Rangers hadn't gone to war since Korea if you didn't count actions like Desert Storm, Panama, Grenada, and Somalia, none of which lasted long enough to be classified as a war. What this meant was that we had few old vets to lead the way. However, almost everyone in my squad had deployed to Afghanistan the previous autumn, which meant there were only about six of us in the platoon, including Ben and me, who had to be blooded.

When you were nineteen, the world was fresher and more exciting than it would ever be again. It was like everything was your first time and you saw with eyes that hadn't been jaded while you incorporated new thoughts and impressions onto the blank slate of your mind. So far, the war was just one great adventure for a small-town kid. It was Joe's and Ben's Amazing Adventure.

By platoons and squads, the companies of the battalion were shuffled off to GP Medium tents erected over plywood floors. Using flashlights that cast shadows and eerie light, we sorted through baggage pallets to retrieve our gear and store it in the tents. Finally, we were allowed to rack out on cots in the tents for a few hours. Winds that had blown across the camel caravans of the old Silk Road centuries before tugged at the flaps of the tents and popped them like distant rifle shots.

I awoke hungry and rushed outside to find a chow hall and get a first look at my new surroundings, trying to take it all in at once. The airfield with its single runway, hangars, tower, support buildings that were either constructed of plywood and tin or renovated mud huts, and various troop tent cities lay in a flat desert valley where everything was gray, brown, or tan. There were no real trees or even grass, only gray tufts of vegetation here and there. Concertina wire or concrete walls called HESCOs surrounded the base. Off in the distance on all sides rose impressive snow-capped ranges of mountains disappearing into clouds. They strung out south toward Pakistan and Iran and north in the direction of Russia and China. CH-47 Chinook helicopters lifted in and out transporting troops of the 82nd Airborne or the 10th Mountain Division on missions outside the wire. The twin-engine, heavy-lift Chinook was the workhorse in a land where few roads were paved and the rest were narrow and pockmarked, muddy in the spring and snow-covered in the winter.

Below one of the mountain peaks and within view of the airbase huddled the ancient city of Bagram, as gray and brown and tan as the rest of the valley. No one knew exactly when it was first settled, but it was probably at least a thousand years before the birth of Jesus. The founder of the Persian Empire, Cyrus the Great, destroyed it during his campaign against the Saka nomads in the sixth century B.C. It was rebuilt only to fall to

Alexander the Great around 330 B.C. One of Alexander's generals, Seleucus, traded it to India in 305 B.C. after Alexander's death. Since then, it had been captured, destroyed, and rebuilt several more times.

Ironically enough, considering that the United States was now using Bagram as a staging site, invading Soviet forces had selected the airbase as their initial staging point in 1979. After the Soviets withdrew with their tails between their legs in 1989, the airfield sank into a battleground in the civil war between the U.S.-supported mujahideen of the Northern Alliance and the Taliban. Many of the support buildings had been destroyed, leaving only mud-brick foundations and crumbling walls. Opposing sides often controlled opposite ends of the base.

By the time the 3rd Battalion landed for its second tour, Bagram was the bustling home of more than seven thousand members of the U.S. and allied armed services. Numerous tent cities with impromptu names like Viper City and Sandtown quartered the various units. Although I couldn't see how anything less than a modern army could hope to tackle an installation of this size, which I assumed al Qaeda didn't have, we were nonetheless required to carry loaded weapons wherever we went. Occasionally, I learned, the air base was shelled.

"Dodge City," Hunter commented wryly. "People are a lot politer to each other when everybody carries guns."

I remembered how it was said that Afghanistan with its high mountain ramparts and its fractious and warlike nomadic tribes had often been invaded but never conquered. The Brits and the Russians had learned that lesson the hard way in recent history.

Now the Americans were here.

"The war is *out there*," Lieutenant Wence said, pointing toward the mountains. "Don't get comfortable here, and don't bother to unpack your rucksacks. We're not staying."

8

John J. Edmunds and Kristofor Stonesifer were the first Rangers to die in-country. That was in October 2001.

Operation Anaconda five months later, in March 2002, claimed the first Ranger casualties inside Afghanistan when three fell in the most intense firefight spec ops had been involved in since six Rangers were killed in Mogadishu, Somalia, in 1993. I didn't know the three guys; they were members of 1st Batt from Hunter Army Airfield. News of the fight spread throughout the regiment back at Benning, where it was widely discussed and debated.

The Rangers were operating as a QRF (quick reaction force) out of Gardez southeast of Bagram when Anaconda began as a major joint push-in-force into the mountains by Americans and Brits. U.S. commanders decided to insert special operators onto the crest of a 10,000-foot mountain peak called Takur Ghar, which would serve as a superb observation point over action in the valley below. "Unfortunately," the after-action report lamented, "the enemy thought so too." A sizable number of al Qaeda fighters were already dug in on the same mountain.

SEALs triggered the shit storm. A team of them accompanied by an Air Force Combat Controller lifted off in a Chinook helicopter shortly before 0300 hours. The bird followed the river in the dark and rose steeply to flare for a landing on a flat spot at the top of the mountain.

As it settled toward the ground, hovering, machine-gun fire suddenly erupted from the surrounding rocky terrain. A swarm of green-tracer bees ripped through the aircraft's thin skin. A rocket propelled grenade (RPG) penetrated the side of the chopper. SEAL Petty Officer First Class Neil Roberts, who was preparing to go off the open back ramp, took the brunt of the explosion. It blew him out the opening onto the snow 10 feet below.

The Chinook pilots threw some power and lift to the crippled chopper and managed to nurse it to a crash landing on a ridge about 4 miles away. By then, the other SEALs had discovered Roberts missing. He was now alone on Takur Ghar, surrounded by enemy fighters.

A second Chinook quickly responded to the emergency by plucking the SEALs and the Air Force Controller off the ridge and delivering them back to the mountain to rescue their teammate. The helicopter touched down just long enough for the rescuers to bail out into the snow, weapons blazing. They fought off a brief counterattack and then looked around for Roberts. He was already gone, dragged off by the enemy.

"Based on forensic evidence subsequently gathered from the scene," the battle report later surmised, "we believe Roberts survived the short fall from the helicopter, likely activated his signaling device, and engaged the enemy with his squad automatic rifle (SAW). He was mortally wounded by gunfire as the [enemy] closed in on him."

U.S. forces later found his helmet nearby with a bullet hole in it. His body was never recovered.

Unable to find Roberts, the SEALs decided to disengage. They moved down the side of the mountain toward the valley below. Enemy fighters tailed them, barking like a pack of hounds on a blood trail. Covering fire from a circling AC-130 gunship was the only thing that prevented their being overrun.

The Ranger QRF at Gardez received an alert at 0345 hours. SEALs under heavy fire were requesting reinforcements. Nineteen Rangers, a Tactical Air Control Party, and a three-man Air Force Special Tactics Team scrambled in two Chinooks.

Because of a communications FUBAR (fucked up beyond all recognition), the first chopper, Razor Zero-One, assumed the SEALs were in defense on top of the mountain where Roberts was last seen. Dawn was about to break, the sun red behind the Hindu Kush and reflecting like blood off the snow, when Razor Zero-One flared for touchdown. It immediately took ground fire. Bullets riddled the door gunner, Army Sergeant Philip Svitak. He slumped mortally wounded in his harness.

An exploding RPG took out the chopper's right engine. It crashed to the ground, hitting hard, smoke and flames belching from it. Passengers and crew scrambled from the wreck and ran into a withering hail of lead that cut down three Rangers almost immediately. Private First Class Matt Commons, Sergeant Brad Crose, and Specialist Marc Anderson fell dead in the snow. Surviving members of the QRF and crew took cover on a hillock as the firefight flared into a full-scale battle.

In the meantime, Razor Zero-Two, the second Chinook, carrying the QRF's Chalk 2, a second load of troops, landed at its proper location down the side of the mountain. Rangers began to hustle upslope toward Chalk 1, arriving at 1030 hours to relieve the beleaguered defenders. By then, full daylight had broken upon the mountain. Al Qaeda fighters didn't have the stomach to take on a bunch of pissed-off Rangers in full light. They fled as the linked Ranger teams assaulted enemy positions through knee-deep snow.

SEALs and Rangers on the ground aided by Coalition air strikes killed at least two hundred Taliban and al Qaeda foot soldiers before the action ended that afternoon. Seven Americans died in the battle, including the three Rangers and SEAL Neil Roberts. Eleven Americans were wounded.

• • •

That fight was on everyone's mind as the Chinook arrived to airlift 1st Platoon from Bagram. Platoon Sergeant Ray Reid paced nervously up and down the chalk of troops preparing to board the bird as it warmed up its engines. Propellers started to whir.

Wright could be something of a smart-ass at times. I suspected he was attempting to mask his own jitters. He snapped off a pretty fair Brit salute with the palm turned outward as Sergeant Reid walked by.

"Yes, sair, Guv'nor Sergeant."

"Wright, there's been more than one court jester strung up by his balls at the king's court for being a wise donkey."

"An' your point would be, Sergeant?"

"Get on the damned bird, Wright." He turned away. "All right, people. Assholes and elbows. The war waits on nobody."

This was our first *real war* mission. Everyone was a bit on edge, but we covered it well with bravado and bullshit. Everything we owned we carried either on our backs or in our hands, locked and loaded. Curved NOD mounts strapped to foreheads beneath our helmets made us look like rhinos from the neck up. PL Wence took the lead, pointing at the chopper's open ramp and shouting back over his shoulder.

"Get it on. You've done this before, people."

Sure, but only in training, not when there was a possibility that some of us might not be coming back. I glanced around at the other guys, my buddies, as, laden with an awesome array of machine guns, explosives, and other weapons, we made our way toward the lowered ramp of the Chinook. Rotor wash from its whining blades tugged at our desert-camo field uniforms while the same blades seemed to puree the morning sunlight, like one of those Veg-O-Matic things hawked at the Durham Fair.

When it came to killing the enemy, I thought I could do it when the time came. Killing was a conundrum every warrior had to confront at some point. On the one hand, most of us grew up being taught that killing another human being was wrong, even a crime, but in the Rangers killing was almost a job description, like plumbing was for plumbers or welding for welders. Sometimes during PT we jogged along in formation chanting *"Kill! Kill!"* in cadence.

"It's war," Hunter rationalized. "We have to do it to protect ourselves and our country."

Pretty good words, pretty easy words when uttered in safe territory and when killing remained merely theoretical—but how about the reality of it when you had some guy in your sights and the only thing between him and paradise or hell was the pressure of your finger on the trigger?

I could do it. I knew I could. I was a Ranger.

I was less certain about my reaction if the tables were turned and some guy on the other side solved *his* conundrum by killing one of my buddies, Hunter or Kopp or the smartass Wright. Hunter and I pushed each other through the heady, muddy days of RIP. It was hard to imagine the platoon with him gone.

I refused to think about it. I turned my mind off as the platoon finished loading the chopper and the pilots applied liftoff power. More than thirty of us with battle gear were jammed into the bird's belly, many of us sitting on the floor or on our rucks. Hunter and I latched onto each other to steady ourselves against the helicopter's movement.

The back ramp remained down. A machine gunner sat in a metal folding chair on each side of the ramp, tethered to the helicopter by an umbilical. I gazed out past them as the chopper climbed into the air. Nearby rows of tan tents shuddered from the rotor wash as the Chinook gathered speed and flashed over the wire into enemy territory. It darted over low hills and through the valleys of eastern Afghanistan, flying fast and ultra low to evade enemy ground fire. It ascended a ridgeline, popped down on the other side, and flared to land in a flat, low area.

I spotted an Afghani man standing on the top of a low hill outside a small brown village next to a dry streambed. Just standing there wearing a black turban and a dirty man-dress. He was the first indig I had seen.

He looked at us as we off-loaded on the sand. We looked back. He turned and disappeared down the other side of the hill.

"You suppose—?" Hunter ventured.

I shrugged. Here, the enemy wore no uniforms.

Captain Wence pointed out a hilltop about a half mile away, our destination. On it sat an outpost, a patrol base consisting of a couple of mud huts and two GP tents surrounded by concertina wire and sandbags. It was a healthy hump to the top, burdened as we were with enough beans and bullets to sustain us through anything short of a D-day invasion. The sun bore down on our backs and heads like one of those old heated flatirons Grandma Churchill told me about. We were sweating profusely by the time we arrived.

The team sergeant in charge of the Special Forces team outpost grinned when he saw us. As well he might. We were his relief.

"Welcome to God's Little Acre," he quipped. "Where the living is easy."

"How about the women?" Wright asked.

The sergeant laughed. "See that farm down in the valley? He's got a real pretty female camel."

Guys mostly stripped down to T-shirts were hanging out, some reading, others playing cards or just sitting around chatting. The somnolent buzz of flies vibrated the hot air, but even insects lacked the energy in the heat of the day to take the trouble to bite us.

"How bad is it?" a Ranger asked an old Special Forces hand, who sat up, scratched himself, and yawned.

"Quiet," he said.

"As in *too* quiet?"

"You ain't from around these parts, are ya? I been here two months and I ain't capped a round yet."

Captain Wence posted watch while the rest of us settled in and prepared for combat patrolling. The Special Forces guys had the mud huts; we took the tents.

So this is war? I thought. I once heard it described as "hours and hours of utter boredom followed by sudden stark terror." There didn't appear to be much of the latter in this area of operations.

As dusk arrived in spidery purple shadows, Hunter and I found a couple of sandbags to rest on while we ate MREs and looked down over the valley. Farmer fields in the lowlands occupied a series of steppes. Low rock walls separated the individual plots. I had read that something like 90 percent of Afghanis were rural.

Fires started to sputter in the little town by the dry creek, an indication that the villagers were settling in for a quiet night. I experienced an eerie moment when it occurred to me that we were at last in "Indian Country," something for which I had trained for most of the past year. I imagined us surrounded by radical killers waiting for the opportunity to jump out of the dark and put holes in us. They might be all around us; we just couldn't see them. Like the actors in Hunter's old B-movies liked to say, "The night has a thousand eyes."

Sergeant Smith came by to talk a few minutes. He got up to continue his rounds. "Better sack out," he advised. "I want everybody alert when you go on watch."

Hunter got up and stretched. He gazed out toward the little village and its flickering fires. Everything seemed peaceful. You wouldn't even know there was a war going on.

"Underwhelming," he decided.

9

I expected war to be something other than "hours and hours of utter boredom." What time the platoon wasn't pulling guard inside the wire at the patrol base on the hill or scanning the valley below with binos checking for hostile movement, we patrolled up toward the Pakistani border in GMVs. A Ground Mobility Vehicle was a Hummer (HMMWV or Humvee) modified for use by spec ops. It had an open flat bed, like a pickup truck, into which good ol' boys stashed fuel, ammo, MREs, and other supplies before we left the area on what some of the guys dubbed a "camporee."

Each GMV mounted either a .50 caliber machine gun in the middle of the cargo area or an MK-19 automatic 40 mm grenade launcher. Squads were armed with at least one M-240 7.62 mm machine gun and individual weapons that consisted of a 5.56 mm SAW, M-4 assault rifles, pistols, grenades, and knives. Entire companies during World War II, sometimes even battalions, hadn't been so heavily armed.

Armed for bear—only we couldn't seem to find any bear.

Hunter said we were like *Rat Patrol*. Wright said it was more like *McHale's Navy*. I had no idea what they were talking about, as I hadn't seen either one and from what I understood they had been made before most of us were even born.

Roads that existed were dusty and rubboarded with rocks. Kopp didn't know what a rubboard was. I had to explain that the old folks once used them to get laundry clean before there were washing machines. People here, we discovered, mostly laundered in the nearest stream and beat their clothing clean on some big rock. One day while the platoon was on a mission to clear buildings in a village, which meant we descended upon hapless residents without so much as a "by your leave" and went through their little mud houses searching for weapons and explosives, I was surprised to find an old woman doing laundry using a rubboard in a bucket. I pointed it out to Kopp.

"How do you plug it in?" he asked.

I hadn't known any really poor people back home. In fact, I don't think there were any *really* poor people in the United States compared to people here and elsewhere. Inside their little huts maybe you found some thin grass mattresses or some blankets for beds and some wooden cupboards and homemade tables and chairs. Perhaps brother and sister had a change of clothing and a "Sunday" pair of shoes or sandals; they went barefoot all summer. Out back was a pole corral or fenced field made of sticks and posts in which existed a skinny mule or camel and some sheep or goats. The more well-to-do owned cows. Often, four or five families went together to buy an old rattletrap Toyota pickup for transportation and use on the farms. Because of the shortage of medical facilities, many infants died before they were a year old.

The way of life here probably hadn't changed much in hundreds of years. I found it odd that even though no one owned many possessions, almost everyone owned a cell phone.

Afghanistan is one of the world's least-developed countries. It is completely landlocked, bordered by Pakistan on the east and south, Iran on the west, three former Soviet republics on the north, and China off a little gooseneck in the far northeast. One of our "camporees" took the platoon caravaning up as far as the Chinese border. We stopped and looked across and saw nothing more than we had seen on this side. The patrol was uneventful save for our spotting nomads out on the desert flats with their goats and cattle. *Nomads,* for Pete's sake, in the twenty-first century, some of whom I suspected had never seen an American before.

"Like National Geographic Channel," Kopp observed.

In the villages, little dark-skinned kids in baggy cotton pants waved and waved. Men and women in dirty robes, the men wearing turbans, the women short shawls, looked sullen and resentful. Or perhaps they merely accepted that war and soldiers were how life was. After all, armies of the world had for centuries met at these crossroads to fight.

"That scroungy little kid threw a rock at me! The little bastard tried to hit me," a guy from Third Squad complained indignantly.

"It's because you're so ugly," someone else chided him. "Why didn't you shoot him?"

I assumed occupying the patrol base must have been sort of a shakedown cruise for us, to break us in slowly, because after a few weeks, before boredom became terminal, 1st Platoon packed and linked up with the other platoons of Alpha Company at Asadabad. FOB Wright—our Wright in 1st Platoon claimed it must have been named after him—occupied a valley near the confluence of the Pech and Kunar rivers between two mountain ridgelines running northeast to southwest on both sides of the valley. You could see the river from the FOB. It was a shallow, muddy affair for the most part.

The FOB was small compared to Bagram Airfield, about the size of three football fields surrounded by concertina wire and the ubiquitous HESCO concrete walls. This early in the war, as at Bagram, troops lived in tents with plywood floors. It was hot and it was dusty and there was that smell of Afghanistan in the scorched air. Alpha's three platoons rotated duties. While one platoon pulled guard, the other went out on patrol, and the third stood by as a QRF in case somebody got in trouble. All of us expected some action since the FOB was only a few miles from the Pakistan border. Nawa Pass about 10 miles south was the next border crossing north of Khyber Pass and a major heroin-smuggling and Taliban route.

An OP (observation point) had been established a couple of hundred meters outside the FOB on top of a hill that provided a panoramic view of the entire valley. There was nothing up there except a stone-and-wood shack containing pads to sleep on, a couple of radios on which to make comms with the FOB, and an old rusted DShK (Dushka), a wheeled Soviet heavy machine gun left over from when the Russians were here. As the GMVs could not make it through steep or arduous terrain, the only way to reach the OP was by foot. It was a hell of a hump for the OP watch teams, but well worth the effort. It was pud duty, almost like a holiday. Nothing for a team to do except hang out and chill.

One afternoon as the sun was setting, Nate Brown, Donahue, Kopp, and I were sitting on the ground at the OP looking down in the valley as the night rolled in, as peaceful as an evening on a porch back home with my uncles and aunts. Fires were starting to kindle in the village down by the river across from the FOB.

"All Quiet on the Western Front," Kopp meditated.

I *had* seen that movie.

Kopp said, "I thought it would be different than this. Reckon we'll get our Combat Infantry Badges?"

"You haven't come under fire," I pointed out.

"I'm not sure I want to be shot at."

"You're a Ranger, aren't you?" Donahue asked. "Rangers are supposed to get shot at."

"As long as you're not hit," Brown put in.

I nodded in agreement. "Better to shoot the other guy."

Donahue shook out a cigarette, lit one up, and passed the pack around. "Like Patton said, 'We're not here to die for our country. We're here to make the other poor bastard die for *his* country.'"

We had to be satisfied with packaged MREs in the field. At the FOB we generally enjoyed T rations cooked in the mess tent. Most of them still came freeze-dried or packaged, but they were a step up from Mouth to Rear Elements. The chow hall was out in the open air with a couple of tables and a field mess unit where those unfortunate enough to draw KP helped the cooks with their pots and pans and with ladling out the rations. The army didn't have *chefs*. At least not for the common soldiers. The battalion had a handful of cooks and we were lucky enough to have one with us.

One evening around dinnertime, just before dark, some of us from 1st Platoon were smoking and joking and playing grabass in the chow line. I suddenly heard a strange whistling noise coming at us from out of the darkness. We were all standing there dumbly, looking up like chickens waiting for a diving hawk.

"Incoming!"

The alarm spread by immediate osmosis throughout the camp. *"Incoming!"*

Bunkers for such occasions were located here and there, but there wasn't enough time to reach one. I hit the ground, just like we had trained at BCT. Hit the ground with my face in the dirt and arms wrapped around the back of my head. I was curious, too, so I kept one eye open.

Powdered mashed potatoes, green beans, and mystery meat went everywhere as diners and mess cooks either hit the ground or scattered to find cover. One of the smaller cooks—"smaller cook" was pretty much an oxymoron—ended up inside a large iron pot, although the nearest round thunked in more than 50 meters away. Two or three other explosions walked over the base in bright flashes of light, black smoke, and quick bursts of thunder before the shelling ended as abruptly as it began. No one was injured, the only casualty was a tent that a squad from 2nd Platoon lived in but was empty at the time. One of the guys bitched for a week afterward that the "dirty little cocksuckers" had blown up his Pink Floyd CDs. Fortunately, none of the shells landed on the chow site to really piss us off.

It was the first time under fire for the company's new guys. Well, *sorta* under fire. We began to laugh and joke about it, especially about the cook in the iron pot and *What's for dinner?* We were pumped and ready for something else to happen. Maybe a mass suicide charge or a camel cavalry attack. Hunter said he had seen that in *Lawrence of Arabia*.

Since 1st Platoon was currently QRF, we got all geared up and, accompanied by 2nd Platoon, jumped into GMVs. Bristling with weapons and bad intent, we descended in a cordon and search upon the nearby little village like God's wrath unleashed. Normally at that time of the evening people were outside their little huts gossiping about their neighbors or whatever. Tonight, not a soul was in sight. Even the fires were extinguished.

Troops herded everybody out into the street for interrogation. As far as I could tell from my post at the edge of the village, nobody knew shit. Then again, privates didn't know shit either. We just did what we were told.

Somebody in the village must have finally snitched. We jumped back in our vehicles and scooted over the rickety old bridge to the other side of the river where several caves honeycombed the slope of the mountain. Inside one of them we recovered a cache of mortars, rockets, small arms, and ammunition. A substantial find that indicated *somebody* was preparing for war. Demo men blew the cache in place with an explosion so tremendous it rocked the mountains and opened a fiery portal into the maw of hell.

That ended the excitement. It was a pretty good night's work, even if we didn't find the people all that stuff belonged to. Nobody was hurt, and we destroyed a big arsenal of weapons the bad guys could have used against us. The only crappy outcome was that we wound up eating MREs again for dinner.

Next day, "hours and hours of utter boredom" returned. It was too hot for fishing, too dry to plow, and the Talibs and terrorists were apparently shacked up out of the heat somewhere with all their wives and concubines.

One blazing afternoon on vehicle patrol while we were rolling around in the GMVs wearing our battle-rattle armor and gear, sweating in absolutely brutal terrain, the platoon came across a little creek flowing out of a spring in the side of a hill to form a pool at the bottom. Lieutenant Wence called a halt. Damn, that water looked inviting, what with the desert sun glaring down and nothing around except baked rock, scorching sand, and scorpions.

The PL glassed the terrain and made up his mind. He stood up in his seat. "Anybody for a swim?"

The average age of the platoon was about twenty; boys and a swimming hole went together like, well, ducks and water. Sergeant First Class Reid set up rotating security while the rest of us, whooping with youthful enthusiasm, stampeded toward the water, stripping down to bare skin as we ran. The water was so cold that jumping into it almost stopped our hearts. It was wonderful.

"War ain't so bad after all," Hunter decided.

10

FORT BENNING, 2003

"War ain't so bad after all" fairly well summed up my first deployment with Alpha Company to the front lines of the War on Terror. Nothing went wrong. There were no shots fired other than when Third Squad fired up a couple of armed guys while out on patrol. Other than that fast little encounter, the only contact made was that night when the mortar rounds came in at chow time. It was a good rotation for most of us.

Third Battalion saddled up and returned to Fort Benning. Its troops had gone into the wilderness and returned unscathed. Morale and confidence were at an all-time high, although I felt a bit disappointed. I think every young man at some point harbors the urge to prove himself in battle. Kind of a primordial need. So far, I hadn't proved anything. It even appeared that the heavy fighting was all done and the War on Terror over except for the shouting and the fat lady singing.

Then again, what did privates know?

Things had been heating up on another front while 3rd Batt Rangers were in Afghanistan. It seemed American and British aircraft were bombing the hell out of southern Iraq. Rumor around post was that the bombing was a clear indication that we were trying to destroy the country's air defense systems in anticipation of an all-out attack.

Regiment gave 3rd Battalion Rangers two weeks leave to go home on

R&R and decompress after Afghanistan. I almost decided to stay on post but didn't. It was okay to see the family again, hang out with Erin and Randy and some of my old high school buds. Otherwise, everything was different, things had changed—or perhaps *I* had changed.

Dragging Bristol's main street or sneaking off to the woods with the guys and a case of beer seemed so, well, *juvenile*. Now that I had enlisted in the army and gone to war, such as it was, people at home treated me like a man. I had more confidence, I felt like a man. Randy, seventeen, was going into his senior year and getting into a little trouble. He talked about going into construction. I told him I thought it was a good idea.

"Joe, you really have grown up," he noticed.

I caught up with my high school sweetheart Kristin while I was home. I knew when we saw each other the last time before I left that our paths were diverging. She was attending the University of Connecticut and enjoying her new life. Me, I jumped out of airplanes and played army. Better to leave our paths diverged.

I was ready to return to Fort Benning by the time my leave expired. Back *home* where I belonged.

The battalion jumped right into a new training cycle as soon as it reassembled. Rumors flew all around Benning as the no-fly zone in Iraq continued to heat up. *You guys are going . . . No, no, you're not going . . .* We were getting prepared with lots of NBC (nuclear, biological, and chemical) warfare training. The writing was on the wall. Saddam Hussein supposedly possessed weapons of mass destruction and supported international terrorism.

The warning order came down at the end of the training cycle in February. We had a date: 3rd Batt was deploying to Saudi Arabia within the month to prepare for the invasion of Iraq. This one promised more action than we had seen in Afghanistan.

On a Friday night before the 3rd Battalion's scheduled rotation to Saudi on Sunday, a bunch of soldiers from the platoon and company descended on the soldiers' bar called Coach's Corner for a last hoorah before marching off to war again. My fire team leader, Buck Sergeant Josh Kuhner, was a big thick man in his early twenties with a fleshy nose and the heavy jaw of a linebacker. Not only did he have the looks of a barroom bouncer, he *was* one part-time at Coach's. Some of us weren't old enough to get in legally—I was twenty—but Kuhner got us in, no sweat. Cops rarely bothered with soldiers unless we got drunk and made asses of ourselves.

Coach's Corner was one of those dark dens with smoke, beer fumes, loud honky-tonk music, and lots of testosterone. After a few beers, some of the guys, being horny Rangers, started to hit on a couple of good-looking blond college girls sitting by themselves at a table. I could hardly take my eyes off the one with the dark blond hair and blue eyes. She was absolutely gorgeous—but every time she looked my way I ducked my head over my beer.

Kimberly tells the story best:

I was twenty-two, drinking age, and was driving home from Columbus State University, where I studied communications, when my best friend, Melanie Lymburner, cell-phoned to ask me to meet her at Coach's Corner for a drink. I had never been there before, but it was only two miles from home. I lived with my mom, Elizabeth Smithwick, in Columbus.

Melanie and I were just settling in for a good chat when the floodgates opened and a horde of loud, obnoxious soldiers from the base swept through the doors. I knew little about soldiers, but it didn't take me long to discover that these guys were Army Rangers. A few beers and they were loose enough to parachute-jump off the bar, hustle girls, and pick fights with "legs," their term for nonairborne personnel. Either one by one or in reinforced pairs, they worked their way to our table armed with appalling pickup lines.

"You're an angel. I must have died and gone to heaven."

"There can't be any more like you at home. You're one of a kind."

"I'm a lonely soldier going off to war. You wouldn't begrudge me a last kiss, would you?"

Every soldier at the bar eventually made his way to our table, where Melanie and I shot them down as gently as we could. Only one guy kept his distance, he a lean, sober-looking fella with an Auburn Tigers baseball cap pulled down tight over his almost-shaved head and a shyness that stood out in this crowd like a blush.

"I wonder what's with him?" Melanie observed.

I kept watching him. The quiet type, seemingly out of place, the only guy in the joint I really wanted to talk to, and all he did was cast quick glances in my direction and then look away whenever I attempted to catch his eye.

I was a cheeky Southern girl, more Scarlett O'Hara than Melanie Hamilton, and I finally had to take matters into my own hands. Since the mountain wouldn't come to Kimberly Smithwick, Kimberly Smithwick must go to the mountain. I marched right up to him at the bar and stood shoulder to shoulder next to him. My mom would have considered me awful forward.

"Why is it everyone in this bar has come to talk to us except you?" I asked him bluntly. "All your buddies have hit on us."

He blushed. I swear, he actually blushed.

"I, uh, I guess I'm shy," he muttered, ducking his head and smiling like a little boy.

That did it. This guy was genuine. Joe Kap was his name. We stayed in the bar until it closed at 3:00 A.M., Joe and me, and Melanie and Joe's buddy Griffin Hoover, a slender guy with dark hair and elastic features who liked to talk about riding bicycles. I did most of the talking at first, but Joe began to open up toward the end. I could tell he liked me, that we were hitting it off.

After the bar closed, Melanie and I drove the soldiers to the post to keep them from taking a cab. On the way, we stopped off for breakfast at Denny's. I gave Joe my phone number before he and Hoover got out at their barracks.

"Ummm . . . Can I call you tomorrow?" he asked.

He seemed to be operating pretty fast for a shy guy. What happened to waiting for a couple of days?

I was still in bed the next morning, Saturday, when the telephone rang.

"Kim . . . uh . . . Kim, can we have lunch or something?"

I hesitated. I still had sleep in my eyes.

"It doesn't have to be just the two of us," he added hastily. "Hoover's a nice guy. You reckon your friend Melanie would like to go with us?"

Things were moving a little fast, but . . . Why not?

I hung out with Joe all day, beginning with miniature golf and lunch and ending with dinner and a movie. The movie was *Old School,* a comedy starring Will Ferrell, about three guys in their thirties trying to recapture their college days by starting a fraternity. It was pretty raunchy, with nudity, sex jokes, and the F-word popping off like firecrackers. Joe looked embarrassed, but it was still a funny movie.

Several times during the day, Joe remarked something to the effect that "We're going to be leaving." I had no idea what he was talking about until late that evening before we parted.

"Kim, the battalion is leaving in a few hours for Saudi Arabia," he said. "Can I call you when I get back?"

That was all he told me. Perhaps it was all he *could* tell me. A few days later I saw it on TV. "Shock and Awe" had started. The United States was invading Iraq—and Joe Kap was in the middle of it.

11

The written history of Iraq extends back to before the Old Testament of the Bible, the oral history even further back to the days of Sargon the Empire Builder. During the last five thousand years of hosting empires, of invading and being invaded, Iraq has been conquered more times than practically any other country in the world. For a land that was the birthplace of two "peaceful religions," the "Land Between the Rivers," as it was known through its ancient name, Mesopotamia, suffered almost continuous warfare for most of five millennia. A list of its various rulers and invaders read like a geographical *Who's Who of the World:* Sumeria, Assyria, Persia, Greece, Rome, Mongolia, Turkey, and Britain, among others.

Some of the world's greatest civilizations thrived in this area. Baghdad served as the intellectual center of the Muslim world between the seventh and thirteenth centuries, renowned for its scholars and artists when few people in Europe could even read, much less write.

Many historians and biblical scholars say Iraq, the "Cradle of Civilization," was the approximate location of the Garden of Eden, where mankind began. Although Israel is cited in the Bible more times than any other nation, Iraq runs a close second under such names as Babylon, Mesopotamia, and Shinar. The Euphrates River is mentioned in the Bible more than fifteen times, beginning with Genesis, the first book of the

Old Testament, and on up through Revelation, the last book of the New Testament.

Satan made his first cited appearance in Iraq. Abraham hailed from a city in Iraq, as did Isaac's wife. Jacob spent twenty years in Mesopotamia. The Tower of Babel was erected there. The events in the Book of Esther took place in Iraq. The Euphrates River marks the eastern boundary of the land God promised Abraham. The prophet Muhammad, founder of the Muslim religion, was born 500 miles away in Mecca in what is now Saudi Arabia. By the end of A.D. 638, Muslims had conquered Iraq and all the western provinces in the neighborhood.

According to the Book of Revelation, God warned that the Antichrist would return to a resurrected Babylon to rule over the world. Saddam Hussein was now reportedly undertaking the task of restoring the ancient city.

Nebuchadnezzar II, ruler of Babylon, conquered and destroyed Jerusalem in 586 B.C., carrying away over fifteen thousand captives and sending the rest of the Judean population into exile in Iraq. The Persian Empire seized Iraq under Cyrus the Great in 539 B.C., then gave it up to Alexander the Great in 331 B.C.

Iraq became a satellite of the Roman Empire in A.D. 115 and remained under Roman rule until Arab armies conquered it in 637 and brought it into the Muslim fold. As capital of the first caliphate, Baghdad reigned as a center of learning known for its achievements in the arts and sciences for the next six hundred years, until the Mongols invaded from the east in 1258 and cast the region back into another Dark Ages, a collapse from which it never fully recovered.

Ottoman Turks ran off the Mongols in 1534 and ruled as the Ottoman Empire until 1918, after the Ottomans chose the losing side in World War I by siding with Germany and the Central Powers. The League of Nations divided up the empire at the end of the war and gave Iraq to England to rule under a British mandate.

Iraq was granted independence in 1932, only to again choose the losing side when World War II erupted. Allied forces led by Brits quickly defeated Iraq in May 1941. They occupied it and thereafter used it as a base for attacks against the Nazi-allied Vichy French and Germans in Syria. Under new rule, Iraq dutifully declared war against Hitler in 1943 and in 1945 helped form the Arab League.

Unsuccessful uprisings against the Iraqi government in 1948 and 1952 eventually led to success in 1958. Army officers overthrew the monarchy under King Faisal II and replaced it with a "republic" that was actually a military dictatorship under General Abd al-Karim Qasim. Qasim reversed the country's pro-West stand and began siding with Communist countries.

Coup followed coup until 1968, when the Arab Socialist Ba'ath Party took over. "Ba'ath" means "resurrection" or "renaissance." The goal of the Ba'ath Party was to "resurrect" the glory of the Arab nations that had been destroyed by Ottoman and Western imperialism by unifying all Arab countries against the West.

In 1979, General Saddam Hussein, a Ba'ath leader, assumed the offices of both president and chairman of the Revolutionary Command Council. That made him Iraq's sole ruler, a dictator so ruthless that he had murdered an estimated three hundred thousand of his own people so far.

War and strife continued its pattern of violence in the region throughout the twentieth century and into the twenty-first. Some people say that of the more than one hundred shooting wars raging at any one time on the globe, only two or three do not involve Muslims. The Iran-Iraq War of 1980–88, between rival Muslim countries, was at the time the longest conventional war of the twentieth century.

In 1990, two years after his truce with Iran, Saddam invaded Kuwait. The Gulf War of 1991, Operation Desert Storm, ensued when he refused to comply with United Nations demands to withdraw. As many as one hundred thousand Iraqi soldiers died before one of the shortest conventional wars of the twentieth century ended with Kuwait freed and an uneasy truce established between Iraq and the UN.

The region heated up again after the 9/11 terrorist attacks against the United States. American foreign policy began calling for the removal of Saddam Hussein and the Ba'ath Party, accusing Iraq of producing weapons of mass destruction, harboring and supporting terrorists, and repeatedly violating UN Security Council resolutions to disarm. On November 8, 2002, the Security Council offered Hussein "a final opportunity to comply with disarmament obligations" and threatened "serious consequences" if he failed to comply.

On March 20, 2003, the United States and Britain, with military assistance from a number of other Coalition countries, joined the list of empires and nations that had, over thousands of years, invaded the Cradle of Civilization, the land of Adam and Eve.

The 75th Ranger Regiment was being handed a piece of the action. Its units began air landing at Prince Sultan Air Base in Al Kharj, Saudi Arabia, to prepare for jump-off into combat.

12

IRAQ 2003

While Alpha Company Rangers cooled our heels at Prince Sultan, it began to seem that we were going to *watch* the war, not fight it. I was as restless as the other men as we hung out in a tent and watched Fox News and
CNN on satellite TV. We were stoked, edged, and ready to kick ass, yet all
that happened was that we sweated our asses off. And we waited. And we
competed in squad competitions to include lunge races, a kind of exercise
in which one squats and repeatedly leaps like a frog for maybe a quarter
mile or so, undoubtedly a torture devised by the platoon leadership to try
to keep us occupied.

"Invasion of the Killer Frogs," Hunter commented sarcastically.

Captain Wence was still PL, and Sergeant First Class Ray Reid was
still the platoon sergeant. Big Jeffrey Rembold had replaced Staff Sergeant
Smith as squad leader for the platoon's First Squad after Alpha Company
returned from Afghanistan. Ben Hunter's younger brother Ian completed
RIP toward the end of our last training cycle. He transferred into Alpha in
time for battle deployment to Iraq, a rather insignificant event to the unit
but a big deal to Ben to have his brother with him. Ian was detailed to
Weapons Squad in 1st Platoon while Ben and I were in First Squad.

Ian was a younger, lighter version of Ben, tall, the same build, with
that inherited crooked, wise-ass grin and a sunny nature to go with it. He

and Ben were one of the few sets of brothers that I knew of in the Rangers. They were tough Alabama boys from Birmingham.

Ian viewed his assignment to a different squad as a mercy role. "They wanted to put me in another squad so I wouldn't be showing up you old-timers," he chortled.

Most of the other ground outfits departed the base when the invasion began, leaving mostly air support and security behind on the 80-square-mile American enclave of the Royal Saudi Air Force Base. Stripped down to skivvies and boots, skivvies and a cap, or shirt and boots, we cheered as our guys on TV as they raced through Iraq like green grass through a goose. It was like the biggest Super Bowl of all time.

The game had kicked off at 0534 hours on March 20 with the heavy armor of the U.S. 3rd Infantry Division moving west and then north through the desert toward Baghdad. The U.S. 1st Marines fought through Nasiriyah to seize Tallil Airfield and the major road junction there. The 3rd Infantry beat hell out of Iraqi forces entrenched around the airfield, bypassed the city, and with the support of the 101st Airborne Division hightailed it north toward Najaf and Karbala. By the end of the first week, Karbala Gap was secure, as were bridges over the Euphrates River. American forces were passing through the gap, a key approach to Baghdad. At the same time, the 1st Marines fought their way onto the eastern edge of Baghdad and prepared to enter the city.

Ol' Saddam had to be getting nervous in the service.

And the Killer Frogs waited.

What distinguished Rangers from the milling herd was our willingness to take chances and risks. Rangers attracted the army's largest collection of adventurous men with supreme faith in our ability to take on the odds and win. Guys like me came from everywhere in the United States—tough guys from city slums, good ol' farm boys, spoiled rich kids (not many), big-city dudes, kids like me from small-town America . . . all ready to jump into the fray.

And the Killer Frogs waited.

Even the name Prince Sultan Air Base conjured up images of heat, sand, dust, scorpions, and snakes. It was said you weren't exactly in hell, but you could feel hell from there. Ten to twenty knots of wind blowing almost constantly across the sand made 115 degrees feel like you were in a big hair dryer. Scorpions and nasty camel spiders were always seeking shade in the tents. You never put on your boots without shaking them out.

Living conditions elsewhere on post weren't that bad. There were even air-conditioned rooms, showers, a gym, and a base theater—but not for the Rangers. We had been promised a combat parachute jump, but it never seemed to happen. A warning order would come down, only to be canceled. Rangers weren't much on spectator sports; we were players.

Sore from lunges and a little put out at missing all the action, we had even got tired of talking about women and ribbing a couple of guys who, at least by their accounts, got more ass than a merry-go-round pony. Language kept getting rougher, more irreverent, and more obscene the testier we got.

"Eat me, monkey meat."

"Spread your cheeks. We're about to get the green weenie again."

"Damn! When did you take a shower, numbnuts? Last August?"

All the Ranger combat jumps so far had been made in Afghanistan. Two of them had been in 2001—at Helmand Desert in October and near Alimarden Kan-E-Bagat in November. A third jump went down just last month in February at Chahar Borjak. Meanwhile Alpha Company sat around on our asses and did frog jumps. We had been promised the first combat jump in Iraq—but that combat star on our jump wings seemed to elude us.

Charlie Company 3/75, not Alpha, made the first jump in Iraq on the night of March 24 when it parachuted in to secure H-2 Airfield in the northwestern desert near the town of Al Qaim on the Syrian border. We learned about it the next morning on Fox News. *Fox* knew about it before we did. We were really pissed.

Jermaine Wilson, my squad's sole black guy, sprang to his feet and hurled a plastic water bottle at the TV. Squad leader Jeff Rembold stalked out of the tent muttering to himself.

"We got good losers and bad losers," Wright groused, "and then there are downright fucked losers like us."

That observation inspired a quartet to chant the refrain from the old Mickey Mouse Club theme song, altered for the occasion: *"F-U-C-K-E-D A-G-A-I-N. Boys and girls, can you say 'fucked again'?"*

"We'll get our chance," Platoon Sergeant Ray Reid promised, but the expression of perpetual skepticism he wore was less than reassuring. "I got a feeling this is going to be a long war."

"Kee-rist, Sar'ent! We're almost in Baghdad already."

The *second* combat jump in Iraq wasn't ours either. That was also on Fox News. A thousand paratroopers from the 173rd Airborne, "the Herd," landed in the dark on March 26 near Bashur to secure Harir Airfield. It was the biggest combat jump the army had made since the invasion of Panama and the first real wartime drop in thirty-five years.

Where the hell was *our* airfield?

13

Squad leaders and fire team leaders returned to the tents after the morning meeting on March 28. Something was coming down; you could tell from the expression on the faces of Staff Sergeant Rembold and Buck Sergeant Josh Kuhner, my fire team leader. They were all business.

"This is your warning order," Sergeant Rembold announced. "Make sure your weapons are clean and you got all your shit in one ruck. Team leaders, go over the equipment checklist with your people."

"Is it a jump, Sar'ent?"

"You'll get the op order."

It *was* a jump. It just had to be. If it didn't get canceled again. Joes in the company started to get excited and a little quieter when the company officers were summoned to the Tactical Operations Center. We knew it was the real thing when Captain Wence returned to the platoon. He looked pale, and his lips were compressed like they had been glued. He took a long breath and looked us over one by one.

"It's a go, people. You've always said you were tough. We're about to find out."

The PL assembled 1st Platoon in the operations tent and spread a map on a tripod. Alpha Company's mission—"Whether we choose to accept it or not," Hunter cracked—was to parachute onto H-1 Airfield in western Iraq near the Haditha Dam and seize and hold it as a launching pad for further allied operations. Takeoff time: 1835 hours *tonight*.

You could almost hear Adam's apples bobbing.

Captain Wence produced a blow-up intel photo of the airfield showing buildings, hangars, and airstrip, all of which were enclosed in a 10-foot-tall chain-link fence. Using a pen, he designated the platoon assembly area once we hit the ground.

"Our task," he said, "is to cut through this fence—*here*—where we will clear and hold these buildings—*here*."

Somebody asked the big question: *What about enemy resistance?*

"It's a combat jump," the PL replied. "Expect anything."

He turned the platoon over to Sergeant First Class Reid.

"It's assholes and elbows time, people," the platoon sergeant said. "We don't want to miss our flight."

Alpha's sector of the airbase crackled with excitement. Forgotten were the long boring days of the past week. Tough young men bustled about packing stuff, loading rucks, issuing ammo, drawing parachutes, conducting precombat inspections . . . You couldn't let the other guys know about the knots in your stomach, so you concealed your jitters with bluster and wisecracks. The nearer we got to H-hour, the quieter everyone became, as though in recognition that we were about to receive what we had hoped for. What was that old axiom? *Be careful what you wish for* . . .

Some of the guys paced and chain-smoked. I came upon Hunter sitting on his cot writing a letter, all his gear nearby ready to go. That mischievous grin he generally wore had disappeared. He finished his letter, sealed it, and stuck it into a breast cargo pocket.

"Kap?"

I knew what he was going to say and didn't want to hear it. This was that part in the war movie where the guy asked his buddy to deliver the letter if he didn't make it. In the movies, he never made it.

"It's to Lori," he said, and I nodded.

I hadn't felt the need to contact home.

My nerves were surprisingly settled as the sun arced west toward 1835 hours. I always liked to watch the activity on base. I stood outside in the lowering sun, with still an hour or so to go before last muster, and watched fighter aircraft zipping off the 15,000-foot, parking-lotlike landing strip. B-17s and C-130 gunships roared in and out. Chinook and Apache and Black Hawk helicopters hovered before kicking in their power and lift, noses down as they boogied to war. The airbase with its modern concrete hangars and towers and support buildings and its bustling tent ghetto suburbs was a major launching site for a variety of outfits, including Rangers, SEALs, Green Berets, armor, infantry, and marines. It was an awesome experience to watch America go to war.

I thought about the blonde I met at Coach's Corner the day before 3rd Batt deployed. I considered calling her or maybe dropping her a note—but I couldn't. I had cut all ties with my high school girlfriend Kristin when I enlisted in the army and left Connecticut. That was the kindest thing a soldier could do for a woman when he knew he would eventually go to war. What applied to Kristin then applied to Kimberly now. Or to any other woman I met, for that matter. What kind of an asshole would I be to get romantically involved and then get killed? Worse yet, what if I were maimed or screwed up physically? How fair would that be to a girl waiting at home if I went away a man and came back a vegetable?

I vowed to forget all about her. Forget about everything except tonight's operation.

Saddam Hussein, we learned, had the capability to use chemical, biological, or radioactive agents through Scud missiles or artillery. Therefore, we were jumping garbed in padded MOPP-4 (Mission Oriented Protective Posture) moon-man suits that were heavy, hot, and restrictive. My job in the squad was the SAW, which meant I also had to load myself down with ammunition for it. My ruck weighed 115 pounds. Some of the bulkier guys like Kuhner and Rembold had to download some gear in order to meet aircraft weight and balance tables.

With such a load, it was excruciatingly painful just to walk from the hangar to the C-17 and climb aboard. We resembled spacemen on our way to Mars. The sun was setting as my stick on the outboard side buckled in. Everything I saw outside through the airplane's lowered tail ramp assumed a reddish tint. We packed into the bird so close in the canvas seating that our knees meshed with the knees of the guys across from us. We sat with our rucks in our laps. It was hot and stuffy, and my legs fell asleep. Some guy would move to try to get comfortable, and then everybody had to move.

Our bellies began to tickle from that old familiar feeling of mounting tension. Hardly anyone spoke, not only because we had said everything that needed saying but also because you had to shout to be heard above the warm-up roar of engines. Military aircraft had few of the amenities available on commercial aircraft.

The ramp lifted, sealing more than one hundred paratroopers inside the two aircraft. The planes began moving. They picked up speed, engines turning, and then we were in the air. I assumed fighter jets were escorting us. The darkening desert passed smoothly beneath the plane, a vast near-wasteland spotted with Arab villages, camels, goats, horses, cattle, wheat fields, and death lurking like a mugger.

Men rustled in their parachutes as they broke open packs of chewing tobacco or gum. It got dark. Interior lights remained off. Down by the door glowed red lights that would turn green when it came time to jump. The monotonously thrumming engines lulled some to sleep—or they pretended to sleep. Most of us hunkered into ourselves and sat brooding and trying not to think about antiaircraft fire, surface-to-air missiles, or MiGs as we awaited word to exit. Three hours to go on a one-way ticket.

All I wanted was to get out of this flying tin can.

After what seemed an eternity, the C-17s plunged toward earth in a wild death spiral to discourage enemy AAA (antiaircraft artillery), circling tightly on the way down as they dropped from 30,000 feet to a jump level of about 700 feet. You didn't need a reserve parachute at that level. It wouldn't have time to open anyhow if your main malfunctioned. I heard someone getting airsick and chucking into a barf bag.

Nerves vibrated like plucked violin strings when the aircraft leveled off and the order to "Stand up!" was issued. Sergeant Kuhner stuck out a hand to help me to my feet on the moving platform. I reached and pulled Ben Hunter up. Ian Hunter with Weapons Squad waved and grinned at us. The lights by the doors still glowed red. Reeling under the weight of parachutes and battle equipment, we hung on to the jump cable to keep our balance, pulling it down to chest level instead of where it was supposed to be above our heads.

"Hook up!"

Adrenaline pumped when the doors opened into blackness and fresh air entered.

"Sound off for equipment check!"

"Okay . . ."

"Okay . . ."

And so forth all the way back toward the doors now open for the exit. We were in such physical pain that all anyone wanted was to get out that door and to hell with anybody waiting on the ground.

The jumpmaster hung into the slipstream to check for the drop zone. The night was so black I wondered how he saw anything. I hoped the pilots were good navigators.

"Stand by!"

Green lights flashed on with terrible presence. First into the air out of the planes would be 2nd Platoon, followed by 1st Platoon, with 3rd Platoon and Headquarters Company bringing up the rear, the jumps staggered from both doors of each C-17 in order to place the respective elements on the ground in a position to accomplish their assigned objectives.

"Go!"

The airplanes dumped each platoon in almost a single swift movement, boots stamping on the metal deck, static lines banging against the sides of the plane as they jerked loose from parachute packs. I soared into space with 1st Platoon. It was so dark that I only knew I was out because I felt myself falling. The 'chute opened with a *pop,* as though gripped in a giant fist that swung me back up into the sky. I dangled in total darkness and in silence so complete that I might have been drifting in a vacuum of sight and sound. I saw none of the other 'chutes, heard only the faint sussurating whisper of their presence around me.

My stomach muscles tightened against ground fire that I expected must surely receive us when we hit the ground.

14

Floating down like a giant mushroom, I hit the ground hard enough to jar my Kevlar plates. I rolled once on the sand and started to spring up, only to find myself entangled in parachute shroud lines. I fought clear and ripped my SAW free from where I had tethered it to my equipment. I crouched in the dark to listen, half expecting bad guys to pounce on me out of the blackest night I had ever experienced. Every little whisper of sound—wind in the sparse shrubbery, the rustle of some rodent—sent me whirling about with my finger on the trigger. For all I could tell I might have been the only living human being dumped into the wastes of deepest, darkest space. Talk about feeling *alone.*

I readjusted my NODs. There was no moon, but desert stars gave sufficient ambient light for the things to work. I hunkered down at the ready in a depression in the ground that provided some cover and looked around to catch my bearings. At first I saw nothing through the NODs other than the nearest liquid outline of some pitiful-looking tree about 3 feet tall with a few leaves stuck to the top.

I thought of how alone SEAL Neil Roberts must have felt abandoned on top of Thakur Ghar with al Qaeda closing in on him.

After a few minutes, I heard rustling sounds coming from the desert, which I assumed, which I *hoped,* were my guys rolling up their 'chutes and gearing up for a fight. A shape appeared in the scrawny trees, through NODs resembling in his bulky MOPP gear the greenish ghost of a spaceman. No self-respecting Iraqi Republican Guard would be garbed out like that.

"Kap, that you, man?" Jermaine Wilson stage whispered.

"Shut up. I'm over here."

We huddled together. I was still dragging my parachute. I hit the quick release and dropped the harness to the ground. Several more spacemen slowly emerged from the dark to join us. Wright was one of them. Kopp, Hoover, and a private from Weapons Squad struggled over wearing their NODs. The platoon seemed to have landed tight, not too shabby for a jump like this in the dark, into strange country.

The squad leader arrived next. No mistaking the formidable figure of Sergeant Rembold, even in the dark. He came up limping painfully. He was pissed and cussing up a storm, having broken his ankle on the jump. He collapsed on the ground and was cinching a first aid cravat around his foot, boot and all, when Reid and Captain Wence brought in some more of the platoon, the Hunters among them. I tapped Ben on the shoulder with my fist, glad to see him. He grinned tightly.

"I don't think we're in Kansas anymore, Toto," he cracked.

This part of the platoon set up a quick defensive perimeter while the platoon sergeant set up a choke point to guide the rest of the men into the designated assembly area. Guys started to trickle in by two- and three-man buddy teams. Except for the NODs we would have had men wandering around out there in the dark all night—like the clusterfuck that the 82nd and 101st experienced when they jumped into Normandy in the predawn of D-day.

A couple of other men had broken bones or bad sprains. With the head count up, the platoon sergeant secured the jump casualties for medevac while the rest of the platoon slipped toward the fence that enclosed the airbase. So far, there had been not a single rifle shot. Apparently, 2nd and 3rd platoons landed under similar circumstances. It seemed the airfield might be deserted.

Sgt. Joseph Kapacziewski and Charles W. Sasser

Either that—or it was a trap waiting to be sprung.

Cautiously, ready for contact, anticipating it, the squads overwatched each other as each crawled through a hole in the fence and approached a cluster of small mud-brick buildings that constituted 1st Platoon's only objective for the mission. It was cool, almost cold out on the desert at night, but I was perspiring heavily underneath my MOPP and combat gear.

Not a sound escaped from the buildings. No lights, no nothing. It was almost like a ghost town. There were rows of buildings with multiple rooms in each building. We took them one at a time, stacking up and kicking in doors, rushing in with NODs at full power and red-dot lasers jumping all over the rooms, seeking a target. A rat ran out of one of the buildings. In another, a snake lay coiled in the middle of the floor. Sergeant Kuhner stomped its head.

The buildings appeared to have been office space, some kind of minor headquarters, along with several barracks. They hadn't been used in quite some time, judging from the patina of dust on the desks and chairs left behind. Anything of intelligence value had been packed up and evacuated with the previous occupants of the airfield. We learned later that the only thing in the hangars was a MiG that had been scavenged for spare parts.

H-1 Airfield was firmly in U.S. hands within a few hours after we landed. So much for a "combat" jump. Squads took over the buildings in our sector and waited for daybreak to reveal our easily acquired prize.

"They knew the Rangers were coming," Wright opined, "and decided they'd better haul ass."

The sun rose to reveal the airfield flat and literally in the middle of nowhere. Dry brown hills rose on all horizons with no signs of habitation. A shout would have had to travel a long distance to find an echo. Alpha began establishing a defensive perimeter in anticipation of receiving additional troops and equipment. Josh Kuhner, the bouncer from Coach's

Corner and my fire team leader, put his five men to digging fighting positions outside the wire behind what we considered *our* houses.

"Kee-rist!" Jermaine Wilson protested. "They ain't coming back. They didn't want this place the first time. Why would they want it now?"

"You know how people are," Sergeant Kuhner said. "They might want it back if they see we got it."

I was disappointed. Rangers kicked ass; we didn't dig holes like a bunch of rodents. Ben Hunter and I teamed up. Our foxhole was almost knee deep. He stood up and stretched a kink out of his back and wiped sweat. His shirt and Kevlar lay on the ground nearby next to mine. Our weapons were propped against the helmets out of the sand. Together we gazed out across the heated desert with its scrubby gray-green growth toward the brown roll of distant hills. Nothing moved out there.

"Kap, you realize this is the second war we been to?" Hunter mused. "We get more action playing dominoes."

"Underwhelming," I said. He chuckled.

Josh Kuhner sauntered up.

"I was going to ask you, Kap," he said. "How'd you make out with the good-looking blonde that night at the bar?"

"She's back there," I replied. "I'm over here."

C-17s began airlifting heavy equipment into H-1—GMVs, mortars and artillery, pallets of ammo, chow and water, even a bulldozer . . . An army on the move required a lot of supplies. While all this was going on, Alpha Company baked in our new holes during the day and, since we had jumped in without comfort items, froze our asses off when the sun went down. A few of us slipped out onto the drop zone where we had discarded our parachutes and cut up some of the canopies to fashion sleeping bags out of. The company XO riding his little Gator vehicle came around the next morning and raised hell about it.

"Those parachutes will come out of your paychecks," he threatened.

This was *war*. War was *hell*. Things got messed up in war.

The platoon hid in our holes on perimeter security and watched

Bravo Company 3/75 airlift in and establish an assembly area to plan for an operation. We learned, with some jealousy, that Bravo had a fighting mission coming up. Its task was to caravan to Haditha Dam and secure it before the hajjis blew it and flooded southern Iraq, creating a huge humanitarian crisis and major problems for the 3rd Infantry Division's march north into Baghdad.

We watched and bitched and froze our asses off at night and baked them off during the day. We swatted at flies, organized scorpion races, played "rock ball" with an old ax handle for a bat and a round rock wrapped in 100 mph tape for a baseball. We watched the war go by while Bravo prepared to go out and fight the war.

15

Bravo 3/75 breezed in and out of H-1, pausing only long enough to get off the plane, check out their prearrived vehicles, load up, and move 'em out. Members of Alpha Company, still in the process of digging in, watched with a mixture of resentment and envy as the column of GMVs pulled out through the airfield perimeter into the sunset of Saturday, March 29. It was the ninth day of the ground war. The heavily armed company soon disappeared into the twilight wastelands, leaving Alpha behind to sweat in the sun and watch buzzards soar.

"Into the sunset—just like the Lone Ranger," Hunter noted.

Accounts of the fight at Haditha Dam filtered back to the airfield as the battle unfolded day by day, but we only learned the full skinny of what went down when Alpha platoons began running resupply missions to Haditha a week later.

The earth-filled dam closed off a stretch of the Euphrates River about 150 miles northwest of Baghdad, near the farming town of Haditha. It stretched 5.6 miles across the river and rose 187 feet, collecting Lake Qadisiyah behind it to generate hydroelectricity and provide irrigation water. Bravo Company knew in advance this was going to be a fight. Army intel reported the dam heavily guarded by at least two hundred Iraqi soldiers equipped with armored vehicles, T-55 battle tanks, and more than fifty AAA, mortar, and artillery pieces.

Against this formidable force rode Bravo Company, supplemented by a platoon from Charlie, a little more than 250 soldiers lightly armed in comparison to the tanks and artillery that awaited them at the dam. Army planners were concerned the Iraqis might blow the dam and lay waste by flooding the farms, villages, and towns downstream, while blocking the approach to Baghdad from that quadrant. Objective Lynx—the dam—had to be taken before that occurred.

Traveling under the cover of darkness, the Ranger task force reached its daytime rest site in a wadi less than 20 miles from its objective just as the sun came up on Sunday. The company CO and platoon leaders smoothed out the operation plan, conducted rehearsals, and let the men sleep. The desert-camouflaged convoy pulled out at sunset on the final leg of its journey, speeding determinedly toward the dam using blackout lights.

Due to darkness and the necessity for light and noise discipline, the entire element actually drove one-third of the way across the dam before someone realized it and called the movement to a halt. Even the best-laid plans on paper often go to pieces in the fog of reality. So far, the Rangers had received no resistance; it was almost as if the dam, like H-1 Airfield, were abandoned.

Charlie Company's platoon and Bravo's 2nd Platoon missed the turn that would have led them to the main power facility at the base of the dam, their immediate objective. They broke off from the main body and reversed course to locate an alternate route.

At the same time, the commander detailed 1st Platoon in the opposite direction to establish security with an M-240 machine-gun team off on a side road that ran up a small hill alongside the lake. Twelve large concrete buildings on top of the hill overlooking both the lake and the upper dam appeared deserted until the platoon surprised two civilian guards apparently taking a nap. The guards immediately surrendered.

The platoon set up its machine gun in the first building as security, while it moved to clear the rest of the buildings. The Rangers were more than halfway through the process when they received their first indication that they were not alone after all. From below-dam at the main power facility erupted a quick sharp exchange of small-arms fire, topped by a burst from a heavy-chugging .50 cal machine gun. That ended the engagement.

The enemy security element occupying the power facility fled downstream; Bravo's two platoons secured the powerhouse and established a hasty defense. Everything turned quiet again. Frogs and insects filled the darkness with their peaceful chirping.

Having taken the dozen concrete buildings on the hill, 1st Platoon Rangers moved in the night across a narrow open paddock toward a billboard displaying a huge mural of Saddam Hussein. The paddock dropped off toward the desert on the other side of the billboard. That was when everything suddenly went crazy.

Darkness at the far crest of the hill split open with the muzzle flashes of rifles and machine guns. Rockets exploded amid the Rangers in quick white blasts of light. Farther out, 82 mm mortars began chunking high explosives at the Americans. Apparently, Iraqi soldiers had seen what was about to happen and pulled back from the top of the hill in favor of more-survivable positions at its base. Now they were returning with bad intent.

Rangers called up GMVs mounted with 240s, .50 cals, and MK-19 40 mm grenade launchers that provided higher platforms for firing downslope over the top of the hill. Tactical air support fired a Javelin missile at a mortar site on a small island out on the lake, then followed up with a pair of 1,000-pound bombs. The island went silent again except for the crackle of fires ignited by the explosions.

The enemy attempted a couple of halfhearted counterattacks before sunrise but were readily beaten back to lick their wounds. As daylight seeped into the world to replace the Rangers' first night on the dam, they were stunned to discover interconnecting trench lines and bunkers carving the open desert from a few hundred meters away all the way to the horizon. It seemed the Iraqis may have intended to defend the dam in force, but, for some mysterious reason, there seemed to be little movement out there in the earthworks.

Below the dam at the power station, Charlie Company's 3rd Platoon sent a patrol of several GMVs to investigate two isolated reinforced concrete buildings set out on the flats back from the river. As the patrol approached the structures, fire from heavy machine guns opened up, sending the Rangers to cover. They radioed for air support. F-16 fast movers thundered in over the top of the dam, swooped down, and dumped their loads directly on the buildings, creating a spectacular display of smoke, sound, and fury for 1st Platoon spectators on top of the hill. They cheered as the F-16s waggled their wings in a flyover and returned to base to rearm.

The bombing appeared to accomplish the goal. After a few minutes, a GMV occupied by four Americans drove toward the smoking buildings to conduct a battle damage assessment. Watching from the hilltop, 1st Platoon saw a Ranger get out of the truck and start toward the first of the two buildings.

"Bad move," someone muttered just as small-arms fire from the building engulfed the Ranger and the halted GMV. The man on the ground wheeled and jumped a running mount on the vehicle. It dug out and left a contrail of dust in a lap around the end of the dam that would have qualified for the Indy 500.

Riddled with bullets, the truck lost momentum as, barely chugging along, it climbed the hill to 1st Platoon's position. Smoke billowed from the engine. The transmission left a trail of fluid on the road. Medics and Rangers ran out to take care of casualties and push the truck the rest of the way up the hill before it deadlined.

One of the Rangers in the backseat had taken four rounds in his Kevlar armor plate, which saved his life. The driver was hit in the right foot when a bullet pierced the side plate. The other two Rangers escaped unscathed except that, as one of them put it, "I might have ruined a good pair of skivvies."

Rangers claimed total control of the dam complex by the end of the first day, having captured twenty-five civilian dam workers and nine soldiers after a brief but sharp firefight. Two of the prisoners died; one had had his lower jaw blown off by a .50 cal. Two halfhearted attempts by the Iraqis to assault the dam proper ended badly for them.

For the next two days, Bravo Company consolidated positions to hold the dam and prevent attempts to sabotage it. The hill with its overarching view of the dam, the surrounding terrain, and all roads leading in and out proved to be the key to the entire defensive system. Rangers of 1st Platoon sandbagged in 120 mm and 81 mm mortar positions while Bravo's CO augmented the platoon's strength with squads drawn from 2nd and 3rd platoons. Their orders were to hold it at all costs.

One night, an enemy assault element approached past the Saddam billboard with weapons slung over their shoulders as though they intended to simply walk right up on the Rangers. Obviously, they knew nothing about NODs or thermal imagers. The Rangers sliced them down like ripe wheat.

They were more circumspect the following night. A group of more than fifty rushed the hill with weapons blazing. Rangers threw them back, inflicting heavy casualties.

On Wednesday morning, 1st Platoon spotted a kayaker on the lake paddling hell-bent for the small island that had been bombed the first night as an enemy mortar site. A warning shot across the bow failed to stop the guy. Since he had clearly been sent to gather intelligence on Ranger positions, the platoon leader ordered his .50 cal gunner to engage and sink the little boat.

The heavy machine gun splintered the kayak. Frightened and slightly injured, the Iraqi surfaced, spitting water, and swam to the nearest shore, where a Ranger fire team secured him. In his possession were a number of sketches of Ranger defensive positions.

Direct attacks against the dam ended. Iraqi infantry was observed loading into twenty or thirty vehicles, mostly pickup trucks and the like, and fleeing south toward Haditha City. Mortars, batteries of 155 mm artillery, and tanks with big guns replaced them.

Three high-explosive rounds impacted either on the hill or against the dam on Thursday. On Friday, more than four hundred artillery shells in strings rained down on Ranger battle points. One struck a 120 mm mortar pit behind a concrete wall next to one of the buildings on the hill. The concussion hurled a Ranger into the air and over the wall.

The platoon sergeant, a medic, and another Ranger raced to his aid in a GMV. Leaving the vehicle behind the building, they dismounted and hugged the wall as they made their way to the wounded Ranger. He lay on the ground unconscious and severely injured. Enemy artillery zeroed in and added to the drama by walking rounds toward the rescuers like exploding footsteps.

Under fire, the medic promptly stabilized the wounded man before the Rangers loaded their buddy in the GMV and sped toward a casualty collection point located on the road near the center of the dam. Enemy artillery and tank fire continued to pound the hill, scoring a near-direct hit on a vehicle parked in a dugout. Overpressure from the round bounced the truck 2 feet off its base and blew the weapons squad leader, a heavy gunner, and an air force forward observer over *that* wall. They were uninjured other than being shaken up and a little hard of hearing for the next few days.

Fast movers and Apache helicopters with Hellfire missiles enjoyed a busy day as they swept for artillery pieces, tanks, boats, and any other movement on the terrain above and below the dam. Things began to settle down. Only a few rounds came in on Sunday, April 6. The fight for Haditha Dam was over.

Resupply missions from Alpha Company and H-1 Airfield began arriving. A platoon of M-1 A1 Abrams tanks passed safely across the dam toward continued operations in the north.

During that single intense week, Bravo Company, using direct arms fire, mortars, and various aerial platforms, killed or captured more than 230 enemy soldiers, 29 Russian-made T-55 tanks, 3 heavy cargo trucks, 2 motorcycles, 14 AAA and 28 155 mm artillery pieces, 17 82 mm and 60 mm mortar tubes, 8 ammo caches, 10 military boats—and a kayak.

Back at H-1 Airfield, I scored a home run at "rock ball."

16

Bravo Company required resupply after the fight at Haditha Dam was over and won. Alpha got tapped for the job. The long, desolate route to the dam was fraught with peril; there were no friendlies between H-1 Airfield and the dam. Convoys were ambushed on nearly every run, usually by a mortar round or two or by hajjis hiding in a wadi or behind a hill with a couple of AK-47s to get in a little sport before heading for the hills. So far, we had managed to fight our way through with no serious casualties— but activity seemed to be picking up out in the wastelands. At least Alpha Company was finally getting in on some of the action, sporadic and piecemeal though it might be.

H-1 served as a kind of St. Louis, which in the days of the pioneers was the gateway for settlers heading west. Aircraft delivered provisions to the airfield, where one of the Alpha Company platoons took over to complete the transport to Bravo Company. Columns of GMVs bristling with weaponry and loaded with chow, water, and ammo lined up in marching order at the perimeter gates waiting for the signal.

The sun rose over the horizon on our left flank, like the angry red eye of some giant Cyclops. The leafless desert stretched out to near-forever in all directions, those low, brown, threatening hills rising off in the distance, beyond them here and there rugged mesas and ridgelines. Geronimo would have appreciated this country. All it lacked was smoke signals drifting in the hot air, a band of redskins riding spotted ponies on the horizon, and John Wayne.

The PL and his platoon sergeant, E-7 Ray Reid, stalked up and down the convoy, Captain Wence looking young and self-important, Reid wearing his usual cynic's scowl beneath his helmet. Today was 1st Platoon's show.

"Oscar Mike in three minutes," Reid called out. Translation: on the move in three minutes.

Beneath big Sergeant Josh Kuhner's earlobes, his jaw bunched and relaxed, bunched and relaxed. It was like watching his heart beat in the sides of his face. He had taken over as leader of First Squad after Staff Sergeant Rembold medevaced out with his broken ankle.

"Mount up!"

Cigarettes were stubbed out, gear rechecked quickly. Men climbed aboard their vehicles. Kuhner's First Squad had the last two trucks in the convoy. Ben Hunter was driver on my GMV. He slipped behind the wheel and sat there grinning and seat-bopping to the sound of music in his head. I clambered into the open cargo bay behind him with my SAW and made a place to sit among piled boxes containing MREs, water, and ammunition. Kurt, the machine gunner, checked the action of the mounted .50 cal machine gun and made a place for himself next to the pintle. Kuhner strode up and shook his head at us with dry humor.

"You can dress 'em up but you can't take 'em out," he said. "Stay alert. They're out there."

The PL stood up on the fender of our vehicle and waved like an Old West wagonmaster before slipping into the front seat of the vehicle with Kuhner and Hunter. Griffin Hoover, Kurt, and I settled into the truck bed.

The convoy rumbled through the gate and stretched out at safe intervals across the burning desert in the direction of Haditha. The wagon train was on its way. Hunter wondered aloud if "Apaches" might not be watching.

About midmorning we approached a pair of mud-brick buildings on the outskirts of a village with an unpronounceable name through which the unpaved road twined, one of the few examples of civilization along the route. At the tail end, my truck, Rico 4, was about a quarter mile back from the point vehicle.

I heard the spiteful sputter of machine-gun fire from the buildings, followed by the *splat-splat* of bullets slapping sand around the convoy. Indian attack! This was my first time under actual hostile direct fire; my impulse was to jump out of my truck and unleash the SAW. Except my vehicle was too far back and out of range of weapons less than a 240 or .50 caliber.

My first firefight and I was effectively out of it.

Captain Wence jumped on the radio with a situation report, *"One-Six Actual, we're taking fire at—"* He provided coordinates. He sounded cool under fire. That was good.

"Roger, One-Six. Keep us advised."

Point vehicle manned by a Second Squad fire team returned lead for lead with its .50 cal. A .50 caliber bullet was about 2 inches long and designed for use against vehicles and reinforced structures. The buildings blocking progress sat in lowlands alongside the road about a half mile downrange. Even from that distance, I heard the methodical *chunk* of the big rounds eating at the buildings and saw puffs of mud and rock dust erupting from their walls. Shot long enough and concentrated, the heavy machine gun could actually destroy the huts. The guys in there must not have been serious ambushers or they would not have engaged us at such long range.

"Sergeant Kuhner, take the squad in bounding overwatch off to the right and approach on foot," Captain Wence ordered.

"Roger that, sir."

First Squad's two vehicles whipped out of formation and raced out across the rough desert floor in an enveloping movement, jouncing passengers and cargo until my teeth popped. We circled wide, using a shallow arroyo as protection against fire from the buildings.

Hunter skidded to a halt behind a rocky knoll almost directly opposite our objective. Kuhner ordered everyone to dismount except for the truck drivers, who followed a short distance to our rear in case we needed transportation quick. The rest of us on foot began to snoop and poop toward the buildings.

Oddly enough, I felt as calm as if I were out for a stroll in a park. I felt energized and ready; my heart rate was almost normal. I scanned 180 degrees across the front seeking a target for my mean-spitting little SAW as we edged to the top of the knoll and looked over.

The two buildings and the village on down the road from them looked quiet, almost deserted. Residents always ducked for cover when the shit started and tried to stay out of sight and out of the crossfire. Firing had ceased. The rest of 1st Platoon's trucks were scattered on the desert to either side of the road, their drivers and crew out and down in the sand. It looked like an old-fashioned standoff.

I spotted a huge flock of sheep and goats spread across the hills off to our right flank about 500 meters away. Several shepherds stood among the flocks watching. It reminded me of a scene from the Old Testament.

Two mortar rounds in quick succession splatted on the flats about a quarter mile to our immediate front, erupting geysers of sand and dust and sounding muffled over the distance. I couldn't determine where they came from. Apparently, the shooters couldn't see us, either; they were just shooting in our general direction, hoping to get lucky. Nothing to get alarmed about yet. These guys couldn't shoot for shit.

We resumed movement, trotting along at the bottom of the arroyo as we anticipated getting near enough to the two mud huts to do some serious ass kicking on the hajjis who shot at us.

The next mortar round landed long but nearer, about 150 meters to our rear. The pucker factor went up a few notches. I realized we were being bracketed. One short, one long, and then the next directly in the middle. That meant we had an observer watching us and calling in corrections to the gunners. Things were about to get serious.

I shot a look at the shepherds on the nearby hills. I yelled at Kuhner and the PL and pointed. They understood immediately.

"PL wants us to collar the sheepherders," Kuhner shouted and motioned for our vehicles to pick us up on the fly.

The two GMVs sand-slid up. We tumbled into the cargo bays on top of each other. Hunter dug our vehicle out in a sharp, sand-throwing turn toward the flocks of sheep and goats, followed by the second vehicle in enfilade.

It was one hell of an exciting ride. Adrenaline pumped in my veins as if through water pipes as more mortar rounds lobbed in on us, stomping eruptions in a crazy zigzag pattern around the two fast-moving GMVs. The laws of physics say a moving target is not easily hit, especially not by area weapons like mortars and artillery, but you couldn't always count on that. Murphy's Law said that anything that could go wrong, would.

A shell exploded 50 meters or so ahead. The two trucks burst through the dust and smoke and kept moving. A box of MREs bounced out of our truck and hit the sand. Incredibly, the next mortar shell struck it dead center and splashed spaghetti and meatballs all over the terrain.

"Did you see *that*?" Hunter whooped.

I was too busy to look. Frightened livestock scattered out of the path of our charge, noisily bleating. Instead of dispersing with their animals, however, the three shepherds in their dark robes and turbans knelt and opened fire with AK-47s. Caught foolishly directing fire for the mortars, they now wanted to make a stand.

On my knees in the back of the truck, I braced my SAW across a stack of boxes and lay down on the trigger. Kurt, with his feet spread wide, hung on to the handles of the mounted .50 cal. His hot casings pinged off my helmet.

A SAW is a smooth weapon, not much recoil, but it can put out an awesome amount of firepower for a weapon of such relatively small caliber. Hunter compared it to a lightsaber from *Star Wars*, only with a much longer reach. I sprayed the shepherds with 5.56 mm hot lead.

The shepherds found themselves in a fierce dust storm kicked up by fire from both vehicles. One of the three jumped up and took off down the other side of the hill out of sight. The remaining two held their ground, firing wildly while a barrage of lead chewed off the top of the hill around them and then chewed them down. Nothing could have survived that cavalry charge. All it needed was drawn sabers to make it perfect.

We ceased firing, and circled wide. We came up the back side of the ridge out of sight of the village and its mortars, skidding to a halt while dust boiled. The two shepherds lay broken in pools of blood and gore, literally ground into hamburger. One was young, seventeen or so, the other older with a beard on what was left of his face. He might have been the younger guy's father.

They were the first dead enemy I had seen so far in two wartime rotations. I stared at the men I had helped kill. My bullets may even have been the fatal ones. I didn't know how I should feel about it, how I might eventually feel, or even if I *would* feel. They were trying to kill us. We killed them instead.

A pair of fast movers, F-16s, zoomed low above our heads and dropped eggs on the two buildings from which we had initially received fire. They must have been in the vicinity when Captain Wence called for air support. After the aircraft finished the job and left, two Toyota pickups loaded with bad guys squirted out the back side of the nearby village and sped toward Haditha City, where they could get lost in the population.

Down on the flats by the road, black pillars of smoke climbed from the buildings and etched scowls across the sky. There was no further movement in the village after the Toyotas left. Everything turned preternaturally quiet. I turned away from the fresh corpses of the two sheepherders.

"If they were the Three Wise Men," Hunter drawled later in a flat voice, "one of them must have been wiser than the other two."

17

Alpha 3/75 remained at H-1 Airfield for most of our three-month rotation in country. You could tell how long we had been there by the way everyone started referring to it as "home" over their real homes in Denver or Tallahassee. Unlike more conventional troops, say the 101st Airborne or the 3rd Infantry, who came prepared to slog out the war month after month after month, special operations forces pulled about three months at a time in a combat zone, sometimes less. Rangers were mission-oriented strike forces designed to do a job, then withdraw to prepare for the next mission.

Isolated outposts like H-1 weren't getting any mail at this early stage in the war. There were no satellite phones or computers as there would be later when the war settled down into "occupation" phase. Everything was still in basic combat mode. Sometimes I thought we were lucky to get MREs and water. Still, hardships for me weren't really *hardships*. I think I would have made a good Spartan or Apache warrior. I rarely wrote letters and disliked talking on the phone so much I doubt I would have used it even if we had one. I was in my element. Doing exactly what I was born to do.

Like most soldiers, perhaps even like most men, or at least those with testosterone, Rangers long to be tried and proven in combat. It has to be due to something in our genetic makeup, perhaps extending all the way back to the caveman. War, not peace, is man's normal condition on earth. Until Jesus came again, I supposed, nations would need warriors to defend and pursue collective goals. Call it job security.

Alpha Company platoons continued to make enemy contact at some level almost every time we ran beans and bullets up to Bravo Company at the dam. The clashes were never anything sustained. Most of them were hit-and-run, usually in the form of a far ambush like that 1st Platoon encountered at the two buildings. A burst of fire from the top of a hill, a couple of mortar rounds generally impacting too far away for any real alarm, and the hajjis responsible shagged out of Dodge before we could unlimber on them. These guys were awful marksmen, at least so far.

These were the days before IEDs (improvised explosive devices) became popular among the jihadist elements, before the "martyr" rage caught on and every raghead with access to a stick of dynamite tried to take an American with him when he went to meet Allah and claim his seventy-two virgins.

You couldn't say at least some of them didn't learn by experience, however. Sheepherders in the hills all turned into wise men after what happened to their two soul mates who stood their ground on the hill to fight. From then on, they ran like the devil with his burning pitchfork was poking them in the butt if we so much as stopped a convoy to look in their direction. They didn't seem all that interested in receiving their virgins. Wilson said they had a lack of faith.

Heat and hellish desert conditions claimed more casualties than hostile fire, hampering a combat soldier's fundamental function: to move, shoot, and communicate. Soldiers during the First Gulf War in 1991 described the indescribable heat as like standing in the boiler room of hell. Such heat could not be ignored, only endured. You never stopped sweating. Talcumlike dust in the air mixed with sweat to coat your skin. You had to wear dark sunglasses against the brilliance of the sun that was like a photographer's flash going off continuously. After my first Iraqi tour, I never saw a plastic water bottle again without thinking of summers in the land of Saddam Hussein and Adam and Eve.

Arabs dressed for the heat by donning layers of clothing to prevent loss of body fluids. The hotter it got, the more layers they added. Their garb, however, was lightweight compared to the heavy battle-rattle armor, helmets, and full uniforms Americans wore. You saw no T-shirts and headbands like the guys in Vietnam sometimes wore against the humid jungle heat. Our heat was dry. A corpse left out in the sun mummified within a few days. Exposed skin on the face and hands burned like an overdone steak on a grill. Why was it that wars almost always seemed to be fought under such unpleasant conditions?

We conducted patrols and resupply during both the night and the day. Each had its advantages and disadvantages. Say what you will about the advantages of NODs and infrared, your vision was nonetheless severely reduced at night from your normal daytime vision. On the other hand, although you could see for miles across the wastelands during the day, the sun took its toll as the heat settled in, vehicles got too hot to touch with the bare hand, ammunition swelled, and radios lost range. Everything was a trade-off.

While Bravo Company had lost men during the big fight at the dam, the only casualties 1st Platoon suffered during the weeks at H-1 were Sergeant Rembold and two other guys injured in the parachute jump. Second Platoon was not so fortunate.

One morning, I straggled in from midnight watch to find 2nd Platoon saddling up to move out. Specialist Ryan Long of 2nd Platoon, a friend and drinking buddy who had been at Coach's Corner the night I met Kimberly, told me his outfit was being chopped over to man a road checkpoint somewhere up around the town of Haditha. We shook hands good-bye; in war you never knew how final a good-bye might be.

"Take it easy, man," I said.

"I'll take it any way I can get it" was the standard response.

A few days later, the radio net funneled the bad news to every Ranger in theater. Platoon Forward Observer Captain Russell Riptoe, Staff Sergeant Nino Livaudais, and Specialist Ryan Long were killed when an Iraqi vehicle passing through their checkpoint detonated. The "martyr" phase was about to begin.

You start thinking of the past when something like that happens, when someone you know dies suddenly. It jolts you into facing your own mortality, even if you are only twenty years old. I suffered the shock of Ryan's death in private, in silence, walking off by myself and squatting to draw figures in the sand to keep from thinking. Things like buddies getting killed happened in war. It came with the territory.

Rangers don't cry, but I saw tears in eyes that day. Some of the guys took it hard, this first KIA with whom we were all acquainted.

"You know something," one of them commented miserably, "they'll hold a memorial service for Ryan back in his hometown and he won't know nothing about it."

I started thinking about Kimberly, someone alive and normal and away from the abnormality of war. I thought about her, and then I commanded myself to stop thinking about her. After all, we had had only one night and a day together before I deployed. Why should I expect her to remember me, much less wait for me? She owed me nothing that should make me expect her to put her life on hold until I returned.

No one at home waited for me other than my grandparents and my brother and sister. I didn't need anyone else. Ranger Battalion had become my home, Rangers my brothers, my family. Best to forget all about Kimberly. The war was beginning to look like it might last a long time after all.

18

COLUMBUS, GEORGIA, 2003

Kimberly:

We really hadn't had time to get to know each other. An evening at a noisy bar and a day playing miniature golf and watching a movie together failed to qualify as much more than getting acquainted. That was it—and then he was gone off overseas. Nonetheless, I couldn't help thinking that maybe fate was at work here. Even in so short a time, I sensed in this man a quiet strength and simple sincerity that I had encountered in few other men—and certainly not in the basic trainees who hung around Columbus or the callow youth at Columbus State who, Joe's age, thought it the height of daring to wolf-whistle at blondes on campus.

The war in Iraq was all over Fox and CNN. "Shock and Awe," it was called. Bombs were exploding, cities were burning . . . columns of armored troops, helicopters, jet fighter planes . . . It was scary, just watching it on TV. I could hardly imagine what it must be like for Joe in the middle of all that. I had never known anyone close who actually went into combat.

I assumed Joe would contact me again after I gave him my telephone number and address, but the weeks passed, then months, and not a call or a scribbled word on the back of a postcard. Nothing.

I googled him. Joe Cap. I thought that was his last name—Cap or perhaps Capp, with a *C.* I finally gave up and assumed that whoever Joe Cap was, I had seen the last of him. For all I knew, he could have been killed over there.

It saddened me to think that way, that we might never have a chance to get to know each other. I decided to dismiss all thoughts of him. I was working my way through college by exercising horses at Midland Farms north of Columbus. What with that and studying nights, I had little time for a social life and certainly no time to brood over some guy who breezed into my life one unusual night and then just as suddenly breezed out again.

Like Joe's parents, mine were also divorced. I was eight years old when my father left. Dad just left one day with hardly a good-bye or anything. I remembered little about those times other than that Mom lost a lot of weight and seemed depressed. My sister, Melissa, was fifteen, a teenager. She married right out of high school, married into a great family that filled the void left by the breakup of ours.

Melissa, I hardly knew ye, what with our age differences and everything. I hardly knew Dad either. He disappeared, and by the time I met Joe neither Melissa nor I had received so much as a telephone call from him in over ten years.

I was eleven when Melissa married. That left Mom—Elizabeth Smithwick—and me. Mom landed a job as administrative assistant at a private school in Columbus. We moved from Moultrie, Georgia, where I was born, to Columbus, not far from the Fort Benning army base. Soldiers were always hanging around the area and sometimes being rowdy in Columbus. I never dated them and seldom went to soldier bars and clubs. That wasn't my scene. Just look what happened the first time I went out to one. I met an Airborne Ranger. Talk about irony.

After graduating from Columbus's Hardaway High School in 1999, I immediately enrolled in nearby Columbus State, thinking I might get a degree in communications and work in TV or public relations. Mom hadn't the money to pay my tuition, and Dad wasn't in the picture. Fortunately, my grades were good enough for a HOPE scholarship. HOPE and a part-time job were enough to see me through.

I loved animals and was good with them, especially horses, and was always hanging out on friends' farms. I met another girl my age, Suzanna Lampton, whose family owned Midland Farms of Georgia. Suzanna hired me to help with the horses.

Midland Farms was right out of the pages of some romance novel. It took my breath away the first time I drove onto its grounds. It was like entering another world, a horse heaven. Miles of black rail fencing enclosed rolling hills of green trimmed in forest and green-manicured paddocks dotted with coops and other jumps. Multiple Old English–style stucco stables out of *National Velvet* were home to about sixty beautiful, spirited horses trained for various activities—steeplechase, polo, foxhunting, show, and Thoroughbred racing. Their kennels of hounds for hunting fox—or, in this country, coyote—were renowned throughout the world.

I had owned ponies before, but never horses like these. They were tall, shiny, muscular. I was so excited about working there that I took on any chore just to be able to stay longer. Two of my favorite horses were Vigor and Ivor. Suzanna's husband, Mason, was a steeplechase jockey and had hopes that Vigor and Ivor would be his next champions.

Not many people were familiar with steeplechase horse racing. I know I wasn't, although there were about two hundred steeplechase tracks in the United States.

The steeplechase originated in Ireland in the eighteenth century as a cross-country Thoroughbred race that went from one church steeple to the next, thus "steeplechase." The first is said to have occurred as a result of a wager between Cornelius O'Callaghan and Edmund Blake in 1752, who raced their horses four miles cross-country from Buttevant Church to St. Leger Church in County Cork, Ireland.

Earlier races were contested cross-country rather than on a prepared track. Today, horses and jockeys run a prepared course of 2 miles or sometimes 3, jumping fences and ditches and other obstacles. For me, steeplechase racing was much more exciting than conventional oval-track Thoroughbred racing.

My job at Midland was to help with the riding, exercising, conditioning, feeding, and care of the animals. It was one of the most exhilarating experiences I had ever known to fly through a course on one of those tall, magnificent creatures with the wind whipping in my face and all that power underneath me. I could never imagine a life sitting in a stuffy office somewhere.

I confided in Suzanna about the Ranger I met at Coach's Corner. For a while after Joe left, she kept asking if I had heard from him. She stopped asking when she realized I hadn't.

Leaves on the ancient live oaks of Georgia were not yet on display with autumn's greeting when a group of friends and I went out for dinner one evening. As we left the restaurant, a young man as drunky as a skunky staggered across the street hollering about how he had just returned from Iraq. He wore jeans, his shirt was all mussed up and unbuttoned, his eyes were red-rimmed, and his nose was running. Really messed up.

I knew little about the army, how big it was and how the chances were slim that any one soldier from Iraq might know any other particular one. I might not have approached him otherwise. I ran up to him on a whim. His eyes lit up. He must have thought for a moment that he had struck gold. Blonde, that is.

"Do you know Joe Cap?" I asked him breathlessly.

What were the odds?

"He'll be here tomorrow," the guy slurred. "What are *you* doing tonight, pretty girl?"

I laughed. My heart was pounding. "Waiting on Joe Cap," I replied.

I kept expecting Joe to call all the next day. My cell phone was never out of reach while I was in the barn mucking stalls.

"He'll call, you'll see," Suzanna kept saying with her reassuring smile. "He's a fool if he doesn't."

I hadn't taken Joe for a fool. Quite the opposite, in fact. Still, there was the possibility that I hadn't made the impression on him that he had on me.

I jumped every time the phone rang.

One of our horses, Mason's steeplechase runner Ivor, a big quirky sorrel, had just recovered from some tendon issues. I had devoted hours to hosing his legs and administering electrotherapy. I spent so much time getting him fit for action that as a reward Suzanna and Mason invited me to go with them to see Mason and Ivor run at the Maryland Hunt Club, one of the biggest steeplechase races in the nation. We flew out that afternoon.

Unfortunately, Mason took a spill on one of the jumps and failed to finish after having cleared the high wall. Ivor was spectacular, for his part. After the race, we piled into a cab for the ride back to the airport. I noticed on my cell phone that I had missed two calls, both from the same unknown number. My heart raced. I just knew it had to be him.

A few minutes later, my cell phone rang.

"It's . . . him. I know it's him." I seemed to have frozen.

Suzanna giggled. "Aren't you going to answer it?"

I finally caught my breath and punched the little RECEIVE CALL button.

"Do you know who this is?" a shy voice asked.

"Absolutely I know who it is," I gushed, trying to control myself.

"Are you free tonight?"

"I'm in Maryland, but I'm coming home tomorrow."

"Tomorrow night, then?"

"Don't you dare hang up, Joe Cap, without telling me your name. I've looked everywhere for you."

He pronounced it phonetically, then spelled it. K-A-P-A-C-Z-I-E-W-S-K-I. "I'm the only Joe Kapacziewski at Fort Benning."

"That," I laughed, "I don't doubt."

Suzanna made sure I got back on time by loading me up in her family's private plane and flying me back to Columbus after the race. My car was at the airport in Atlanta where I'd left it for the flight to Maryland. I called Joe.

"I have to go to Atlanta to get my car. You want to go with me?"

That was our second date. My friend Melanie Lymburner drove Joe and me to Atlanta in her pickup truck. We talked the entire trip, never an awkward silence. Mostly about horses and Ivor and the race. Joe told me about his childhood and how he loved the outdoors and horses, but he said nothing about the army or the war. We made plans to visit Midland Farms and spend lots of time together.

Joe and I brought my car back together. I knew after that that we were together from now on. We were never one of those on-again off-again couples. We had a destiny together.

19

Kim and I had about four weeks together after I returned from Iraq, hanging out, dating, all the usual things young couples do when they're "courting," as my grandma would have put it. Miniature golf again, movies, riding horses, even a dance or two, although I wasn't much at dancing. Too many feet.

Experts say 93 percent of all communication between people is through body language. That was a good thing. I was never much of a talker. I was one of those guys who, at a party, found a wall that needed holding up and that was where I planted myself until I came up with an excuse to leave. Sometimes, though, with Kim, I became what you might call downright gabby. I confided in her, after only that short time together, secrets that I would never have shared with anyone else.

We were serious about each other. Maybe it was selfish of me to want to hang on to her, what with my being a soldier already deployed twice to war within my first two years in the army, but the thought of letting her go was too painful to bear. She was the woman I wanted to take home with me. I felt sure she saw me the same way. She had to know what she was in for, though. I had pretty much decided on the army as a career.

In the movies and in books, the romantic hero lets a girl know how serious he is by buying her roses and candy and falling down on one knee.

That wasn't me. You might say I was low-key. After a movie one evening—a Clint Eastwood, I think—we took a walk around the block together, holding hands. It was a clear, cool night, and older couples passing by smiled at us. Kim smiled back and often paused long enough to exchange pleasantries. When Grandma Churchill finally met Kim, she said Kim was the type of wholesome girl-next-door who never met a stranger and who could talk the leg off a store window dummy. We complemented each other that way—she could do the talking for both of us.

"Kim?"

"Joe."

"Kim, I think I'll be reenlisting in the army."

"That's nice."

What was the matter with her? Suddenly she had lockjaw or something, leaving the next move up to me.

"Uh . . . ?"

"Joe."

I glanced sidewise at her as we strolled along. A little smile played on her lips. She wore almost no makeup to mask the expression that opened her heart for the world to see. The girl was actually *enjoying* this.

"Uh . . . a lot of time a Ranger only comes home long enough to wash a rucksack of dirty clothes before he's gone again."

We continued to walk. She continued to smile. The girl had patience, I had to hand her that. Out at Midland Farms she often wore that same patient smile when she worked with the horses she loved. I would watch her as she eased into a corral with some high-strung gelding to coax him with kindness and a gentle hand into doing exactly what she wanted him to do. The horse would be following her around nuzzling the back of her neck within a few minutes.

"That's the army," she said presently.

We stopped long enough to look at a storefront window display.

"I've been to Afghanistan once and just got back from Iraq," I pointed out. "Uh . . ."

"Joe."

"It's not much of a life."

"It's according to how you look at it."

She pulled me around to face her. "Joe, are you trying to say you love me?"

"Uh . . ."

Of course I loved her. I supposed she could take it or leave it.

She laughed softly. "I know what I'm doing," she said.

She took my cheeks between her two hands and kissed me firmly on the mouth. If I hadn't been the self-controlled reticent type, I might have been fast-popping with joy all over the street like some wacky cartoon character. She took my arm and we resumed our walk. Both of us were smiling.

One thing I was discovering about Kim. Not only was she gorgeous and sweet-tempered, she was as tough as the horseshoe nails out at Midland Farms. The girl was long-haul material. She had the "right stuff." Kim was Ranger quality.

You might have called ours a whirlwind, between-wars romance. We met and I left immediately for three months in Iraq. Now I was back and orders came down for me to attend Ranger School, which meant I would be gone another three months. Hadn't I warned her?

As I explained to Kim, I had pretty much settled on the army—more specifically, the Rangers—as a career. I was still a private first class, a PFC E-3. In order to advance in rank and responsibility, I had to complete Ranger School. Less than 30 percent of those who began the course completed it with their starting class. Over half never earned the coveted black and yellow Ranger tab.

The stated goal of the training was "to produce a hardened, competent, small-unit leader who is confident he can lead his unit in combat and overcome all obstacles to accomplish his mission."

"You're a combat vet," Staff Sergeant Rembold reassured me as he recuperated from his broken ankle. "You'll do fine."

Men who had already completed the Ranger Indoctrination Program and actually served in Ranger Battalion, as I had, possessed an advantage over cherry candidates. I wasn't exactly cocky going into Ranger School, but I felt confident I could do it. It turned out to be my most challenging undertaking so far in the army. Once you earned that Ranger tab, you knew you were able to do anything, even if you had never done it before and knew absolutely nothing about it. You were a Ranger. You could do *any damned thing*.

20

Ranger School was established in 1951 near the beginning of the Korean War, the first class graduating in March 1952. Any member of any branch of the military or from allied nations was eligible to attend. The idea was to transmit Ranger training to individuals who then returned to their parent outfits to teach what they had learned.

All training was conducted in realistic environments designed to simulate the stress of actual combat. That meant a grueling physical setting, hunger, lack of sleep, and constant pressure. When you didn't have anything else to do, say five minutes here and there, the instructors had you on the ground knocking out push-ups or flutter kicks. "Drop down and give me thirty!" By the end of the course, the average student was beat down and in the worst mental and physical shape of his life—and that was those who succeeded in passing it.

Ranger training had been reduced from four phases to three, the second phase of desert fighting and survival at Fort Bliss, Texas, having been eliminated. It seemed to me that phase would have been particularly relevant to the wars in Iraq and Afghanistan. Be that as it may, training began at Fort Benning with the Ranger Assessment Program (RAP).

Students who survived RAP at Fort Benning went on to the second phase in the forested mountains of Dahlonega, Georgia, to learn mountaineering—rappelling, climbing, and survival. After that, the third and last phase was the toughest phase of all: jungle warfare training at Eglin Air Force Base, Florida.

Everyone arrived at RAP wearing plain BDUs and field caps without rank or service insignia; students were considered equal, from a colonel down to a private. Just like in RIP, the first order of business after "drop down and give me thirty" was to be assigned in pairs as "Ranger buddies" who would work together throughout the course, or at least until one flunked out. If a man fell behind, his buddy was expected to help him. No Ranger did anything alone. That went back to Darby's Rangers' "Me and My Pal" training of World War II.

Although the course trained individuals, teamwork within platoons was essential in order for individuals to make it through. Experience showed that platoons with the most cooperation had the highest rates of graduation.

"Self, Chris."

"Sar'ent!"

"Your buddy is . . . is Kap . . . Kapa . . ."

"Kapa-*chess*-ski, Sar'ent."

"Whatever. You and Kap, Self."

Chris Self was somewhat older than me, in his early thirties, a thick, athletic-looking man and, like me, a combat veteran. He was stationed at Fort Campbell, Kentucky, with the 5th Special Forces Group, a Green Beret sergeant first class with ten or twelve years in service. He stalked over to me after formation.

"A Batt Boy?" he asked with a grin. A "Batt Boy" was a soldier already assigned to a Ranger Battalion.

I grinned back. "A Green Weenie?"

He laughed and stuck out his hand to commence not only an immediate personal friendship but also a good-natured rivalry between two spec ops forces represented by several Green Berets in the platoon on one side and, on the other side, the Batt Boys, who significantly outnumbered them. As Ranger buddies, Chris and I became virtually inseparable. We balanced each other, he the robust Special Forces operative, me the quiet but equally determined partner. Ranger buddies often became lifelong friends. It wasn't unusual for a colonel and a private buddied up in Ranger School to remain friends afterward.

Ironically enough, Chris and I would end up together at Walter Reed Army Medical Center a few years later, both of us suffering from combat wounds.

RAP training at Benning wasn't so much different than RIP. Basic stuff like the Combat Water Survival Test, proficiency exams in weapons, mines, grenades, and commo, obstacle courses, crawling in the mud while artillery simulators exploded, compass courses and map land navigation, unarmed hand-to-hand combat . . . and a lot of PT to get us ready for the following two phases.

"Build us up to break us down again," Chris observed. "You really eat this shit up, don't you, Kap?"

Hunter had said the identical thing to me back during RIP. Hey, I had found a home with the Rangers.

Further training included survival techniques and a parachute drop from helicopters into a forest clearing as part of a field training exercise to demonstrate combat skills in reconnaissance, patrolling, and mission planning. The Darby Queen obstacle course, up a densely wooded hillside, was one of the toughest anywhere in the army. You had to crawl, run, jump, climb, and slide through a variety of obstacles with your Ranger buddy, helping each other because one of you could not continue without the other. Chris and I, both competitive and in good physical shape, were among those with the fastest time through it. We dropped down off the last slippery wall neck-and-neck, raced across the finish line, and gave each other a hearty high five.

"You eat this shit up, don't you, Self?"

After one phase ended, the next began immediately. While I might have looked upon the canceled Fort Bliss training as necessary, I couldn't say I regretted not participating in the parachute jump that traditionally preceded it. I had heard stories from the old hands of flying NOE (nap of the earth, low to the ground) to Texas and rigging the jump in flight. NOE always made jumpers airsick. Every paratrooper remembered participating in at least one NOE "barf jump."

I had had mine a year or so earlier. Rigging in flight wasn't as simple to accomplish as it sounded. The C-130 Hercules was crowded with troops, and it was rough riding, which complicated getting to your feet to don 'chute and gear up for the equipment jump.

Across from me, a kid from Texas or Arkansas started the epidemic by barfing his guts into one of the little bags provided for such events by the air force loadmaster. He looked up, all flushed and greenish around the gills. A half-digested spaghetti noodle from the MRE he consumed before we took off hung from one nostril like an anemic worm.

"Way-ull," somebody observed in an exaggerated Texas drawl, "that thar boy is so inner die-rected. Us-all jus' luuve him on account of he knows what he wants out of lahf."

Another kid took one look at the dangling spaghetti participle and grabbed for a barf bag. Pretty soon, the air reeked of vomit and the aircraft's steel deck turned slippery with it. I had never wanted to get out of an airplane so desperately. Rather than actually *jumping* from the plane, we slipped and slid to the doors when they opened and *fell* out. Airsickness did not exempt you from going out. You went out into the slipstream carrying your little bag in one hand and dropped it on the way down. Watch out below!

Everything in the training ran in high gear. We received two or three hours' sleep a night—if we were lucky. Battle drills, reconnaissance, ambushes, flanking movements, reaction to direct and indirect fire, survival training, assaulting fortified bunkers, clearing trench lines and buildings, penetrating barbed wire, more airborne operations and helicopter assaults . . .

Instructors placed increasing emphasis on tactics, planning, and leadership as the course proceeded. The formula for planning missions seared itself onto the front lobes of my brain. METT-T stood for the factors of (M)ission, (E)nemy, (T)errain, (T)roops, and (T)ime. What was the duration of the (M)ission? Who were the (E)nemy and how many? What kind of (T)errain was it? How many friendly (T)roops and what type? What was the (T)imeline? Leadership positions rotated among students so each could be evaluated at least once during each stage of training.

The hard-ass instructors never let up.

"Drop down! Give me thirty! If you can't take it, we don't want you here."

Traditionally, the mountain phase around Dahlonega, Georgia, claimed more medical drops than either of the two other phases, due largely to sprains, torn muscles, dislocations, and broken bones from climbing, rappelling down cliffs, and patrolling around the mountains in the dark. Hoist a 40- or 50-pound ruck on your back—you were already sleep-deprived and losing weight—and rappel down a cliff as high as a six-story building, sometimes face forward Australian-style like you were walking down the cliff, and somebody *would* get hurt.

Afterward, at night, with full combat pack, you helicopter-assaulted into a tree-surrounded mountain clearing not much larger than a football field through which ran a stream and a band of pines to wind up the phase with another field training exercise. Students planned and executed recons, ambushes, raids, and other actions while the "enemy" harassed your ass and brought fire and brimstone down on the best-laid plans of mice and men.

"*Baaaa!*" McDowell bleated wearily.

"You even smell like a mountain goat."

Due to medical drops and lack of motivation, only a little more than half the students who started remained to begin the last phase—a Florida vacation in the sun at Eglin Air Force Base. Even the survivors by now were so beat up we were operating on instinct, training, and sheer willpower. Chris and I were still hanging in there. We were grungy, tired, and hungry, and the most grueling phase of the training lay ahead. When a Ranger thought back on it, what he remembered most vividly, and most painfully, was the jungles and swamps of Gulf Coast Florida. Dazed and exhausted, we expended what strength we had left moving through swamps inhabited by mosquitoes, gators, and snakes. Fatigue and near-starvation made rational thinking almost impossible, planning and reaction to "enemy" elements slow. Some guys hallucinated and saw big juicy steaks, boats, houses, or even their girlfriends. They attacked imaginary enemies. Sometimes, guys had to tether Ranger buddies to their harnesses to keep them from wandering off during a movement. Until then, I would have thought it impossible for a man to sleep while walking or while paddling a rubber Zodiac boat up a narrow, muddy waterway.

It was brutal. The only thing that got you through was mental toughness. I hated every minute of it, but I never seriously thought of quitting. I had never quit anything, and I wasn't going to start now. Rangers were my life.

I developed dysentery. About all that came out was water since we were living on one MRE a day. I remembered stories of guys in Vietnam with dysentery so bad they cut the crotches out of their fatigues so they wouldn't have to take the time to drop their drawers. Miserable and dehydrated, crushed by the various movements, I fought against the oppressive heat and tropical rainstorms.

"You're sick, man," Chris said. "You gotta go in. You'll kill yourself."

"I won't quit, Chris."

"You can recycle."

"And go through this again? No way. Chris, I can make it, buddy. I can make it."

The phase ended with a predawn assault on Santa Rosa Island and its "enemy" contingent. Preparations started before nightfall. We checked and loaded Zodiacs, assembled equipment and weapons, planned and rehearsed the operation. The boats set off under cover of darkness across the open stretch of water between the Florida Panhandle and the island. We arrived an hour or so before dawn.

A barrage of flares simulating supporting fires illuminated the beachhead. With weapons blazing—blanks, of course—students crashed ashore to overwhelm the enemy in a firefight fiercer than anything I had endured so far in Iraq or Afghanistan.

It was over. Even the instructors joined in the blowout. I don't know where the energy came from, but in a burst of post-training exhilaration and good-natured hazing, Batt Boys wrestled the outnumbered Green Weenies to the ground, everybody laughing like madmen, taped their hands and feet together, and scrawled all over their bodies in Magic Marker endearing phrases like *We Love Batt Boys*.

Relief replaced exhaustion as survivors returned to Fort Benning on the sixty-eighth day of training, September 18, 2003, for all-you-could-eat hot dogs and a good night's sleep, the first in over two months. Those of us who made it knew that we had the strength and resiliency to take on anything.

During graduation ceremonies the next day, while field music played and the colors paraded, I glanced up from my place in ranks to the spectator bleachers, my eyes searching. I spotted an old friend, Dave Winters, now retired from the Air Force and a civilian employee of SOCOM out of Tampa. Someone must have told him of my achievement. Josh Kuhner drove down from New Jersey to pin my tab on.

Next to him perched Grandma and Grandpa Churchill, and next to them sat Kimberly. She blew me a kiss. It was one of the proudest and happiest days of my life so far.

The day I graduated, my company deployed to Thailand for up-training to get ready for our next combat rotation. I was ordered to stay behind at Fort Benning to recuperate from Ranger School. I had it easy while the company was gone. I hung out with Kim and put back on some of the weight I had lost.

I still figured I owed it to Kim to give her an exit strategy.

"You don't have to stick, Kim."

"Would you quit?" she asked.

21

Terrorist leader Osama bin Laden had been around on the world stage for at least two decades by the time of the 9/11 attack against the United States. Following the attack, videos of the al Qaeda founder made the entire globe aware of the tall, angular figure wearing a U.S.-type BDU camouflage jacket over a long white robe, a white turban on his head, a long black beard hanging down from his chin, and carrying a Soviet AK-47 rifle he claimed to have "liberated" from a dead Russian soldier.

In his most infamous statement following 9/11, bin Laden declared, "God knows it did not cross our minds to attack the towers [until] after the situation became unbearable and we witnessed the injustice and tyranny of the American-Israeli alliance against our people in Palestine and Lebanon... when Americans allowed the Israelis to invade Lebanon, helped by the U.S. Sixth Fleet... As I watched the destroyed towers in Lebanon, it occurred to me to punish the unjust the same way: to destroy towers in America so it could taste some of what we are tasting and to stop killing our children and women."

Osama bin Laden—born in 1957 to Saudi Arabian billionaire construction magnate Mohammed bin Awad bin Laden and Mohammed's *tenth* wife—and al Qaeda were directly responsible for the deaths of thousands of people worldwide from at least 1979, when he first appeared on the international scene during the long Soviet war in Afghanistan. Using his inherited fortune, he attracted and recruited jihadi fighters from all over the Arab world to battle the Soviets. He even received support from the American CIA. He was a major factor in the defeat of the Russian military.

As the Russians began withdrawing from Afghanistan in 1988–89, bin Laden was not content with his accomplishments so far. He saw himself as a major force in restoring the worldwide grandeur of the Muslim world through a new caliphate. On August 11, 1988, he met with other like-minded jihadists and founded al Qaeda to take up jihadist causes elsewhere in the world, using his considerable wealth to fund it. Although he returned to Saudi Arabia in 1990 as a hero of the jihad, the man who with his Arab fighters "brought down the mighty superpower" of the Soviet Union, his extremist views soon landed him in disfavor with the Saudis and made him persona non grata in much of Africa.

Beginning with the 1992 bombing of the Gold Mihor Hotel in Aden that killed two people, he soon became implicated in a string of ruthless terrorist actions against the United States that included the first bombing of the World Trade Center in New York in 1993. He returned to Jalalabad, Afghanistan, in May 1996, where he forged a close relationship with Taliban leader Mullah Mohammed Omar and began establishing al Qaeda terrorist training camps throughout the country. Three months after his return, he declared war against the United States in a fatwa entitled *Declaration of War Against the Americans Who Occupy the Land of the Two Holy Places,* those being Mecca and Medina.

In 1998, in the name of the "World Islamic Front for Jihad Against Jews and Crusaders," he issued a second fatwa that proclaimed killing North Americans and their allies was an "individual duty for every Muslim . . . in order to liberate the al-Aqsa Mosque [in Jerusalem] and the Holy Mosque [in Mecca] from their grip." North Americans, he asserted at the announcement of the fatwa, were "very easy targets . . . You will see the results of this in a very short time."

FBI and CIA in the United States placed him behind the 1997 Luxor Massacre in Egypt that slaughtered sixty-two civilians, most of them foreign tourists; the 1998 U.S. Embassy bombings in major East African cities that killed hundreds of innocent people; and finally the attack on New York City and the Pentagon on September 11, 2001.

Two profound beliefs motivated "the Lion Sheik," as bin Laden became known, among a spread of fawning nicknames. Raised a devout Wahhabi Muslim in Saudi Arabia, where he was said to have studied economics and business administration, he believed that U.S. foreign policy oppressed, killed, or otherwise harmed Muslims in the Middle East. Only the restoration of Sharia law would set things right. Afghanistan under the rule of Mullah Omar's Taliban, he believed, was "the only Islamic country" in the Muslim world and thus a model for other Arab nations to follow.

In his second core belief, he expanded on the need for violent jihad to right injustices perpetrated by the United States and to destroy Israel and the Jews, whom he regarded as "masters of usury and leaders in treachery. They will leave you nothing, either in this world or the next."

His ideology included justification for targeting innocent civilians, including women and children. Anyone standing near the enemy, no matter who, he said, would find a proper reward in death, going straight to paradise if they were proper Muslims and to hell if they were nonbelievers. Luring large enemies such as the Soviet Union and America into long wars of attrition in Muslim countries, he contended, would collapse them economically and lead to the rise of a world-wide caliphate.

He was dead serious, as the 9/11 attacks proved. President George W. Bush launched the War on Terror almost immediately after the Twin Towers collapsed in Manhattan, a war that would eventually become one of the longest continuing wars in history. The bounty offered on bin Laden's head soon reached $50 million, making him the most-wanted fugitive in history.

"I want justice," President Bush proclaimed on September 17, 2001.

"There is an old poster out West, as I recall, that said, 'Wanted Dead or Alive . . .'" In October he emphasized, "There's no need to discuss innocence or guilt. We know he's guilty."

All attempts to assassinate or capture bin Laden had failed so far. Predator drones targeted him, killing some of his henchmen but missing him. In 2001, shortly after the United States invaded Afghanistan, spec ops troops thought they had him trapped in caves where he was hiding in the mountains of eastern Afghanistan. Somehow, he managed to escape during the Battle of Tora Bora. Apparently, as of 2004, he was still hiding in the mountains, *somewhere*.

During the winter of early 2004, the U.S. Army's 3rd Ranger Battalion deployed for another combat tour into eastern Afghanistan. One of its primary missions was to aid Navy SEALs, Army Green Berets, the CIA, and other special operations forces in running Osama bin Laden to ground and killing him. Freshly out of Ranger School and promoted to corporal, I looked forward to having my boots back on the ground in a combat zone. Rangers were on the way.

22

AFGHANISTAN 2004

I sought rank and responsibility, but I felt a bit guilty about how my promotion came about. Not my promotion to specialist E-4, which I deserved. After all, I had already been to war twice, made a combat jump, completed Ranger School in the top tenth percentile, and was looking forward to reenlistment. Kim and I were sailing along, and although I hadn't popped the question yet, both of us assumed we'd get hitched sooner or later. "Hitched." That was how they expressed it down south.

It was my promotion to fire team leader, not to E-4, that posed the dilemma.

The day Alpha Company returned from Thailand, 1st Platoon turned in its unit gear and headed out to Coach's Corner to do some partying. I noticed Sergeant Jermaine Wilson was boozing pretty heavy. He was one of First Squad's fire team leaders. Jermaine and I had jumped into H-1 Airfield together. He was tough, Jermaine was, a short, wiry, black guy from Maryland and a superfast runner who smoked almost everyone in the company when it came to PT. I liked him. He was a good Ranger, funny, and a goof-off at times.

I slapped him on the shoulder as I was leaving Coach's early to meet Kim.

"Jermaine, want a lift back to post?"

He presented me a knuckle dap and a wide half-inebriated grin. "What it is, what it is, bro'?" he chortled. Nate Brown, Sherlock, and a couple of others were settling in with him to close down the party. I would have had to physically drag Jermaine out of there to get him to leave.

The Columbus police nabbed him later that night and charged him with DUI. He got kicked out of the Rangers for standards violation. Having been promoted to specialist out of Ranger School, I was moved up to take over as leader for Jermaine's fire team. Hunter was still with me. I learned later that Jermaine got out of the army when his enlistment was up.

A fire team leader was the lowest level of leadership in the combat infantry battalion. A battalion commanded by a lieutenant colonel was composed of three line companies and a Headquarters and Headquarters Company, about seven hundred soldiers. A captain or major commanded a company of around two hundred soldiers. The company broke down into three platoons of forty or fifty men each, each platoon led by a lieutenant or a newly pinned captain. Below the platoon leader came the platoon sergeant over four squads or, in the case of 1st Platoon, three squads since we were undermanned. First Squad was dissolved and its members distributed to Second and Third Squads and Weapons Squad. The platoon leader *led* his platoon, but the platoon sergeant *ran* the platoon. A squad of nine men or so led by a staff sergeant further broke down into two fire teams. That was where I stood upon deployment to Afghanistan for my third combat tour: fire team leader in Third Squad, 1st Platoon, Alpha Company, 3rd Battalion, 75th Ranger Regiment. Staff Sergeant Ken Clayton was my new squad leader, having taken over from Staff Sergeant Jeffrey Rembold, who broke his ankle on the jump into H-1.

I was conscientious to a fault in my new leadership status, not the least reason being that I had assumed it because of Jermaine's misfortune. I stuck myself first on most shit details as an example for the other members of the team, to show them that Corporal Kap led the way rather than pushed the way.

Bagram Air Base in Afghanistan still smelled the way I remembered from our first rotation—*distinct*—but with a fresher, colder quality to the winter air off the Hindu Kush. A recent snowfall mantled the terrain in glistening white as Alpha Company unassed the C-17 and loaded up on what appeared to be the same old buses from before to transport us to our quarters. Luckily, the buses passed tents still set up in rows but vacated for the season and dropped us at wooden barracks with kerosene space heaters. I pondered again why they always gave wars in the most miserable countries in the world—in deserts and jungles and snow-smothered mountains. Why not somewhere temperate with sunshine and regular trees and a year-round 70 degrees?

"If they give another war and it's cold like this, I ain't going," Mike Edwards decided right off. "I'd rather be in Iraq."

"It's winter there, too," Eric Franck said.

"Not like this."

Spring and summer were the "fighting seasons" in Afghanistan. The Taliban rarely fought in the winter. They mostly holed up somewhere, stayed out of sight, and waited for warm days. Sounded smart to me.

So, with nobody out there for us to shoot at or to shoot at us, Alpha Company platoons pulled QRF out of Bagram in support of Navy SEALs whose mission was to hunt down Osama bin Laden and capture or kill him. "Kill" was the operative word; none of the SEALs expected he would come in alive. Frequently, they received intelligence from some source that "the Sheik" might be hiding out in this particular village, in this cave, or protected at an isolated farm.

Since Rangers supported SEALs in their quest, we would be going about our business at Bagram when suddenly a modified operation order came down. The platoon on QRF would haul ass in a helicopter assault force or mount our GMVs to link up with SEALs to clear and search houses or sneak up on some cave. All we needed to complete the picture was a cavalry bugle blowing *Charge!*

"He's like the Road Runner," Mike Edwards carped. "The Coyote chases him with all that stuff from Acme and he always gets away."

"You and Hunter are watching too many movies, Mike."

Today, Osama bin Laden was supposed to have been seen tucked in for the winter in a little farm village near a creek at the foot of the Khost-Gardez Pass. Three Chinooks full of SEALs and Rangers leaped from the Bagram helicopter pads and steamed at full power into the chase. We had to be ready at a moment's notice to jump on the slightest piece of information if we ever expected to find the most sought-after HVT in the world.

The objective was a small settlement like hundreds of others in this region, a scattering of a dozen or so mud-brown huts shoved into one end of the valley at the base of a snow-covered mountain tinged with the pink-orange of the sun rising through clouds. The little creek was frozen solid, which meant the villagers had to melt ice for water. Goats, sheep, and camels outnumbered the population three or four to one. People were beginning to stir when helicopters dipped down and deposited troops at either end of the main street. Third Squad's job was to set up a blocking force on our side of the village while the rest of the platoon and the SEALs went through it from the other end.

It was an archaic scene of pandemonium as twenty-first-century warriors with all the accoutrements of the modern world flushed out seventh-century inhabitants from their tenth-century dwellings and stacked them in the snowy street for questioning. You couldn't miss the irony of the most dangerous international criminal in the world, who had terrorized a great nation and brought it to war, possibly living in primitive squalor not far removed from the Stone Age while being pursued by modern technology.

Bin Laden wasn't in the village, probably had never been. He seemed to always be somewhere other than where we were. For over two decades he had succeeded in eluding first the Russians and now virtually the entire free world. Why would a guy like him be hiding out in this little dunghill in the middle of nowhere anyhow? He was probably not in a cave either, but more likely in Hong Kong or Cairo or somewhere else warm drinking beer and cavorting with his four or five wives and concubines, however many he might have.

Sgt. Joseph Kapacziewski and Charles W. Sasser

23

That was how the hunt for Osama bin Laden went. We were out there on cold, dark nights that drove sane people home and to bed, scouring snowy ramparts where bin Laden was still apparently living with the Abominable Snowman. We might have had better luck chasing the Snowman.

First Platoon had been in Afghanistan for three weeks, most of that time on GMV patrols, when an unexpected blizzard struck. It started to snow, thin showers, while the platoon mucked around in some village asking questions of the occupants through our terps (interpreters). You just didn't walk up and blurt it out: *Hey, you people seen Osama?* You asked the villagers about their families, how the world was treating them, anything happening? You snooped around and tried not to look suspicious—but we were about as inconspicuous as an alien spaceman in Manhattan. You acted friendly and pumped the people gently for information. Of course, as usual, nobody knew shit, which may or may not have been the truth.

No one thought much of the snow showers; this *was* winter in the mountains. An hour later, however, up in the pass, the war came to a sudden halt. Called on account of weather when the blizzard arrived with its full fury, leaving the platoon stranded and isolated until it blew over and we could see to drive back to Bagram. Damn miserable country. No wonder no one wanted it. No wonder the Russians left.

Captain Chris Molino, who had replaced Captain Wence as PL, circled the wagons against attack, a precaution unnecessary under the circumstances and more SOP than anything. Snow swirled so fiercely that visibility was cut to near zero and exposed skin froze within minutes. It was like being trapped inside one of those little crystal snow globes and dropped into a deep freeze. Ian Hunter was so bundled in Mickey Mouse boots, parka, and foul-weather trousers that he resembled Ralphie's little brother in the *Christmas Story* movie that played on TV every year. You know, the little kid who couldn't put his arms down to his sides because his mom layered him in so many clothes.

I wasn't the only one who thought so. I kept hearing from the other guys wry remarks like "No, Ralphie. You'll shoot your eye out."

I accepted first perimeter watch for Third Squad, leading the way as team leader. Kyle Butcher, one of my guys, jerked open the door to my Hummer and dived inside, letting in an explosion of blowing snow and the sound of the warm-up tent canvas-popping against itself in the wind. He was shivering, so I cranked over the engine, opened the heater wide, and turned on the wipers to clear the makeshift Plexiglas windshield of accumulated snow. Even then, I could barely discern the outline of the tent in the blizzard only a few feet away. The other trucks on perimeter watch around the tent remained all but invisible in the whiteout. I had never been so cold and miserable in my life. Neither had Butcher, judging from the teeth-chattering sounds issuing from somewhere inside his snivel gear.

"Kap, I seen this movie about buffalo hunters in the Old West," he said, slapping his mittened hands together to encourage circulation. "A hunter gets caught in a blizzard and they find him the next day frozen to death in place, rifle resting across his lap like he was waiting for a shot. I keep thinking that could be us."

"Go get in the tent, Butch. They got a heater going."

"You ain't been in there, Kap. All that fartin' and snorin', I'd rather be in the truck. You and me can relieve each other on watch, if that's okay? It's not like we have to worry about Mongolian hordes riding their camels and elephants and ostriches in on us. Hell, they're probably with Osama bin Laden deep in some warm cave with a fire going—which is where they'll stay until it thaws in the spring."

Butcher and I hunkered in the freezing cab of the GMV while the vapor from our breath frosted ice on the glass and on the dash and even on the steering wheel. Every so often one of the other vehicles kicked over its engine, not just for the heater, which was inadequate in this kind of cold, but also to keep the oil from freezing. Butcher dug out an MRE and offered me the chocolate bar. I chewed on it reflectively, feeling isolated and insulated in the storm from the rest of the world.

"Mind if I smoke?" I asked.

"Mind if I fart?"

"You'll put your eye out."

So the hunt for Osama bin Laden continued. One empty hole after another. We made some progress, however. Just before Alpha Company rotated back stateside, the PL was questioning a peasant huddled with his family around a fire in his little hut. The farmer scratched himself, looked at the interpreter and then at Captain Molino, then nodded thoughtfully.

"Osama bin Laden?"

"Yes," the interpreter said as he translated.

"Seem I hear of him one time, but I not for sure."

24

In the meantime, Iraq was becoming the War on Terror's main effort while Afghanistan, Osama bin Laden or not, was slowly being relegated to a support role. President George W. Bush had stood on the flight deck of the aircraft carrier USS *Abraham Lincoln* on May 1, 2003, about seven weeks after the war began, and declared the end of "major combat operations" in Iraq. The media described a kind of euphoria as the liberated population enthusiastically expressed their pro-American sentiments by toppling Saddam statues and preparing for "democracy."

The war, however, had not ended. It had merely changed its character from the lightning strike that brought U.S. troops all the way to Baghdad in a matter of weeks to a kind of static urban warfare. Never in U.S. history had American forces been required to participate in large-scale urban fighting while simultaneously rebuilding the combat zone. Even as Saddam Hussein's Ba'ath Party disintegrated and his army capitulated, the remaining leaders being hunted down and captured or killed by U.S. special operations teams, elements of the army and secret police started forming guerrilla cells. Calling themselves "jihadists," they began targeting Coalition forces around Mosul, Tikrit, Fallujah, and Baghdad with ambushes, suicide bombings, and IEDs.

Iraq descended into a sectarian hell that claimed the lives of thousands of Iraqis and forced millions more to flee the country. The particularly virulent strain of Sunni Islam called Wahhabism flourished as the nation's Sunni minority backed the insurgency in an effort to preserve the political power and economic benefits it enjoyed under Saddam. Insurgents and terrorists were attempting to impose draconian Sharia law throughout the country. They carried out summary executions in the streets and villages of those who opposed them or who cooperated with Coalition troops and the new Iraqi government. It was not unusual for a town to awake in the morning and have to police up off the roads the corpses of those slain overnight.

A seemingly endless supply of weapons looted from Saddam's old ammunition depots and the collapse of the economy postinvasion acerbated the situation. Jihadists pulled suicide martyr bombings against police stations, schools, and other public facilities. They posted cash bounties for the deaths of Iraqi security personnel, National Guardsmen, American soldiers, and virtually all foreigners. Insurgents kidnapped and publicly beheaded their captives on the Arab TV station Al-Jazeera, one of the first of these being the American journalist Daniel Pearl in February 2002, even before the war began. The savage video showed a black-hooded man later identified as Khalid Sheikh Mohammed using a knife to slice through Pearl's throat while the camera rolled.

American military forces were ill equipped to cope with the new brand of urban warfare founded on raw terrorism. After the Vietnam War ended, the U.S. military focused its training on a doctrine of rapid maneuver and combined arms, the so-called AirLand Battle concept. It worked amazingly well in the quick "conventional" fight to liberate Iraq but then bogged down in the guerrilla jihad that followed. No comprehensive doctrine existed for counterinsurgency outside relatively small units like Army Special Forces and U.S. Army Rangers.

As the insurgency gained momentum after July 2003, U.S. occupation troops pulled back into huge forward operating bases far removed from the population and began executing "offensive operations" to destroy enemy forces. The U.S. military sallied forth daily in search-and-destroy missions against jihadists in civilian clothing whom they could rarely identify and whom the general population concealed and protected. American commanders launched large-scale sweeps to roll up enemy leaders and terrorist members, fired artillery to interdict insurgent activity, and used airpower to level sites suspected of supporting the jihad. Following each operation, Americans retreated to their consolidated FOBs and, instead of attempting to secure and hold ground, conceded the cities and countryside back to street-thug insurgents.

Predictably, the situation throughout Iraq deteriorated. Attacks against Coalition forces continued to increase.

The Coalition Provisional Authority made up of members of the allied governments and the limited Iraqi Governing Council under military occupation ceded "sovereign and independent" power to the Interim Government of Iraq in June 2004 pending free elections. The first post-Saddam prime minister, Ayad Allawi, and his successor as president following the elections in April 2005, Jalal Talabani, faced challenges of increasing unrest and violence throughout the war-ravaged nation. While relatively small hardcore cadres of Sunni fundamentalists and foreign bomb makers and sympathizers plotting and operating in selected areas had little chance of winning militarily, their aims were not to win through battle but instead to succeed by destabilizing the society and creating an atmosphere of generalized fear and chaos. The growing insurgency, combined with the poor state of the Iraqi army and the nation's police and security forces, hampered all efforts to gain and maintain control of the nation. Militant Shiite (the minority Muslim sect but not in Iraq) bands and former Ba'athist elements engaged in open rebellion in more than a dozen cities.

The United States offered to leave the nation to its own resources if that was what the Interim Government desired. "If that's the wish of the government of Iraq," said John Negroponte, U.S. ambassador to Iraq, "we will comply with those wishes."

The Iraqi government all but begged the United States to remain.

April, May, and June 2004 represented the bloodiest months of fighting since the end of the initial invasion a year earlier. On March 31, four Blackwater USA security contractors were ambushed and killed in Fallujah, their corpses desecrated on Al-Jazeera TV, dragged through the streets, and hung off the side of a bridge over the Euphrates River to decay. As a result of increasing violence such as this, U.S. forces launched a spring offensive against "Muhammad's Army of al-Ansar" in Fallujah and Najaf.

More than two hundred resistance fighters were killed and forty Americans died in Fallujah before the Iraqi Governing Council got cold feet due to negative media coverage led, naturally, by Al-Jazeera and called a halt to the operation. Coalition forces withdrew, ringed off the city against either exit or entry, and waited. Fallujah fell completely into the hands of the insurgents, who, unhampered, began killing off all local civilian opposition.

June produced a coordinated series of car bombings in Mosul that killed sixty-two people, most of whom were Iraqi policemen. For a while, militia leader Muqtada al-Sadr and a thousand men of his "Mahdi Militia" took over the capital. Finally driven out of the city, al-Sadr and his "army" sought refuge in the nearby holy city of Najaf, where they went to ground in the gold-domed Imam Ali Mosque. Since, for public relations reasons, Coalition nations were unwilling to attack and perhaps destroy the holy relic, they besieged it instead and fought a series of minor skirmishes in the surrounding streets until peace was brokered in late August and al-Sadr accepted a cease-fire.

The bloodiest single battle for the United States in the war so far began in November 2004 when U.S. Marines launched Operation Phantom Fury, the Second Battle of Fallujah. This time the Americans took and secured the stronghold, capturing hundreds of insurgents and killing over two thousand of them. The Marines lost ninety-two dead and several hundred wounded.

In an apparent attempt to foment a nationwide uprising, insurgents in Mosul launched their own offensive on November 10 to coincide with the beginning of Phantom Fury in Fallujah. It started with a series of coordinated attacks on police stations in the city. Those policemen who survived fled Mosul and left the city lawless for nearly a month, during which it suffered tremendously due to the unprecedented violence level and destruction of the city's infrastructure. Many scientists, professors, academics, doctors, engineers, journalists, lawyers, clergy, and other "intellectuals" were either murdered or forced to flee—a common enough occurrence throughout the world whenever tyranny supplanted freedom.

The U.S. 25th Infantry Division from FOB Marez, supplemented by Kurdish Peshmerga fighters, took the offensive and maneuvered into the more dangerous sections of the city to restore control. Beginning in 2004, U.S. Army Rangers were inserted onto FOB Marez in Mosul to track down high-value targets and deprive the insurgency of its leadership.

Mosul would be my fourth combat deployment.

25

MOSUL, IRAQ, 2004

Kimberly asked me one time, "Why do you *want* to deploy?"

"It's my job. It's what I do best. It's about the guy to your left and to your right."

I didn't know if that was the true reason or not. Mosul was my fourth deployment to a war zone, and I still pondered her question. Sometimes I thought there must be something wrong with me, character-wise, like that guy—Steve McQueen, I think—in the old movie *The War Lover* that Hunter told me about. It happened in World War II, the Army Air Corps. Steve McQueen, the guy he played, kept flying more and more missions, like it was an obsession or something. You see, he *liked* war and didn't want it to end.

Had I become *that*? A war lover?

Whenever I recalled the two dead shepherds on the hill, the young kid and the older one, probably his father, the image always failed to stir emotion in me one way or another. The killing was necessary. It was my job, and I was going to get better and better at it.

Perhaps war was something in the Ranger character? Something in the hearts and souls of men who gravitated to ultrawarrior confederations. I understood the elite brotherhood of the Plains Indians, the Cheyenne and Comanche and Apache for whom warfare was the ultimate test of their manhood. Or the Spartans, especially the Spartans. Old guys from World War II and Vietnam often spoke as though their time at war had been the high point of their entire lives. Even when they hated the fighting and killing, they recalled with nostalgia and affection the closeness of brotherhood and the sense of belonging. That was why they attended the reunions of their old outfits year after year while they seldom showed up for a family reunion.

"I was closer to the guys on my team than I was to my own brothers. They *became* my brothers," a Green Beret who fought in the Northern Highlands of Vietnam confided in some of us once. "It's a primitive, masculine world where a man can *be* a man."

It was understandable why so many Rangers preferred the old movies like *True Grit*, *The Longest Day*, and *Rocky*, movie heroes like John Wayne, Clint Eastwood, and Sylvester Stallone. These old guys were comfortable with their masculinity and it showed, unlike in recent movies that so often depicted the American male as some kind of sensitive, compassionate wimp or dolt enslaved to feminist values. I mean, *Leonardo DiCaprio*!

Almost every action movie you saw anymore had some 5'1", 100-pound dame leading teams of men and whipping the hell out of half a dozen brutish apes four times her size. She takes 'em all down *in the same fight* with her martial arts prowess, courage, and determination. Even in the sitcoms, the woman was the head of the household, the husband some kind of bumbler who keeps getting into messes from which the woman has to rescue him.

Give me a break! In the real world, one of those brutish apes would tuck that little slip of a girl underneath his arm and walk off with her, no matter how many black belts she owned. There were becoming fewer and fewer places left for real men, at least in the "civilized" world. Even my own army was sending its women into battle, and if you think that's not fucking up the natural order of things then you don't know anything about men, war, and the real world. At least, so far, there was no GI Jane in the Rangers, SEALs, or Green Berets.

I was no philosopher. I barely completed high school. I had common sense, though. Maybe it really was about the guy to your left and to your right.

Only the 1st Platoon of Alpha Company rotated into Mosul, with a couple of staff guys, a major, and a sergeant major chopped over from Battalion to run the ops shop. FOB Marez under the control of a battalion from the 25th Infantry Division was located next to an airport and on the site of one of Saddam Hussein's palaces, which became headquarters for the 25th. Saddam had dozens of palaces scattered all over Iraq; the guy lived the high life what time he wasn't gassing Kurds, murdering the opposition, or sending his two moronic sons out to rape women.

He wouldn't need his palaces anymore. Our guys had nabbed him the previous December hiding in a hole in the ground like a 'possum or skunk. The Iraqis held him prisoner and were bound to hang him sooner or later, an end befitting a tyrant.

Marez was a good-sized compound, about a half mile square, surrounded by HESCO barriers and concertina. Rangers had our own living quarters, but we shared a chow hall, a gym, and even a movie theater and PX with other troops stationed at the FOB. It was easy living compared to H-1 Airfield during my last rotation to Iraq. A soldier could get soft living like this.

Except Rangers had little time to enjoy the amenities. We were too busy targeting networks of jihadists in the city, going after them where they lived, blowing in doors, throwing bangers, shooting. After all, they were only a half hour away at the most. A platoon operation order was a straightforward thing, emphasizing speed and simplicity. Intelligence would come down from the TOC: So-and-so code-named Bugs Bunny or Elmer Fudd is believed to be at so-and-so location. The order went something like this: This is who we're going after; this is where he is; this is how we're getting there; these are actions on target; and this is how we exfiltrate. Now get in there and make Mama proud.

26

We Rangers did our best work at night. Two Black Hawk helicopters fanned the black air and lifted off the pad from FOB Marez, banked sharply, and sprinted low out across the city. Flying fast to avoid ground fire from enthusiastic hajjis tanked on too much hate, they wouldn't slow down until we reached our destination.

Seats in the birds had been removed to make room for chalks of armed Rangers, ten in each chopper. I rode in the right door of the first Hawk with big Nate Abrams and Kyle Butcher, my feet dangling out above the skids as I watched the city pass rapidly below. Those not in either doorway squatted on ammo cans or on flak-proof Kevlar panels spread out on the deck. Eric Franck was always afraid of getting shot in the ass.

Everyone wore desert cammies, Kevlar vests and helmets, leather gloves, and NODs that gave us the rhino appearance. Over the vests hung load-bearing harnesses to which were attached equipment and ammo we needed for the raid. Next to me in the doorway lay a coil of 2-inch-thick nylon rope.

Below, haze had settled close to the ground, part blown sand and part fog. The catastrophe that was Mosul stretched out toward the horizon on one quarter and toward the Tigris River on the other. There were lights in the city, but not like in Atlanta or anything. It was more like a blackout in which nearly every building cheated by leaving a bulb or two burning.

Mosul was a world gone totally to hell since the war started a year ago. All the streets were crumbling and strewn with trash and debris, piles of garbage infested with rats, the rusted hulks of abandoned Toyotas and assorted foreign-made pickups and trucks. Telephone and electric line poles leaned like tired old men while walls and buildings were battle-scarred and pockmarked from bullets and exploding shells and rockets. In the beginning, we had fought soldiers—Saddam's Republican Guard or the al-Ansar battalions. That phase of the war had ended and eroded into the Fedayeen and al Qaeda, Shiite versus Sunni, martyrs wearing dynamite vests and suicide trucks filled with high explosives. Everything was complete chaos. It was dangerous work if you could get it—and we got plenty of it.

Ben Hunter had shaken his helmeted head as chalks loaded onto the birds at the FOB. "This remind you of anything?" he drawled.

"I forgot to take out the trash before we left?"

"Dumb-ass. This is like *Black Hawk Down*. Remember how it started in Somalia with Rangers fast-roping down onto a building to snatch some of Aidid's aides."

Rangers had died at Mogadishu. You went out on a mission, you never knew what kind of hornets' nest you were going to stir up.

Staff Sergeant Ken Clayton, Third Squad leader, knelt inside the helicopter between the banks of installed radios where he could look out either open doorway. He was built like a spark plug, short, barrel-chested, with wide shoulders, a dozen tattoos, and a fierce countenance. Like Rembold, my previous squad leader, Clayton knew his stuff, his Seven-dash-Eight Infantryman's Bible. You never doubted his technical and tactical proficiency. It was always reassuring to have him in the lead.

He passed the word, *"Get ready!"* A raid like this depended on split-second timing. Below us on the ground, Humvees full of other Rangers raced toward the target to seal it off and prevent the HVTs smelling a rat and squirting before we trapped him between us. Tonight's mark was code-named Elvis. Elvis, we trusted, had not left the building.

The helicopter crew chief thrust his fists over his head. "One minute!" he shouted above the sound of rotors and engines.

"Ready to go!" Clayton responded.

"Let's do it!"

Air blew cold through the open doors. Desert nights were always cold. No matter, sweat still tickled my cheeks. I quickly brushed it away, all my senses concentrated on the excitement ahead. *Rangers lead the way.* Rangers were the army at its gung-ho best. This was where I *belonged.*

The target house hove into view, the most obvious landmark on the street. It was a four-story, block-shaped building that reminded me of a skid row rooming house. Sooty yellow light squared out a few windows on each floor. It was after midnight. Most of the residents who weren't out causing mischief should be in bed by now.

A couple of pedestrians walking by in a pool of light from a street-level window jigged a comical little double take and took off running when they spotted the choppers swoop in low toward the roof of the building. They did an even more zany double take when they ran into the well-timed arrival of our ground support. Rangers were everywhere, or so it must have seemed to the two misfortunates who really *should* have been home in bed. Looking as bulky and menacing as space invaders, Rangers quickly sealed off all escape exits from the building and cuffed the two pedestrians to hold for questioning.

Few targets retained the presence of mind to resist if a raid went down with speed and authority. The more time you gave them to sort things out, the more apt they were to fight. A building beginning to fill with armed invaders delivering explosions, smoke, and flashes of light momentarily frightened and disoriented most people. They generally dropped where they were, stunned and startled and willing to follow simple commands without question. Those stupid enough to fight back were shot.

The first Black Hawk skidded to a hover directly over the flat roof while the other bird made a tight circle to give us time to off-load. I tossed out the coil of rope, one end of which was attached to the inside of the chopper, and shook it a couple of times to make sure the other end hadn't drifted off the roof. Everything looked dense and impenetrable down there, even through NODs.

Men started burning out on the ropes from either side of the bird, sliding down two or three on each rope at the same time like firefighters on a fire pole, to shouts of "Go! Go! Go!" Eric Franck, my redheaded fellow team leader in Third Squad, swung out on a handful of rope and dropped out of sight into the darkness. I followed behind him, M-4 slung across my back and the rope scorching my gloves.

Below me, I heard men crash-landing, all kinds of racket, enough to alert every hajji within a square block, if not the dead themselves. Franck the Tank, often so-called because of his build, added his roar to the other expletives flying up at me. "Fuck! Fu-uck!"

I landed on top of Franck, the both of us tumbling ass over teakettle, entangled with every other Ranger in the chalk in a snarl of telephone wires, cables, electrical wire, clotheslines . . . Wire ran everywhere across the roof. We had landed in the middle of it. Cursing and scrambling marked our efforts to break free and reach the roof door to start clearing the place. Knives flashed as men lashed out to cut themselves loose. Luckily, no one was electrocuted.

Most houses and buildings in Iraq had doors that opened onto the roofs, built that way so that during the summer months residents could sleep in the open air to get some respite from the heat. I didn't step on anyone as I fought myself free from the wires, so I guess it wasn't yet hot enough for people to be bedding out.

Franck and a couple of other guys reached the door first. Nate Abrams wrecked it with a big "donker," at which point the entire raiding party overtook them and stormed inside to the top floor. The action after that was fast and furious. We had done this lots of times before. It was almost routine. Well, not exactly routine—operations were *never* routine— but it was at least familiar. Running with weapons ready, stacks of three or four Rangers took each door on the floor. It was like a police drug raid in New York or Chicago, only on steroids.

Down went the splintered doors, almost simultaneously, kicked in or donkered. You never knew what surprise waited behind Door One or Two or whatever. It could be hajjis armed with AK-47s or a PKM machine gun. That was why you had to hit them hard and fast. First into each room flew a flash-bang to confuse and disorient. Before the occupants had time to recover, before they knew what was going on, Rangers were rolling them up and flex-cuffing their hands behind their backs. One man stayed behind to consolidate and guard the prisoners while the rest of us blitzed down to the next floor.

Most of the residents were probably insurgents, but it was difficult to tell in a country where it was a male thing to go armed with at least an AK-47. You took no chances; you never knew which of them might be as crazy as a shithouse rat and want to fight. Cuff 'em all, sort 'em out later.

Thus, in a mad stampede, Rangers cleared the building room by room, floor by floor, working down the levels so quickly that Elvis and his cronies hopefully wouldn't have time to resist. What you heard was soldier noises of breath coming in excited gasps, gear rattling almost silently, the sharp thump of exploding flash-bangs, and finally shouted commands to "Get down!" in fractured Arabic.

There were only one or two women in the entire building, no children, which was suspicious in itself. The rooms, pitch dark because of window coverings, resembled cluttered and musty caves. For the most part, Iraqi bedrooms were furnished with only thin mattresses and piles of rags on the floor. No Ranger was especially nasty to prisoners. We just didn't particularly care what happened to them, especially not in the middle of the action when you had no idea what you would find behind a door when you kicked it in. We were prepared to shoot to kill.

The only thing we knew about Elvis from the mission briefing was that he was supposed to be inside the building, in one of the rooms. Nothing else, except he was an Iraqi or Syrian man in his late twenties or early thirties, a description that fit almost 90 percent of the jihadists in Mosul. Fortunately, the PL had a mug shot of the guy, which he compared to the captives as we cleared the building.

On the third floor, a door went down in a crash like all the others. In went a flash-bang, followed by Rangers on the prod shouting commands. The room was full of men wearing robes or naked from sleep, all of them caught off guard and blinking from the noise and smoke. As soon as we had them spread-eagled on the floor, the PL walked among them, lifting their heads to compare their faces to his photograph.

Elvis wasn't alive in Des Moines or Kansas City working in a Burger King after all. There he was in Mosul, a scruffy little beggar with a beard and his trademark sideburns. Captain Molino jerked him off the floor by the scruff of his neck. It was him, all right, but the guy was already waving his hand back and forth at shoulder level and shaking his head at the same time, the Iraqi equivalent of "What the fuck you talkin' about?"

It was a good night, a good operation, and a good haul. Sometimes we ended up in firefights and people got hurt. Tonight, no shots were fired, and the only injury was to our dignity when we fast-roped into the wires on top of the building. We rounded up thirteen or fourteen prisoners, including Elvis, whose real name I never cared to learn and probably couldn't have pronounced anyhow unless it was Mohammed. It seemed every Muslim somebody and his cousins were all named Mohammed.

Searching Elvis's cave, we recovered contraband that included about $150,000 cash, American; several pistols and AK-47s; wooden boxes of the sort that once contained rifles but were now disturbingly empty; manuals on Apache helicopters and U.S. M-1A1 Abrams tanks; computer components; and a training video on how to target convoys with IEDs.

I later found out Elvis was a top-level operative in the insurgency hierarchy. Now we had him. One more guy taken down who wouldn't be killing Americans.

"You gotta love this job," Hunter joked, but I knew he meant it.

27

Mosul, situated 250 miles north of Baghdad on Iraq's upper plains, was Iraq's third-largest city, with a population of around 1.75 million, most of whom were Kurds sprinkled with a sizable minority of Sunni Iraqis still sympathetic to Saddam Hussein's regime and therefore a prime target for Rangers out of FOB Marez.

Described as the "Pearl of the North," Mosul possessed an Oriental character noticeably absent in Baghdad and other Iraqi cities. Extravagant old mansions in the prosperous suburbs ubiquitously displayed marble around windows and door frames; many of them added pillars and dramatic balconies of the same beautiful material. Even the Old City on the western banks of the Tigris River retained some of that character in gracious if simpler terms in its narrow, shady alleys and constricted streets and mud-plastered houses.

Opposite the Old City on the other side of the Tigris survived remnants of the ancient city of Nineveh, where the Old Testament prophet Jonah lived and died and was buried. Jonah was the guy swallowed by the whale so God could teach him a lesson. That would have taught *me* a lesson.

"Man, do you know how *old* this is?" Ben Hunter marveled. "I mean, like Adam-and-Eve old."

"It's not much of a paradise now," I said.

Hunter shrugged. "Blame it on the serpent. How many armies you reckon have been right here where we are now and seen this country?"

Turkey lay a few miles north of Mosul. When the United States originally planned its 2003 invasion, generals intended to launch troops out of Turkey to capture Mosul and northern Iraq. After the Turkish parliament refused to grant access, the United States confined its military action in the north to strategic bombing and strategic covert operations. Army Special Forces parachuted in to organize the Kurds and operate with them to create a "northern front."

Under pressure, Saddam's 5th Corps in Mosul abandoned the city on April 11, 2003, two days after the fall of Baghdad, and eventually surrendered. Kurdish fighters took over the city and looted it before ceding control to U.S. forces. The 101st Airborne Division, the Screaming Eagles, moved in to pacify the region.

Since then, Syria on the west and Iran to the east, both of whom were less than cordial to the United States, had opened their borders to allow the infiltration of al Qaeda insurgents, who flocked to Mosul to destabilize the city and organize resistance to Coalition forces. In July 2003, Saddam Hussein's sadistic sons Uday and Qusay were caught hiding in Mosul. They refused to surrender and went down in a blaze of gunfire.

Now, a year later, Mosul was a hotbed of insurgent activity. Guys in my pay grade rarely saw the Big Picture, but even I recognized the way the character of the war had changed and was continuing to change. Used for surgical and strategic operations such as seizing airfields and dams, Rangers missed out on the big "Shock and Awe" movements at the beginning when the furious race across the country put our troops in Baghdad and most of Iraq's larger cities within weeks after the fighting started. Ordinary people poured into the streets to hug our guys and pull down Saddam Hussein's statues and burn his posters and billboards. Everybody—even the president of the United States—thought the war was over when, in fact, as we were discovering daily, it was only beginning.

The insurgency spread like cancer and, like cancer, increased in potency as it gained strength and turned more life-threatening. The population seemed to be settling into it, accepting the pain of cancer and waiting for it to either metastasize or go into remission. What the media initially described as "euphoria" when freedom first presented itself was turning into a grudging and resilient form of resentment against the "occupiers." Human nature was a matter of conditioning. The old life might not have been a good life, but it was familiar and you could get by and it was *our life*. People hated it when "normalcy" got fucked with.

The 25th Infantry Division or, at various times, the Screaming Eagles of the 101st were handed responsibility for the Mosul area of operations. Their job was to tame and rebuild the city. They had teams out trying to keep the electricity and water going and to encourage the new government to take charge and kick the insurgents the hell out of the city and the country. Americans seemed to care more about the nation than most of the people did, even though we didn't eat lambs' heads and pray five times a day toward Mecca. This was our neighborhood, and we didn't like al Qaeda and jihadist assholes from Iran and Syria coming in to trash it.

Rangers did little mixing with the population since we mostly worked the night shifts. Insurgents also did their best work at night, sneaking out like vampires to suck blood by blowing up something or maybe shooting an American if they were lucky. We chased them all night and let conventional troops chase them during the day while they rebuilt the city. Rangers and jihadists mostly went to our mattresses before the sun rose and the more-or-less normal routine of city life began, punctuated now and again by a bombing at the market or an ambush against local police or an American patrol or convoy.

Rangers suffered from mild cultural shock on those occasions when we ventured into the daylight city, like grumpy bears emerging from hibernation to support the troops in some civic action project or other. Unlike in the United States, where every family owns two or three cars and a healthy teenager won't walk a block to see a friend, almost everyone in the third world traveled by foot. Everything a household needed to survive was within walking distance.

The open markets presented great piles of parboiled sheep heads keeping watch with boiled eyeballs through swarms of black flies. Next door stood a booth selling jihadist CDs and other anti-American propaganda. On every corner, it seemed, some kid or some old man—it was difficult to tell age in Iraq since people aged before their time—hawked flatbread kabobs of goat meat, peppers, cheese, and Lord only knew what else. Some of our guys were gutsy enough, or foolish enough, to try anything.

At the FOB we slept next to where we shit and shit next to where we ate. That wasn't close enough. Our gastronomic daredevils tried to make it out of quarters to get some privacy before they collapsed. Most of them failed to make it to the latrine before they had to drop to their knees to puke and shit at the same time. Osama bin Laden's and Saddam Hussein's revenge.

Women in town were always the first to rise with the seep of dawn. They ventured timidly out of their houses to look up and down the street to make sure nothing was going on before they hurried to the market to buy goat cheese and unleavened bread for breakfast. If a military patrol went by, they ran up to their roofs to beg with outstretched arms and a kind of keening wail. Guys sometimes tossed them MREs, but if we didn't you could look back and see that they had learned the universal sign language of "the finger."

None of the women dared actually talk to an American. Her reputation was shot immediately if she so much as smiled at one of us. I heard of "honor killings" when a husband so dishonored had the legal right under Sharia law to stone the bitch to death. A daughter legitimately raped could also be "honor killed." What the hell was the matter with these people?

"Wonderful folks," Hunter observed sarcastically.

"You suppose some of these babes might be smoking hot if you take those bedsheets they wear off 'em?" Joe Edwards speculated.

"I guess we'll never know."

"I could always convert to Muslim and have five or six wives, fourteen concubines, and seventy-two virgins when it's my turn to go to the Happy Hunting Grounds."

Local children ran out and followed our trucks through the street, cheering and begging for handouts. Cheering turned to rock-throwing jeers if we passed them by.

"Jihadists in training," Kyle Butcher muttered.

Every once in a while a hajji would get inspired enough or drunk enough to run into the street and shout, "Fuck America!" We were admonished to be culturally sensitive and never shout back at him.

Most Iraqis, however, simply stared at us as we went by as though waiting for us to leave. Inhospitable ancient Mesopotamia.

We weren't going to be leaving anytime soon. The buildup was under way. Frontline troops like the 101st and the 25th were backed up by stacked layers of support: military police; armor; artillery; intelligence specialists; radar operators; aviation mechanics; communications experts; aerial surveillance teams; civic action groups; engineers and construction units; linguists . . .

Tons of equipment and sophisticated weapons were pouring in: laser-guided "smart bombs" and deadly JDAMs (Joint Direct Attack Munitions), the "mother of all bombs"; antinuclear defense systems; missiles; air defense batteries . . .

Attack helicopters launched Hellfire or TOW missiles. Ground-attack A-10 Warthog warplanes devoured targets with depleted uranium-core bullets. AC-130 Spectre gunships, revised and updated from "Spooky the Magic Dragon" of Vietnam fame, came armed with 40 mm and 20 mm automatic cannon and 105 mm howitzers. Hellfire-armed drones roared high above to spy on people, cars, insurgent cells, and suspicious men with weapons and blast them if necessary. You couldn't hear the fighter-bomber jets, but you saw their sky trails when they passed over. Sometimes at night you saw flashes on the horizon, like distant lightning, when they bombed targets along the borders.

On the ground, steel behemoths like the M-1A1 Abrams tank and armored fighting vehicles represented by the Bradley, the Stryker, and the 25-ton M-2A3 prowled the ancient land of Adam and Eve, striking new fear where for millennia armies had fought and died.

In the midst of all this were the Rangers, men rather than machines who still operated much as we had since Rogers's Rangers in the French and Indian Wars. Risking everything for the mission, going back out time after time to be tested individually and in small warrior bands.

Funny how when you're young you think nothing can kill you, that you're going to live forever. So far, 1st Platoon was either blessed, charmed, skilled, or just plain lucky. Soldiers often joked that they would rather be lucky than good. Although other platoons in Alpha Company had suffered several WIAs and sent a few men like Captain Riptoe, Staff Sergeant Livaudais, and Specialist Long to be "Airborne Rangers in the sky," 1st Platoon had not lost a single man to hostile action. Specialist Kyle Butcher could be fatalistic about it at times.

"It ain't natural," he said. "I don't believe in guardian angels."

"Sure you do," Forbis teased. "Haven't you seen 'em every time we bust into a house?"

"All I seen is your ass in front of me. I'm just saying that it can't keep on like this."

Ben Hunter walked by on his way to the latrine. "Sure it can," he said.

It was true what they said about war—that there was always more work to do than there were soldiers to carry it out. The FOB compound around Saddam's old palace was rarely idle, not even at night, *especially* at night. Patrols came and went, missions were launched, warplanes took off and landed, guard reliefs replaced each other. Men stumbled to and from their racks to catch a few hours' sleep, exchanging crude greetings on the way.

"Your face looks like my ass, Monkey Balls."

"Might cheer me up if you suck my dick."

Soldiers in combat could be staggeringly disgusting.

We slept in Ranger panties or naked with a bottle of water nearby to keep us hydrated against the heat that constantly wrung sweat from our bodies. An hour or so before sunrise on those nights we stayed in, the damned flies started to swarm, tickling, buzzing, and biting us awake. It was impossible to sleep with the annoying little bastards creeping all over your nose and lips. So we got up ill-tempered and still sleepy and tried to carry on normal activities such as chow and talking about girls and cars and drinking and who was getting married or divorced and whose wife was screwing around or had run off with the kids.

"Fucking pussy! Man, the bitch don't write me no more. It's like she broke her hand and can't read and write no more."

Mostly, we devoted our time to the job. Intelligence would come down, and that meant a mission. It could have come from anywhere—Predator drones in the sky, National Security Agency eavesdropping on cell phones, HUMINT (human intelligence, "snitches") . . . Most Iraqis were more than willing to sell out their neighbors for personal gain. They had been screwed over so much for so long that they had few qualms about how they got what they wanted or needed.

At the Tactical Operations Center during mission briefings, I got to looking at the other guys. Butcher, the Hunter brothers, Abrams, Franck the Tank, Sergeant Clayton, and the others in the platoon, all of them smiling, joking, smoking, moving around, getting things done, preparing to handle whatever hand fate dealt, living in the moment, living as though death, if it came, always came for the other guy. Maybe Butch was onto something; we couldn't keep on like this, immune to the ravages of war. Sooner or later somebody was going to get hurt or killed. How would it be to return to Fort Benning without some of them and have to face their wives or girlfriends and mothers? These guys were my brothers. How did you handle a loss like that?

"Do your job," I gruffly commanded my fire team. "Do it right and everybody goes home. Okay?"

Joe *(left)* is pictured here with his father Bill *(right)* before his dad was killed in a car accident when Joe was twelve. *(Courtesy of the author)*

Joe *(top)* as an athlete wrestling in high school in Connecticut. He was inducted into the National Wrestling Hall of Fame in early 2013 and received the Outstanding American award. *(Courtesy of the author)*

Joe *(left)* as a teenager prior to enlisting in the army after 9/11. With him is family friend Mark Bernier, a Bristol, Connecticut, police officer and army reservist. *(Courtesy of the author)*

Joe *(right)* with his mother, Lori *(left),* during his graduation ceremony from Basic Training in 2002. *(Courtesy of the author)*

(From left to right) Erin, Joe, and Randy Kapacziewski at Joe's Basic Training Graduation. *(Courtesy of the author)*

Joe between grandparents Bob and Alice Churchill following his graduation from Ranger School. *(Courtesy of the author)*

Joe *(far left)* at Ranger School Graduation with Rory Virostko *(third from left)* in 2003. *(Courtesy of the author)*

Joe *(right)* and Josh Kuhner *(left)* at Ranger School Graduation. *(Courtesy of the author)*

(From left to right) Griffin Hoover, Josh Kuhner, Joe Kapacziewski, Jermaine Wilson, Daniel Harrison, Ben Hunter, and Joseph Kopp, who are all squad members, after a combat parachute jump onto H-1 airfield in Iraq in 2003. *(Courtesy of the author)*

Joe with Ian *(center)* and Ben Hunter at Ben and Lori's wedding, 2003. *(Courtesy of the author)*

Joe at the wheel of a "Ground Mobility Vehicle" during a combat deployment to Afghanistan in 2004. *(Courtesy of the author)*

Joe and platoon members prepare "what's for dinner—chicken" during a 2004 deployment to Afghanistan prior to his being wounded in Iraq in 2005. *(Courtesy of the author)*

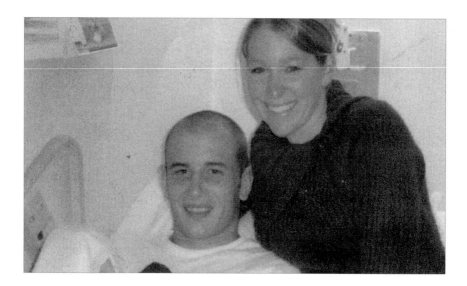

Joe and Kimberly at Walter Reed Hospital in 2005 after Joe was wounded in Iraq. Although it was an ordeal for both, they tried to remain optimistic about their future. *(Courtesy of the author)*

Friends visit Walter Reed: *(top row left to right)* Garrett McTear, Robert Bell, Alex Brenner, Allison and Justin Slusher, *(middle row)* unknown, Kim Kapacziewski, Abby Hunter, Lori Hunter, and Ian Hunter, *(bottom row)* Joe Kapacziewski, Ben Hunter, and Addie Hunter. *(Courtesy of the author)*

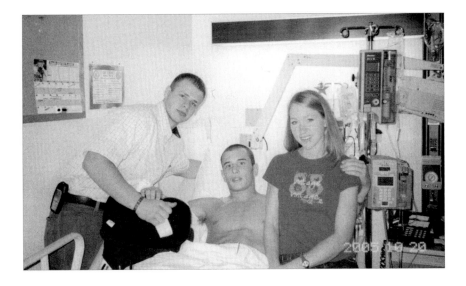

Walter Reed Hospital, October 20, 2005—just a couple of weeks after Joe's injury. *(From right to left)* Kimberly, Joe, and Rex Terpstra. *(Courtesy of the author)*

Joe hunting waterfowl in Chesapeake Bay while still on crutches and in rehabilitation out of Walter Reed Hospital in 2006. *(Courtesy of the author)*

Joe recovering in 2006 after his wounds, by riding with the Wounded Warrior Project on Soldier Ride from Miami to Key West, Florida. Note the "Fixator" supporting his right leg—and the scars. This was prior to amputation. *(Courtesy of the author)*

Joe and Kimberly at their "real wedding." *(Courtesy of the author)*

Joe riding at Midland Farms where Kimberly worked. Joe's decision to have his right leg amputated resulted partly from an incident that occurred at the farm when he was assisting in a pony race and his leg buckled. *(Courtesy of the author)*

Joe *(center)* on a 2007 elk hunt with Brian McCarty *(left)* and Richard Price. *(Courtesy of the author)*

Joe drove himself relentlessly to meet all physical requirements in order to remain as an active duty Army Ranger. Here he is running the 2008 Chicago Triathlon. *(Courtesy of the author)*

Joe *(right)* and 1/75 Ranger Derome West *(left)* at the 2009 Turkey Hunt. *(Courtesy of the author)*

Staff Sergeant Joe Kap adjusts his prosthesis following active combat in Afghanistan in 2009. *(Courtesy of the author)*

Joe and his son Wyatt visit the Ranger Memorial in Fort Benning, Georgia. *(Courtesy of the author)*

Joe with his son Cody before his 2011 Afghanistan deployment. *(Courtesy of the author)*

In 2011, Joe became the first enlisted soldier ever to receive the No Greater Sacrifice Freedom Award in Washington, D.C. U.S. Army Colonel David W. Sutherland *(left)* and Senator Joe Lieberman *(right)* congratulate Joe *(center)*. *(Courtesy of the author)*

Joe and Wyatt at Ranger Rendezvous in 2011. *(Courtesy of the author)*

Joe *(left)* and Randy *(right)* at the 2011 Operation One Voice Honor Run. *(Courtesy of the author)*

Joe *(left)* and best friend, Nick Bientema *(right),* relax on the beach in Northern California. Both are right-leg amputees from wounds suffered in Iraq. *(Courtesy of the author)*

Joe greets Wyatt upon his return from deployment as a platoon sergeant on his latest rotation to Afghanistan in 2012. *(Courtesy of the author)*

Joe *(right)* and Randy Kapacziewski *(left)* in 2012. *(Courtesy of the author)*

Joe *(far left)* and Kimberly *(third from left)* with their sons Cody *(second from left)* and Wyatt *(far right)* in 2012. *(Brooke Garcia Photography)*

Joe and Kimberly in 2012. *(Courtesy of Bill Miles)*

Joe *(center)* with Ian *(left)* and Ben Hunter. *(Courtesy of the author)*

Joe *(center)* with Cody *(left)* and Wyatt *(right)*, summer of 2012. *(Courtesy of the author)*

Joe and William "Pops" Bunce *(right)* riding horses in Wyoming. *(Courtesy of the author)*

Joe *(left)* with Captain Chad Fleming *(right)*. Joe and Chad were in the accident together and supported each other throughout the recovery. *(Courtesy of the author)*

Almost every night we were kicking in doors, blowing up things, shooting a lot of bad guys, making an impact on the insurgency network. Rangers were sent to Iraq to hunt down the enemy, and that was what we did. We became proficient, really good at it. The platoon referred to this period as the "Glory Days" of the war and to itself as the "Glory Boys."

People got bored if things slowed down for a few days. That was when somebody shrugged and said, "Buzzard's bad luck. Can't kill nothing and nothing won't die."

But every buzzard had his day.

28

Thanksgiving was always a big deal with Grandma and Grandpa Churchill. Back in Connecticut, Erin and Randy and some of their friends and their kids would be at Grandma's big table in the kitchen, gathered around the turkey and yams and Grandma's cornbread dressing. There would probably have been frost that morning, the leaves on the trees were already turned, and somebody would ask sooner or later, "Heard from Joe lately? He doing okay in Iraq?"

Kimberly would be with her mom in Georgia, maybe with her sister, Melissa, too. I had no idea what they would be doing; I hadn't been at home long enough to spend a holiday with Kim since we met. Better not to think about it now.

Half the earth away from home, I had turkey at the FOB. The army always put on a spread at Thanksgiving and Christmas to make up for guys not being home for the holidays. No watching the football game or anything afterward, though. Instead, the Tactical Operations Center summoned Captain Molino's 1st Platoon's Glory Boys for mission briefing. Somebody in one of the Old Town neighborhoods had snitched.

"Insurgents are in the house now."

"How many?" Captain Molino asked.

"Unknown number."

"That's enlightening. How reliable is the source?"

"We've used this informant before."

This business, at least during the war's present stage, was a lot like cops and robbers, guys with the white hats and guys with the black hats, only magnified about a thousandfold. You received a hot tip, you rolled on it like gangbusters, like somebody had tugged on Superman's cape or bitch-slapped John Wayne.

Shortly before midnight, eight Humvees loaded with Rangers blasted through the darkened streets along Mosul's riverfront and turned in-city toward the target pinpointed by GPS directions. It was time to kick ass and take names. By this time, with replacements, 1st Platoon was up to full strength with three squads and a Weapons Squad, reinforced by a Ranger sniper team for the mission, a couple of guys with a mortar tube, and a medic. The Hummers sped through the narrow, dark streets with headlights blazing, relying on speed and surprise to avoid ambushes rather than try to navigate with blackout lights. A medic always accompanied an operation, just in case. When people might be shooting at each other, there was always a "just in case."

You made a few raids in a row and nobody shot at you and you shot at nobody, you could let it get routine. You got lax, and that was when the war rose up to bite you in the butt. You had to keep the edge. That was what I preached to my guys. Keep the edge, keep sharp, and everybody completed the rotation and went home alive.

Adrenaline was pumping. Even Staff Sergeant Clayton had that keen look of anticipation. Nate Abrams in the back of my team's Hummer elbowed me in the side. I looked at him, and he nodded toward Kyle Butcher. Butch was a born-and-bred Georgia boy, a good kid on his second overseas deployment. He went home every free weekend when we were at Benning. There was enough light from the headlights to see his face. He was thin in a wiry, rawhide sort of way, and his face, introspective now, made him look as though he should still be in high school. Perhaps he was thinking of the girl back in Georgia he talked about. Whatever, his mind wasn't on the job.

I slapped the back of his helmet. He shook himself out of his reverie. "You with us, Butch?"

"I'm good to hook, Kap."

God, had I ever looked *that* young?

I was barely twenty-one years old. Franck at twenty-two was a year older. With three previous combat rotations under our belts, including the H-1 combat jump, we were two of the old vets in the squad. Sometimes the "kids" in the platoon, wondering if they could be trigger pullers when the time came, asked the vets what it was like to kill someone.

I didn't talk about it much, but I always recalled the sheepherders we wasted on the road to Haditha and how one of them was just a kid, how he lay all broken on the sand with his goats nearby bleating, his eyes open and the moisture drying in them or being sucked at by flies already crawling, his mouth drooling blood on one side. Better him than me.

"It's your job." That was what I always said. "You do what you have to do. It's either you or him."

Like General Patton said, *It's not your job to die for your country; it's your job to make the other poor sonofabitch die for his country.*

Lights out, the cavalcade of armed trucks pulled over in the street short of the target house, behind an old junker Toyota and a French-looking compact dead underneath a eucalyptus tree. Staff Sergeant Clayton held the squad tight for a few moments to allow our snipers time to commandeer a nearby house and set up a hide on the roof to cover the operation with their scoped rifles. Then it was game time.

The squads approached the house tactically, keeping in the night shadows as much as possible. The residence was like most "middle-class" houses in the city. A high rock wall surrounded a two-story house in the middle of a rectangular compound. There was generally a courtyard wrapped into the center of the house where the residents tended a garden of shrubs, bushes, flowers, and sometimes vegetables. I had heard some people actually had courtyard swimming pools, but I had not personally run across any of them.

Stars and a faded streetlamp down the block provided sufficient ambient light for our NODs. It didn't take long to isolate the compound and for the squads to get into position. No lights burned in any of the windows. So we were breaking in on people in the middle of the night and taking over their homes by force—but, hey, this was war and I would have busted a nunnery or a hospital if it provided my guys an edge and helped them go home with all their pieces intact.

The house went down smooth and fast. To our chagrin, it was full of men, women, and kids. That wasn't out of the ordinary for a residence, but you usually didn't run into women and kids if the house was being used as a base of operations for insurgents. Captain Molino and our interpreter took the homeowner aside for questioning while the squads secured the compound and began searching for contraband. According to our snitch, we should find weapons and a mortar tube used to launch indirect fire into FOB Marez.

The women of the household were poor housekeepers; there was spoiled food all over the kitchen area. Under guard, the women watched us with their heads bowed and children clutched tight as soldiers went through the house room by room. We found garden tools in the cellar, a pushcart in a flower bed, butcher knives in the cabinets, a half-eaten duck in an ice chest—but no mortar.

In the meantime, the homeowner was spilling the beans to Captain Molino, Sergeant Barlow, and the interpreter. He took them outside and pointed across the street. We had the wrong house. The guy we wanted lived down there. The Tactical Operations Center confirmed via radio that our informant had fucked up and provided the wrong directions.

Light burned in the windows of the other house; we had lost the element of surprise. Nonetheless, the mission was still a go. The operation simply changed locations. It had to be done quickly before the resistance got organized and summoned reinforcements. Call it the fog of war.

29

Staff Sergeant Clayton's Third Squad rushed the second house to set up the breach while the other squad and Franck's fire team overwatched. As with the first house, a high rock wall surrounded it. Once we reached its cover without being fired on, Clayton held us tight until Franck's team pounded up and displayed along the wall. Clayton tapped me. I flattened myself next to a rusted metal gate. It was unlocked and squeaked on its hinges when I tried it, like the sound a door makes in a haunted house.

Somewhere not far away a couple of dogs yapped. Muslims considered dogs filthy animals, but there was a sizable number of Christians in Mosul, predominately Assyrians, whose ancestors had followed that religion since the second century, if not before. I guessed Christians liked dogs.

Everything remained so quiet I heard fronds rustling on palm trees inside the closure. So far, nothing indicated that we had been discovered or that this operation was any different than dozens of others we had executed, than the previous one across the street, in fact. Lights burning in the house troubled me, however. You had to listen to that little voice in your head—and that little voice was telling me the residents weren't all tucked into their beds with sugarplums and Allah's virgins dancing through their heads.

Sweat trickled out from underneath my Kevlar.

Staff Sergeant Clayton knuckled my helmet. He wore his fierce look. Show time, boys and girls. The tricky part was about to begin.

Tight with my team in a four-man stack, I swung the gate wide and darted through into a small yard of sorts with palms and branching trees overhanging like a grotto, Butcher directly behind me, Nate Abrams behind him, and the kid named Sherlock bringing up the rear. A well-padded dirt path led to a door at the main entrance. No lights shone through it; the lights that were on seemed to be coming from the courtyard.

I felt my stomach muscles tightening at the prospect of running into a hail of rifle fire. My stack reached the door without incident and pressed to either side of it, weapons bristling, while Richards from the overwatch squad took three men and scurried around the side of the house to the back to watch for squirters.

As I gave him time to get set in place, I flicked up my NODs and wiped off the built-up condensation. They were useless when fogged and became more of a hindrance than an asset. I never particularly liked them for close-quarter fighting. Your view through them was greenish and fluid, like wearing goggles and peering through dirty seawater. Muzzle flashes and unexpected lights could almost blind you.

Staff Sergeant Clayton and the overwatch at the gate knelt with weapons aimed at the doors and windows. Good to go. I signaled Abrams. When he applied all those muscles behind the donker he carried, any obstruction short of a steel vault door might as well be matchwood. The door splintered and crashed in under one mighty blow. No need for stealth after that.

My stack rushed inside like a single organism and hugged the right wall. Franck's team vaulted through the outer gate and raced across the yard and into the house to take the left wall across the doorway from me. My eyes scanned for danger. Minimum light shining from the courtyard through bay windows on the opposite side of the room provided sufficient light for my NODs. I quickly assessed the situation.

An open staircase to the left led up to a catwalk around the upper inside wall, a perfect place to stage an ambush. Maybe our quarry had overheard our mistaken first breach at the other house, got cold feet, and squirted before we arrived.

Doorways at either end of the big room next to the bay windows led onto the interior courtyard. Shadows flickered across the windows. Wind in the trees, I thought.

Only a few seconds passed from the time we breached the house until three or four shots cracked open the night from the direction of the Ranger sniper hide down the block, sharp and echoing and high-powered. I heard a muffled scream from above the vaulted ceiling over our heads. Two of our quarry had popped out onto the roof with a PKM machine gun. They didn't last long.

"They're down!" rang through my radio earplug.

Ranger snipers were some deadly motherfuckers.

Franck's stack remained behind to clear the main house and protect our flanks while I rushed my men through the room and out the nearest door into the courtyard. The courtyard was small, rectangular, and studded with a couple of palms and low landscaping. A light hanging on a pole at one end dimly illuminated the front of the building's other wing facing us. A set of outside stairs led from the ground up the side of this wing to the roof.

Our sudden appearance surprised some guy darting out a door on the other side of the courtyard opposite us and thumping up the exposed stairway toward the roof, apparently on his way to a more advantageous firing position. The windows of the room he vacated all at once lit up with the furious winking of angry fireflies and shuddered underneath the heavy pounding of AK-47s. Windows shattered and bullets thudded into the side of the house all around us. Ricochets whined and screamed. We had burst directly into the middle of a shit storm.

The guy on the stairway froze up when the shooting started. He dropped to one knee and looked back and down toward the courtyard. That was his undoing. Abrams and I turned on the lead faucet and hosed him down. He reeled back and bounced off the wall, his outline a darker shadow illuminated from below by the faint light from the patio. I thought he was going to tumble off the stairs, like in an Old West movie gunfight. Instead, he dropped facedown and started sliding down the stairs. I pumped three more rounds into him.

He was still moving, jerking, but a lot of these guys were so high on amphetamines and alcohol that it took a while to know when they were dead. I yelled at the other guys that he was down.

I ducked behind a low double wall that lined a rock path running diagonally across the patio. Using it as cover, Butch and I scooted along it in an effort to approach near enough to the enemy to toss grenades through their shot-out windows. There was a lot of shooting by this time, both theirs and ours as we returned suppressive fire. Explosions, rifle fire, shooting, screaming—bedlam! Smoke and dust caused by firing in an enclosed space hung acrid in the air.

Butch yelped like a dog struck by a car, grabbed his leg, and rolled over behind the low wall.

"Oh, damn! I'm hit!"

I crawled over to him. Best I could tell, a ricochet had ripped through the meaty part of his leg. He was leaking pretty good, but I doubted he would bleed out before we finished this thing. It didn't matter, though. It had to be finished before we all ended up riddled by bad-guy bullets.

"Keep down, stay here," I instructed grimly, patting Butch on the shoulder. "I'll be back."

"I'm good, good . . . I'm good!" You could hear the fear and pain in his voice, but he was game.

I crawled on past him.

"Get them motherfuckers," he said through gritted teeth.

I scooted down to the end of the wall to fire around it. *Shit! Shit! Shit!* That was the depth of my thinking. Everything else was training and instinct. I mean, *Damn!* These guys were serious.

Perhaps 1st Platoon wasn't living the charmed life we had assumed, that Butch had so recently suggested couldn't last. It didn't take long for that alien notion to get reinforced. Bullets were winging from every direction. Suddenly, I winced like somebody had tossed a live hornets' nest across the wall on top of me and they were stinging hell out of those parts of my side and shoulder unprotected by body armor and Kevlar. I knew I was wounded, probably by a ricochet, but I wasn't down, and if I wasn't down, I was still in the fight.

Abrams and Sherlock joined me at the end of the wall. Bullets lashed over our heads.

"Kap?"

"I'm okay. You heard what Butch said. Let's get these assholes."

While the fight might have seemed like it was lasting for hours, in reality only a few minutes had elapsed. Clayton and the rest of the squad in the wing behind us were laying down suppressive fire through their shattered bay windows into the opposite bay windows, forcing the enemy to duck their heads. I radioed Staff Sergeant Clayton what I had in mind, that I was going to plant a grenade on top of the enemy.

"Roger that, Kap. We cease fire on my count . . . Three, two, one . . ."

A sudden, strange hush. I yelled encouragement at the two remaining men in my stack. Abrams, Sherlock, and I sprang to our feet to charge the remaining few feet across the courtyard. As we approached the enemy's bay window at a dead, desperate run, I leaped into the air and slammed a grenade through into the house, like going in for a jump shot in the last quarter with the score tied.

My men and I hit the ground as it exploded with a terrific bang. Fire erupted from the windows, like a brilliant hole ripped through the universe into hell. The building seemed to shudder.

Sherlock, Abrams, and I bypassed the window as an entrance, since shards of glass remaining in the frame could rip us open like gutting a bird, and headed for the nearest door. All in the same motion, without slowing, while the enemy's ears were still ringing, I stiff-legged the door. It splintered. Momentum carried me through.

The room inside was pitch black, the air thick with smoke and dust.

I swept right to get out of the framed door. A jihadist, surprisingly alive in the opposite corner, started shooting. The only reason I picked him out was that his muzzle flash lit up his face. We exchanged fire across the narrow room. I got him first. He went down. I kept shooting him. I shot him so many times his clothing began to smolder.

I directed my attention deeper into the room as Abrams and Sherlock engaged a second surviving insurgent and likewise riddled him with bullets. He went down screaming, wounded. He kept screaming. He was probably high on drugs. Either that or what he saw of Allah made him doubt the attractions of paradise.

The rest of the house was empty. It only took a few more minutes to clear it. There were two dead on the roof, nailed by our snipers. Another lay dead on the stairs. The one I shot in the room made four. The last one wounded by the grenade and then winged by Abrams and Sherlock would likely survive, but he was still screaming like he wouldn't. What a puss.

The floor and much of the walls were splattered with blood. The odor of it was thick in the room. It smelled like when we slaughtered chickens on the farm back in Connecticut.

Platoon Sergeant Barlow took over the scene after the action was over. I made my way outside to the little wall where I left Butch. He was gone. I found him in the outer yard where our medic was working on him and had already called a medevac chopper. Some of the other guys shined lights on Butch's leg so the medic could see to work. The wound was a purplish, puckered hole from which blood and fluid seeped. The neighborhood had been jarred awake. The curious were out in front of their houses craning their necks to see what was going on.

"You're hit, Kap," Clayton noticed.

"It's nothing. A couple of scratches. Let's get Butch out of here."

"Did we get 'em?" Butch asked.

I looked at his leg. I felt blood leaking underneath my jacket. I took a deep breath of relief. All that shooting, it could have been a lot worse.

"Yeah," I replied. "We got 'em."

30

Care packages for Christmas had been arriving all December via Army Post Office from every state in the Union, not just from friends and families, either, but also from support-your-soldier organizations like Operation One Voice. Boxes from these groups came stuffed with items such as toothpaste and underwear, socks and books, and letters, greeting cards, and notes from total strangers like school kids and high school girls seeking pen pals. At least the folks back home weren't calling us baby killers, demonstrating against us on college campuses, and spitting on returning veterans in airports like they had our veterans from Vietnam, my father's and uncles' generation.

Families and friends, now, they knew what we *really* appreciated. Which presents did you open first on Christmas morn? The ones you suspected contained toys and goodies—or the ones from Aunt Bee in Tuscaloosa that you *knew* contained pajamas with bunny feet? Cookies and candy and cupcakes and Aunt Bee's fruitcake made Rangers' tents at FOB Marez look like a troop of potheads with munchies had breezed through. The platoon sergeant shook his head in disgust at the "pigs," received his share of the goodies, and went on in good cheer.

If one guy got a package in the mail, his squad helped him appreciate it. Everybody shared; we were brothers. Kim sent me a box full of baked goods, candy, and other stuff. Naturally, the squad helped me go through it like monkeys.

Cooks at the FOB put up a Christmas tree in the "dining facility." They decorated it with colored lights and an angel with wings perched on top. A little Christmas cheer when you couldn't be home for the holidays. It made some guys nostalgic, others sad, but mostly we liked the friendly colors and the way they made you feel warm inside. You had to realize that a great many of us had been living at home and going to high school one or two or three Christmases ago.

It began to feel like Christmas, what with it being winter and starting to get cold, especially at night. It *does* get cold in the desert. Somebody spread the season by placing wreaths and stringing tinsel around at the Morale, Welfare, and Recreation facility that housed the post weight rooms, movie theater, card game room, beach volleyball court, and a performing stage for when—and *if*—any celebrities ever came over from the States to perform for us. Like they say, war is hell.

The 25th Infantry Division guys got mistletoe from somewhere and hung it at strategic locations where they could ambush the few women serving in their outfit and in the support units. Most Rangers openly scoffed at even the idea of women in combat areas. They were always getting pregnant and bitching, and the guys squabbled over them. I suspect that was why women were considered bad luck on the old sailing ships. If Uncle Sam wanted Rangers to have women, the RIs used to say, he would have issued them to us. Besides, like General Moshe Dayan in Israel said, any country that sent its sisters, mothers, and wives to war wasn't worth defending.

A rumor went around that President George W. Bush would fly in to eat Christmas dinner with us at FOB Marez this year. I doubted there was any true skinny to the rumor. Mosul had become way too dangerous. Guys were still fighting pockets of resistance in the so-called Battle of Mosul that began before Thanksgiving when a bunch of fanatics attacked Iraqi police stations all over the city. The little fight we had at the courtyard in Old Town on Thanksgiving night could be considered one skirmish in the battle. We had engaged in a number of others since then.

The president would probably opt for Christmas at the Green Zone in Baghdad, where security was more reliable. That turned out to be a wise decision for him, considering what eventually transpired four days before Christmas that year.

My fire team was short a man after Specialist Kyle Butcher medevaced to Germany for treatment; we heard he was wounded seriously enough that he wouldn't be returning. The wounds I incurred at the insurgents' house turned out to be minor, nothing really. The post surgeon checked me out and told me to take it easy for a few days. Then it was right back into the harness chasing bad guys and pinning their hides to the wall.

Butch had taken a round for the Gipper on Thanksgiving. Now he was going home to be in the bosom of his family on Christmas, and all that while I was still here halfway around the globe with a bunch of smelly guys crammed together on bunk beds. We were still hunting bad guys, though, and I wouldn't have had it any other way.

"One time on Christmas Eve," one of the guys reminisced, "Dad climbed up on the roof of our house after my brother and I were in bed. Something woke us. It sounded like reindeer hooves. We heard Santa laughing, and he yelled, 'Merry Christmas and to all a good night!' My brother and I jumped out of bed and ran into the living room—and there, right under the Christmas tree, were all our gifts. Mom looked tickled when Dad came running back inside.

"'I thought I heard something out there,' he said. 'Sure enough. I made it out in time to see him. Ol' Santa riding his sleigh off into the night. Too bad you boys were a little slow and missed him.'"

He chuckled a kind of lonely sound. "My brother and I believed in Santa after that until we got out of high school."

"You mean you *don't* believe anymore?" Abrams chided.

"What are you, a heretic? Just wait until *you* see Santa—"

"—riding a camel and hollering *'Allahu Akbar!'*" Abrams finished for him.

On the morning of December 21, the platoon's Humvees returned roaring to the FOB as pink dawn seeped into the eastern sky and Fobbits (FOB rear echelon types) crept out of bed for breakfast before they headed off to fight their daily Battle of the Keyboard, just workaday people shackled to their workaday lives. They stopped to stare. How they must have envied the rough band of warriors they saw returning mornings to our little corner of the FOB compound. Often we had blood splattered on our gear. We looked tough, ready, and rough. *Looked?* Rangers *were* tough, ready, and rough.

"Bad night?" the Fobbits occasionally probed while we shared one of the common facilities on post.

"We gonna have to stop hanging around them old bars every night."

"Whatta you guys do, anyhow?"

"Drink beer. Chase pussy."

Last night had been productive. We took three jihadists off the streets and into the hands of interrogators and sent a fourth into the loving arms of his virgins in paradise. Making the world safe for women and children and Democracy. My ass was dragging. The entire platoon to a man passed right on by the chow tent and headed for our bunks, barely talking. Sleep was more important than eating. Besides, we could always rely on care packages.

"Wake me Christmas morning," Hunter said, yawning.

"I'll go for New Year's Eve," someone amended.

It seemed I had barely racked out, but it must have been about noon when a horrendous explosion shook the FOB and jarred me out of bed. I landed on my feet already running out of the tent in a mass exodus with other Rangers. An ugly black storm of smoke smeared the sky above where the mess tent used to stand. It had been obliterated and what remained of it consumed in flames. Pieces of canvas, along with chunks of flesh, blood, food, clothing, and other equipment, were strewn all over a 200-meter radius. It was early lunch time, and the mess tent must have been full; the aftermath of the explosion was like a tornado had struck a crowded carnival midway. Screams from the burned and wounded resonated from every corner of the compound. Eerie sounding, heartbreaking because you knew they came from fellow soldiers who had people back home waiting for them.

Bodies lay everywhere, tossed around in heaps like broken manikins. Doctors, medics, and volunteers carted the wounded into makeshift ORs, using ponchos when they ran out of stretchers. At first, no one knew what happened. While the FOB got mortared now and again, a high-explosive round or two that mostly landed without much damage, nothing like this had occurred before. It was like you were safe at home in bed when some fool kicked in the door and shot your wife and kids.

Fourteen U.S. soldiers, four Iraqi soldiers, and four Halliburton civilian employees died and seventy-two were injured in the deadliest single attack on Americans so far during the war. Most of the casualties were engineers and Deuce Four Infantry from the 25th Division. No Ranger was in the chow hall at the time since the platoon had been so ragged-out from last night's mission that we were still in bed. It pissed me off nonetheless.

I learned later that a jihadist asshole cleared as a civilian employee on post was the culprit. Twenty-four-year-old Abu Omar al-Museli had worked on the base for two months while spying for the "Army of Ansar al-Sunna." He had entered the mess tent at midchow wearing a "martyr's vest" of explosives underneath a uniform of the Iraqi security services and nonchalantly lit himself off.

This was rapidly becoming a familiar part of the war in Iraq—the suicide bomber, the martyr who immolated himself in fire and brimstone in the belief that to die in the name of Allah transported him instantly to paradise and into the arms of seventy-two virgins charged with catering to his every whim for eternity. As for the enemy he took with him? Screw them. They went instantly to hell.

It was hard to wrap my mind around that kind of mentality. Fighting a war and killing men in battle was one thing; committing suicide as a weapon was something entirely different. I know, the Japanese kamikaze pilots did it, but I still couldn't understand it.

I refused to believe the crazies who flew airliners into the World Trade Center and the Pentagon on 9/11 were now luxuriating in some heavenly paradise populated by comely virgins. It was more fitting to think they were burning in hell for snuffing out the lives of innocent people.

Survivors from the chow tent said they heard the jihadist shout *"Allahu Akbar!"* just before he turned himself into a fireball.

Allahu Akbar! God is great.

"I can understand why a guy would want seventy-two virgins in paradise," Hunter pondered. "My question is, what do the virgins get out of it?"

31

GEORGIA 2005

Kimberly:

Joe was the quiet sort. He never talked a lot. Like in Coach's Corner the night we met. While his Ranger buddies were hitting on Melanie and me, chattering on and on like chickens in a henhouse, trying to impress, Joe stood alone in silence, which most soldiers tended to avoid. The thing about this good, honorable man whom I had come to love dearly in between his going off to war was that you always knew where you stood with him. It wasn't like he had to say it; you just knew it.

"Give him time," Josh Kuhner said. "He'll talk when he has something to say."

He was even quieter than usual when he returned from Iraq this time. Things had happened over there, I knew that. I tried to draw it out of him. No, none of his buddies had been killed. Butcher was wounded, but he was okay and would probably be getting out of the army. I learned Joe had killed people; some of the other guys told me about it, but he and I never discussed it.

"It's my job. You do what's necessary to save your own people" was all he said.

It wasn't until months later that I found out he was wounded in the same battle where Kyle Butcher was hit, on Thanksgiving night. The regimental commander presented him a Purple Heart and a Bronze Star for Valor at an awards ceremony. Joe downplayed it. He simply came in and tossed the medal on a table.

"Look what I got today," he said offhandedly.

"And you were going to tell me about it *when*?" I challenged afterward while we were having dinner at Denny's, the same place in Columbus where we went out for breakfast with Melanie and Hoover the night we met.

He shrugged it off. "It was nothing," he said.

I realized he was trying to protect me. Few of the guys talked about the war to their wives and families—especially since they knew they would be going back. It was better that we not know the raw details. I had to accept that, too.

"Joe, you'll be deploying again?"

It wasn't a question. I knew the answer.

We actually spent little time together, considering his busy training schedule at the base and my working with the horses at Midland Farms. When we were out, going to a movie or whatever, maybe just hanging out on a free Saturday, neither of us wanted to discuss the war. It was almost like we had *now* and nothing else. There was a line from "Class of '57," an old song by the Oak Ridge Boys, that explained it, *Things get complicated when you get past eighteen.*

My friend Melanie and I sometimes talked about it. We called it our "barn talk."

"Are you two serious about each other, Kim?"

I was. I knew Joe was, too. Melanie had driven out to Midland to visit Suzanna and me while I worked. I paused from mucking out the stalls and leaned on the handle of my scoop shovel. Like any well-bred southern girl, I had always dreamed of a classic big wedding.

"What's keeping you?" Melanie asked. "Joe?"

After a few moments, I turned to Melanie and said, "Joe and I are going to the courthouse next week."

Her eyes popped wide. "What? Are you kidding me? Are you crazy?"

I laughed. "I figured I don't want to waste my cute, skinny years waiting on him if I don't have a commitment."

Melanie took it all in. Finally, as any best friend would do, she said, "Okay, let's do it. If he's the guy for you and if you want to keep him, then you have to accept him for what he is. You grab happiness while you can—or you live to regret it the rest of your life. Can I come to the wedding?"

"Absolutely not. This is not a 'wedding.' It's 'paperwork.' We'll have our big wedding someday, and you'll be in it. The farm would be perfect for our real wedding. It's beautiful here in the spring over where the wisteria grows. That's my favorite spot."

Joe and I were right together. I had already waited for him through two deployments and Ranger School. He had been hurt in Iraq, could have been killed, and I didn't even know about it. Ranger Battalion informed you of nothing unless you were listed as a wife or next of kin. You never knew when they were leaving or coming home, or, worse yet, where they were or what they were doing.

With Joe and me, almost from the beginning, it was a foregone conclusion that we would always be together. There was never any deep conversation about marriage between us. We simply accepted the inevitability. No, he was not getting down on one knee with a ring and roses and all that. He wasn't that kind of mushy guy. His proposal and my acceptance went something like this:

"Are you ready to do this thing, Kim?"

"Yeah. Let's do it."

"You know what you're getting into?"

I squeezed his hand across the table where we were having dinner. "I'm not a halfway girl, Joe. With me, it's all or nothing. I'll never ask you to do anything you don't want to do. You'll quit the army when you're ready."

I would definitely be the talker in the family.

We got married before a judge at the county courthouse. We hadn't the money for my big dream wedding, and my mom couldn't afford it. It was the scariest day of my life. I thought I was going to have a heart attack. I kept thinking: *What on earth am I getting into?* Joe wore blue jeans and a button-up shirt; he was never much for getting dressed up. The only time I ever saw him wear a tie was with his dress greens.

I wore a white skirt with a blouse. Besides Melanie, the only people who knew about the wedding—and that after the fact—were my mom, Joe's Grandfather Churchill, and Joe's platoon leader, Captain Molino. One day, maybe after Joe returned from his next rotation, we'd have my big wedding with *"Here Comes the Bride"* and all that. Until then, we promised to keep our paperwork a secret to avoid slighting our families. They wouldn't have to know about it until we had our *real* wedding.

At least I was now on the wives' list for the army to notify me if anything happened. I was a part of it. I hoped I was jumping in without blinders.

We moved into the little condo in Columbus with my mom. There was no sense wasting money on a house or apartment yet, what with Joe being gone so much. During the following six months, he actually spent a total of thirty-five nights at home.

Arriving at the condo, Joe swept me into his arms and carried me across the threshold.

"For better or worse," he said.

Later, that fundamental phrase from our nuptials kept coming back to me: *For better or worse.*

32

I thought becoming a Ranger was the best thing that had ever happened to me—until Kim came along. Our courtship, irregular as it had been between rotations, was never the sweaty variety so common among warriors who never knew if they'd be here tomorrow or not, who, therefore, got as much "pussy and booze" as they could and then left again. I was walking tall, but I was also realistic enough to know that in my marriage to Kim, I would be away from her more time than I actually spent at home. That was the way it had to be for as long as our country remained at war—and we would soon be at war longer than during World War II. I didn't know it then, of course, but the War on Terror in Afghanistan and Iraq would eventually become America's longest war. However long it lasted, I was dedicated to seeing it through.

The rotation cycle at Fort Benning through the first months of 2005, up-training and retraining most of the time, was eventful for the regiment as well as for me personally. Not only had Kim and I married, but there were some major shifts in the leadership structure from platoon level up to battalion. Having been promoted to buck sergeant E-5, I had already been to the board for my next promotion to staff sergeant E-6. All I had to do was get enough time in grade to be promoted since I was already a squad leader. My career was clicking along at a fair pace. I looked forward to becoming a platoon sergeant in a couple more years. After that came master sergeant and company first sergeant, followed by sergeant major. Command sergeant major was the highest rank an enlisted man could obtain. I had no desire to become a commissioned officer. Officers served at the whim and pleasure of the Department of Defense, which meant they could and would be assigned to outfits worldwide. I knew no officers who served out their entire careers as Rangers.

The event that had the most impact on the men of 1st Platoon centered on Platoon Sergeant James Barlow's fuckup during an off-post training event at Fort Campbell, Kentucky, with the 160th Special Operations Aviation Regiment and their helicopters. Sergeant Barlow had never seemed to jell with the men. He had the look of a tough old battle horse, what with his cynicism, thick build, and spiky gray hair, but there the comparison to Lee Marvin or Clint Eastwood characters stopped.

He was overly cautious when it came to a fight. During the shootout in the courtyard where Butch and I were wounded, for example, he remained outside the fray at the front gate until it was over. A leader should, in fact, maintain a command post and a command view of the action, but not every time, not when any other platoon sergeant would have been leading from the front instead of pushing from the rear. Had Sergeant Barlow had his rathers in Iraq, he would have stayed behind the wire at the FOB rather than go out hard-charging, kicking in doors and killing bad guys. Some of the other NCOs had had words with him. A couple of times he ragged on me about my aggressiveness in combat.

"Bravery is stupidity's cousin, Kapacziewski." He pronounced it Kapa-*cheeski*. "You are going to fuck up sooner or later and the CO will be writing a letter to whoever next of kin owns up to a name like Kapa-*cheeski*. You ain't gonna win the war by yourself, boy. A dead hero ain't nothing but another dead man in the end."

As far as I was concerned, being a "live coward" was his non-Ranger philosophy. I couldn't, *wouldn't*, live that way. I always had to do my best, no matter what.

During the training mission at Fort Campbell, the platoon chopper-lifted against an old abandoned jail to rescue hostages from the "enemy." The operation played out according to plan. We shot up the opposing force, whisked the rescued prisoners to waiting helicopters, and exfil'd. We were in the air before someone, not Sergeant Barlow, noticed that our machine gunner had been left behind. Rangers *never* leave a man behind. He was a dead man if that occurred during a real-world mission. It was a black eye on the platoon. One of a platoon sergeant's primary responsibilities was to account for his men.

A week later, the battalion sergeant major relieved Barlow, and he cleared out his desk that night and was gone. In my opinion, it was the best thing the CO could have done for the platoon. Well, second best. The best was that Staff Sergeant Jared Van Aalst moved over from the Ranger Sniper Platoon to replace him. Staff Sergeant Van Aalst was the same man who had been assigned to the Army Marksmanship Unit in 2002 while I was on detail pulling targets and waiting for RIP to begin, who had given us the little pep talk about how the main thing was not to quit, no matter how tough things got.

He remembered me. He shook my hand hard and warmly. "Been hearing good things about you, Kap. You're a warrior, boy. You kept your eye on the prize. I'm looking forward to having you as a squad leader."

"Thank you, Sar'ent."

Colonel Paul LaCamera assumed command of the 75th Ranger Regiment in a ceremony at Fort Benning that kicked off the biannual Ranger Rendezvous. Every two years, thousands of current and former Rangers gathered at one of the Ranger forts in the tradition of the old mountain-men rendezvous of the 1800s for four days of competition, celebration, fun, frolic, games, and drinking. This year, Fort Benning hosted the rendezvous. Rangers from 2nd Batt at Fort Lewis and from 1st Batt at Hunter Army Airfield linked up with 3rd Batt and Regimental Headquarters and with a number of old gray Rangers in their sixties, seventies, eighties, and nineties from as far back as World War II. In this way, units like Rangers, SEALs, and Green Berets formed unbreakable bonds of connectedness to carry on the lore, history, and tradition of their special outfits.

The festivities began with a mass tactical airborne jump onto Fryar Drop Zone. As a brand-new jumpmaster, I pulled my first duty as assistant jumpmaster on the drop. The sky blossomed with parachutes, reminding me how it must have been at Normandy or Anzio with the 82nd and 101st in World War II. It was exhilarating. Troopers came off the field laughing and slapping each other on the back.

The next morning at dawn, about 1,500 Rangers and ex-Rangers participated in the 3-mile formation run. Ben Hunter and I ran together on our good legs, laughing and having a great time. It was like we were back in RIP all over again, except we got to drink beer afterward.

"Hey, we old guys ain't lost it yet," he exulted.

He looked back and laughed harder than ever. Here came this old bald ex-Ranger from World War II in the formation and still running. Ben and I waited at the finish line to present him high fives.

"Rangers lead the way," the old guy panted.

Shooting competitions and various Ranger games, including obstacle course races, football, baseball, tug-of-war, and boxing, filled the next three days. Nights were for eating and boozing, getting together with old buddies and making new ones. Wives and girlfriends often joined us. I found everyone loved my new wife. Not only was Kim good-looking enough to turn heads in a room, she was bubbly and, unlike me, gregarious. She genuinely liked people, and she liked my macho, testosterone-charged Rangers. I could have picked no better wife.

Damn, I was having a good time.

Some of the old vets from World War II distributed copies of a speech President Ronald Reagan delivered on the fortieth anniversary of D-day. One of them read it aloud in its entirety to a large group out on the grinder with the tall parachute jump towers in the background. In it,

President Reagan singled out the men of the 2nd Ranger Battalion who had scaled the cliffs of Normandy.

I could be sentimental about my Rangers. I looked around at the weathered faces of the old veterans of previous wars. Nearly every face was reverent as the speech was read, every eye misted. What was true of this "Greatest Generation" of warriors, I thought, was no less true of today's young warriors. I wondered if someday in the distant future, when I was old and gray and fat, I might not be among these old guys paying tribute to my own generation of Rangers.

HEROES OF WORLD WAR II

SPEECH DELIVERED BY PRESIDENT RONALD REAGAN AT NORMANDY 1984

WRITTEN BY RONALD REAGAN AND PEGGY NOONAN

We stand on a lonely, windswept point on the northern shore of France. The air is soft, but forty years ago at this moment, the air was dense with smoke and the cries of men, and the air was filled with the crack of rifle fire and the roar of cannon. At dawn, on the morning of the 6th of June, 1944, two hundred and twenty-five Rangers jumped off the British landing craft and ran to the bottom of these cliffs.

Their mission was one of the most difficult and daring of the invasion: to climb these sheer and desolate cliffs and take out the enemy guns . . .

The Rangers looked up and saw the enemy soldiers [at] the edge of the cliffs, shooting down at them with machine guns and throwing grenades. And the American Rangers began to climb. They shot rope ladders over the face of these cliffs and began to pull themselves up. When one Ranger fell, another would take his place. When one rope was cut, a Ranger would grab another and begin his climb again. They climbed, shot back and held their footing. Soon, one by one, the Rangers pulled themselves over the top, and in seizing the firm land at the top of the cliffs, they began to seize back the continent of Europe. Two hundred and twenty-five came here. After two days of fighting, only ninety could still bear arms.

Behind me is a memorial that symbolizes the Ranger daggers that were thrust into the top of these cliffs. And before me are the men who put them there. These are the boys of Pointe du Hoc. These are the men who took the cliffs. These are the champions who helped free a continent. And these are the heroes who helped end a war. Gentlemen, I look at you and I think of the words of Stephen Spender's poem. You are men who in your "lives fought for life . . . and left the vivid air signed with your honor."

. . . Forty summers have passed since the battle that you fought here. You were young the day you took these cliffs; some of you were hardly more than boys, with the deepest joys of life before you. Yet you risked everything here. Why? Why did you do it? What impelled you to put aside the instinct for self-preservation and risk your lives to take these cliffs? What inspired all the men of the armies that met here? We look at you, and somehow we know the answer. It was faith and belief. It was loyalty and love.

The men of Normandy had faith that what they were doing was right, faith that they fought for all humanity, faith that a just God would grant them mercy on this beachhead, or on the next. It was the deep knowledge—and pray God we have not lost it—that there is a profound moral difference between the use of force for liberation and the use of force for conquest. You were here to liberate, not to conquer, and so you and those others did not doubt your cause. And you were right not to doubt.

You all knew that some things are worth dying for. One's country is worth dying for, and democracy is worth dying for, because it's the most deeply honorable form of government ever devised by man. All of you loved liberty. All of you were willing to fight tyranny, and you knew the people of your countries were behind you.

The Americans who fought here that morning knew word of the invasion was spreading through the darkness back home. They thought—or felt in their hearts, though they couldn't know in fact, that in Georgia they were filling the churches at 4:00 a.m. In Kansas they were kneeling on their porches and praying. And in Philadelphia they were ringing the Liberty Bell.

Something else helped the men of D-day: their rock-hard belief that Providence would have a great hand in the events that would unfold here; that God was an ally in this great cause. And so, the night before the invasion, when Colonel Wolverton asked his parachute troops to kneel with him in prayer, he told them, "Do not bow your heads, but look up so you can see God and ask His blessing in what we're about to do." Also, that night, General Matthew Ridgway on his cot, listened in the darkness for the promise God made to Joshua: "I will not fail thee nor forsake thee."

These are the things that impelled them; these are the things that shaped the unity of the Allies . . .

We've learned that isolationism never was and never will be an acceptable response to tyrannical governments with an expansionist intent.

But we try always to be prepared for peace . . .

I tell you from my heart that we in the United States do not want war. We want to wipe from the face of the earth the terrible weapons that man now has in his hands . . .

We are bound today by what bound us forty years ago, the same loyalties, traditions, and beliefs. We are bound by reality. The strength of America's allies is vital to the United States, and the American security guarantee is essential to the continued freedom of Europe's democracies. We were with you then; we're with you now. Your hopes are our hopes, and your destiny is our destiny.

Here, in this place where the West held together, let us make a vow to our dead. Let us show them by our actions that we understand what they died for. Let our actions say to them the words for which Matthew Ridgway listened: "I will not fail thee nor forsake thee."

Strengthened by their courage, heartened by their valor, and borne by their memory, let us continue to stand for the ideals for which they lived and died.

33

A week after the Rendezvous ended, a week after the old vet uttered from President Reagan's speech, "Let us continue to stand for the ideals for which they lived and died," I was once more bound overseas with my Rangers to "liberate, not to conquer." Rangers were already the "most constantly deployed" soldiers in the War on Terror. A day seldom passed that 75th Rangers weren't fighting in either Afghanistan or Iraq. Mosul was so active when we were last at FOB Marez that we returned for some more of it, this time with our strength doubled from one platoon of Alpha Company to two platoons, the 1st and 3rd.

Kim saw me off from the company building for the first time as my wife. She clung to me a long moment, but there were no tears. This girl was made of stern stuff. We kept our partings simple and unemotional.

"Joe . . . See you later."

I nodded. "Later."

My promotion to staff sergeant had not come through; this would be my first deployment as squad leader of First Squad. Ken Clayton had moved over to take charge of Weapons Squad. Pavolanis had Second Squad, and Franck the Tank Third Squad. Ben Hunter was now one of my fire team leaders, along with Joe Edwards, no relation to the Mike Edwards of previous rotations, who had since moved on to 3rd Platoon.

• • •

Kimberly:

All the hoopla of Rendezvous had the guys fired up with patriotism and gung ho. They were ready to go out and wrestle alligators or take on bears with a stick. Spending my life with Joe was what I wanted, more than almost anything, but when he left with the platoon for Iraq that hot summer morning with the tarmac giving off hot squiggles and the sun white-hot already, I felt a kind of fear, even premonition.

Women had been seeing their men off to war like this for centuries, for millennia, since the time of mankind began, actually. I imagined they felt the same way I did when the airplane began to thunder down the runway—or the horses disappeared over the horizon.

What if he doesn't come back?

34

MOSUL, IRAQ, 2005

In the normal workaday world, say in an auto plant or as a firefighter, you worked with the same people for ten, twenty, or even thirty years. It wasn't like that in the military where guys were always leaving at the end of their enlistment or transferring to other outfits. They trickled in and they trickled out. I got to looking around on the flight to Iraq for my fifth deployment in four years and remembering all the guys from previous rotations who were no longer with us. Guys like Mendez and Kopp and Wright; like Ryan Long, killed on his and my second rotation; like Platoon Sergeants Ray Reid and James Barlow; Specialist Kyle Butcher, wounded in Mosul the last time we were there; Platoon Leader Chris Molino, promoted from PL to Alpha Company's executive officer; Jermaine Wilson, kicked out of the Rangers on account of his DUI; Morris and Moore and Josh Kuhner . . . Not many of us originals remained in 1st Platoon since 2002 when we went to Afghanistan on my first rotation.

"Only the truly committed stay," Ben Hunter decided.

This 1st Platoon was strike as far as leadership went, with Captain Chad Fleming as platoon leader and Staff Sergeant Jared Van Aalst in the platoon sergeant slot. Captain Fleming was born and raised in Tuscaloosa, where he graduated from the University of Alabama. While attending classes during the day, he worked nights at the Tuscaloosa County

Sheriff's Office as a deputy. After a short stint with the U.S. Secret Service Office in Birmingham, he enlisted in the U.S. Army in 1999 as an Airborne Ranger. In build and facial features he resembled a younger, thirtyish version of the actor Lee Majors, who starred as the Bionic Man on TV back in the 1970s. The platoon liked his no-nonsense attitude when it came to business, higher-higher liked him, and he seemed to be on a career path to becoming a general some day.

Both the 3rd Battalion's commander and Alpha Company's CO accompanied Alpha's 1st and 2nd Platoons to Mosul. Alpha's First Sergeant Eddie Noland came along as well. He was a tall, stocky twenty-year man with big hands and a growl in his voice. Like Hunter said, the hardcore remained—and the hardcore were all hard-charging, kick-in-the-doors, shoot-bad-guys soldiers. Things had to be going to shit in Mosul for the Batt CO to go over with us.

"That's what Rangers do," Staff Sergeant Van Aalst commented wryly. "We're plumbers. We go in and clean up the shit."

"When I grow up, Sar'ent," Ben Hunter teased, "I wanna be just like you. Only better-looking."

Ben's genial, kidding tone let him get away with poking at superiors.

Hopes for an early end to the insurgency and the withdrawal of U.S. combat troops had faded as jihadists gained strength and spread hate and discontent. The year 2005 was more of 2004, except magnified. Suicide bombers like the nut who blew up our chow hall tent last December at FOB Marez killed seventy-nine U.S. soldiers and seven hundred Iraqis all over Iraq, including General Waleed Kashmoula, head of Mosul's anticorruption unit. U.S. Marines had responded two months ago with Operation Matador to cut off and clean up ungoverned regions of western Iraq used as supply and reinforcement routes out of Syria into Iraq. They killed 124 insurgents and drove the rest back across the borders. Marines suffered 30 casualties.

The jihadists appeared to become more sophisticated with time. Soviet-manufactured machine guns and RPGs were abundant, as were

SA-7 missiles for bringing down helicopters. Their urban guerrilla tactics improved. Intel reported that our friends the Russkies not only supplied weapons to the insurgency but also provided Spetznaz instructors for jihadist training camps in Syria and Iran, repaying the United States for its support of Afghanistan mujahideen during the Russian excursion into that country. There was definitely a real shit storm brewing.

Our Humvees, even the new steel-plated ones, provided a rich target environment for jihadists' IEDs, RPGs, and rockets. We were forced to fall back on the old axiom, "If your opponent comes to a fight with a knife, you bring a gun. If he brings a gun, you show up with a cannon. If he . . ." You get the drift.

The heavily armed and heavily armored eight-wheel-drive Stryker M-1126 Infantry Carrier Vehicle, the first new military vehicle to enter the United States Army since the Abrams tank in the 1980s, proved to be the equivalent of bringing a cannon to the gunfight. First appearing in Iraq in late 2003, the steel behemoth weighed 19 tons and scooted along a hard-surfaced road at 60 mph while hauling a crew of two and a nine-man squad in its belly. In appearance, it resembled the amphibious Duck of World War II and Korea, or some kind of weird outer space tank as it tooled down a hostile road in tandem with others.

Hard steel armor augmented by appliqué panels of lightweight ceramic/composite armor provided protection against small-arms fire, most machine-gun rounds, and mortar and artillery fragments. In 2004, units began outfitting the Stryker with "cages" of slat armor as defense against RPGs. Given enough traction, a Stryker could climb the Empire State Building—and kick ass when it got to the top with either a mounted .50 caliber machine gun, an MK-19 40 mm automatic grenade launcher, or a 240 7.62 machine gun.

A squad nestled down inside on the way to a raid felt secure as never before in a Humvee. However, as I eventually discovered the hard way, you had to keep the hatches sealed.

At the airfield Alpha Company's two in-country platoons rotated back and forth on missions, one or the other of us going out nearly every night. The setting sun signaled "hunting time." By the time full darkness fell, the duty platoon was up and geared to receive its operation order. We went to work when the town went to sleep and the day-shift insurgents holed up somewhere while the night-shift jihadists took over. You killed the night shift during the day and the day shift after dark.

During our first hundred-day period in country, the Strike Force ran more than eighty missions and detained or killed an astronomical number of bad guys. Intel would come down with a target. Say, a jihadist in charge of a particular area of the city or in command of a certain cell. We went out, we killed him, and we killed whoever happened to be with him. A week or two later, we went out and killed whoever replaced him. It was a bloody game of cat and mouse; the cat always won. We packed up our gear afterward, and everybody went back to the airfield and went to the gym or played video games at the Morale, Welfare, and Recreation Facility.

No one ever seemed to get hurt on our side. The Glory Days for the Glory Boys just went on and on.

35

Typical night out on the town chasing thugs and goons. Lights burning inside the house backlighted the figure who opened the door and peered suspiciously into his darkened front yard. Hinky hajji, he knew something wasn't right, he just didn't know how unright. He wore a black turban and a dishdasha, one of those long, white, flowing Arab robes. A man-dress. He appeared about thirty, with an Osama bin Laden beard and a crooked bulb of a nose. He looked mean. Anyone who hated your guts and wanted to shoot you looked mean.

I watched him from the top of a ladder on the other side of the outer wall. Amazing what you could see through NODs with just a smidgen of available light.

I figured the information on this particular cell of terrorists came from one of the three-letter agencies. They took huge risks to detect and identify HVTs; they were usually reliable. The report stated this house and the one next door, the two separated by a low rock wall, were the headquarters and hangout for a gang of Sunni jihadists that had been planting IEDs all over the city and may have been behind the assassination of the commander of Mosul's anticorruption unit last May. Our Tactical Operations Center received word that they were home plotting and scheming and available for us to call on them and pay our respects. Never say Rangers failed to follow social protocol.

I kept low at the wall, only the top of my helmet and NODs exposed and largely concealed by creepers growing wild on the rocks. I listened for the signal over my PRC-148, a radio a little bigger than a cell phone. Captain Fleming and Sergeant Van Aalst had the squads in place for the assault. When they were ready they would give the word to go. Staff Sergeant Pavolanis's Second Squad and my First Squad would take over the first house, the one I was looking at, while the other squad busted its neighbor.

This was always the worst part of an operation, waiting for action to begin. Tension wore my nerves thin as I waited for the signal and watched the hajji in the doorway blinking and glaring into shadows. He was unarmed, as far as I could determine, but these guys generally kept a weapon within arm's reach. There was no telling how many other terrorists might be inside the two houses. The houses might rupture like twin red-ant hills when we started probing.

Like the majority of Iraqi houses in this neighborhood on the outskirts of Old Town, both our targets had two stories and flat roofs. From my vantage point at the wall, using NODs, I looked through the windows and into the house's large common area. Iraqis seldom had much furniture, especially those on the run in safe houses where all the spoilers and killers required was a few mattresses for beds and a table around which to intrigue. The members of my squad concealed at the bottom of my ladder were getting restless. I heard them shifting their weight.

The hajji at the front door turned back inside. Maybe he was just paranoid.

He shouted something in Arabic. The door slammed shut. We had been made. He had either seen something or thought he saw something. Immediately, looking through the windows, I spotted men carrying weapons running across the room and up the stairs toward the roof.

My radio squelched, followed by the crackle of Captain Fleming's voice, *"All elements! Go!"*

No need for any more sneaking and peeking.

Our snipers initiated the action. Snipers were equalizers, force multipliers. Even as I used the ladder as a springboard to vault over the wall into the yard, my fire teams scrambling after me, I became acutely conscious of the sharp cracking of high-powered rifles picking off the hajjis on the roof before they had a chance to lay fire down on us. Stupid fuckers always ran for the roof; they never seemed to learn.

I discovered the front door heavy and bolted when I reached it. Joe Edwards came prepared. He slapped a charge of C-4 to the locking mechanism. The rest of us ducked to the sides to avoid the minor explosion when Joe set it off.

The door banged open, smoke boiling out. My combat stacks charged through and into the room before the occupants knew what was going on. Urban fighting was the worst possible scenario of battle as well as the most dangerous. Just ask any World War II veteran. Shooting distances could be measured in feet, sometimes even inches. The action was fast and furious. There was no time to think. You ran on instinct, training, adrenaline, and guts.

The hajji with the big nose I had watched at the door ran back into the room. This time he was armed. He fired several rounds and missed. Bad on him. Bullets from my team's weapons molded a kinetic cone in the room with the apex sucked into the guy's torso.

The man thumped to the floor. He was still moving, so one of my guys stepped up and shot him through the head. Blood exploded. The Ranger jumped back.

"Fuck!"

You couldn't leave 'em in the rear to shoot you in the back or self-detonate.

Glass shattered as a second Iraqi—or perhaps a Syrian or

Iranian—appeared out of nowhere, sprinted across the room before we had a chance to fire him up, dived through a window onto the back courtyard, and disappeared like a ground squirrel. He wouldn't get far. We had the houses sealed off.

Next door, 1st Platoon's other squads were cleaning house. Muzzle flashes and the sudden white-red explosions of grenades and flash-bangs lit up the windows and the courtyard. People were screaming and yelling, in English and in Iraqi. Doors and windows splintered and shattered. A firefight in enclosed spaces was exceptionally noisy, the *tat-tat* of automatic weapons and the *bang* of grenades magnified tenfold. However, it became mere background white noise compared to the roar of adrenaline pumping through your veins. You were so focused on kill or be killed, on primitive survival, that even when you were moving at fast-forward the rest of the world seemed to go into slow motion. Every detail of the fight etched itself into your brain, but both then and afterward it seemed unreal. It was like you participated in it while at the same time you stood off to one side and watched yourself participate.

After clearing the house, quickly, I led my fire teams out the back door onto the tiny courtyard where the low rock wall separated our house from the one next door. Opposite the dividing wall between the two houses, a narrow alleyway led past the end of our house, the opening to which was partially blocked by some kind of concrete structure about three feet high. I glimpsed a fist with a pistol in it pop up from behind the concrete. *Pop! Pop! Pop!*

The ground squirrel! He was afraid to stick his head up to see what he was shooting at. It was crazy. Hunter said later it reminded him of the gangster scenes from the movie *Pulp Fiction*.

"Cover me!" I shouted back over my shoulder. I hit the ground face forward and began low-crawling toward the concrete barrier like a lizard while Hunter fired cover.

Part of my squad became engaged with insurgents fleeing the house next door, who were now shooting over the top of that wall into our courtyard. We had them squeezed between our two squads with nowhere for them to go—and the shit was coming down on their heads.

Hunter lit up the cubbyhole behind the concrete every time Pulp Fiction stuck up his hand to shoot. Not his head, only his hand. Hunter's bullets felt and looked as though they were lashing inches above my head, but I knew they were at least a couple of feet high and that he wouldn't put rounds into the concrete that might produce ricochets that could take one of us out with "friendly fire."

I wormed up to my side of the concrete whatever-it-was. Pulp Fiction was on the other side, a foot or so away. I heard him breathing hard and making strange little frightened mewling sounds. *Whassa matter? You wanna go to paradise and get your virgins, but you don't wanna die?*

Fuck him. I yanked the pin on a frag grenade and tossed the little bomb from my side over to his. I buried my helmeted head underneath my arms and my face in the dirt.

I heard an ear-piercing scream as the guy realized how his life was getting fucked up. The grenade went off with a terrific blast at close quarters that rang my ears, left me temporarily deaf, and shook the ground underneath me.

I sprang up, rifle at the ready to take out whatever the grenade missed. No need. There wasn't much left of the hajji. He looked like raw hamburger, almost unrecognizable as a human being. The grenade must have landed in his lap. I had seen dead men before, but none mangled to this extent. Bad on him.

That did it for the enemy on our side of the wall. Captain Fleming, Sergeant Van Aalst, and Third Squad were mopping up in the other courtyard. Their last holdouts, two of them, went to ground inside a small basement catch space with a half-door from the outside to the inside of a root cellar. Armed with AK-47s, they were giving a good account of themselves. Two Rangers received flesh wounds that put them out of commission.

Seizing an opportunity, Captain Fleming hugged the shadows at the side of the house and approached the cellar door in the insurgents' blind spot. After getting near enough, he slammed a grenade into the catch space. That ended the fight. While I came away unscathed from my grenade adventure next door, the captain ended up with pieces of shrapnel buried in his legs and arms, none of the wounds critical. He walked away from it.

"I don't have time to bleed," he commented.

Everything went quiet again, a silence like a blanket falling over the houses. You might have called it deathly quiet. Dogs began barking again after a moment; it seemed the same damned dogs followed us wherever we went. Nobody spoke or shouted for an inordinately long time, like athletes catching our breath following strenuous competition. I couldn't have heard anyone anyhow; I was still deaf from the grenade.

We took no prisoners. All the insurgents opted to die in Allah's name rather than surrender. The body count stood at eight. Three Rangers were slightly wounded, including Captain Fleming. A good night's work. Time to clock out and go home.

"Ben," I commented to Hunter, "I haven't heard you say 'underwhelming' in a long time."

36

Imagine a war where you could relax with a smoke and an Xbox hooked up to a TV at the end of a bad day, where you could even call home. "Say, babe, how's your day going? Here? Same ol' same ol'. You know, keeping busy. How's the kids . . . ? You tell Arnold he'd better buckle down and study . . . Honey, I know Darla needs to go to the dentist . . . Okay, gotta run. Duty calls . . . Yeah, love, I'm always careful."

It was indeed a different kind of war when a soldier could stay in touch with family and friends through satellite phones, the Internet, and Skype. It made the war seem less dangerous—like we were back on base at Fort Benning instead of in a war zone on the other side of the globe.

It was all part of the Pentagon's effort to make war at least "civilized" in Iraq, if you could put "civilized" and "war" in the same sentence without their being an oxymoron. What with the Morale, Welfare, and Recreation Facility at the airfield and attendant movies, computers, and other amenities—even washers and dryers—life off mission wasn't that bad. Still, even if we had had shopping malls and Disney World on post, war would still be war, people would still be getting killed, and some crazy martyr would probably try to blow up Mickey Mouse and Donald Duck while shouting *"Allahu Akbar!"*

The 2/325 (2nd Battalion, 325th Regiment) of the 82nd Airborne

Division had been ordered to Marez following the chow hall suicide bombing last Christmas. Paratroopers had pretty much taken control of the FOB and the surrounding area, although elements of both the 25th Infantry Division and the 101st Airmobile remained. Marez was like a fort in Indian Country, a virtually impregnable base outside the city. U.S. forces had been instructed to stay out of dangerous urban areas except for patrols, heavily guarded civic action incursions, and missions by Rangers and other SOCOM teams. This was before the "surge" and General David Petraeus's taking command of the Multinational Force in Iraq. Petraeus was to initiate a new philosophy of counterinsurgency he called "clear-hold-build." As he was to write, explaining it to the troops, "Accomplishing the mission requires carrying out complex military operations and convincing the Iraqi people that we will not just 'clear' their neighborhoods of enemy, we will also stay and help 'hold' the neighborhoods so that the 'build' phase can go forward."

In 2005, however, we were still in "strike" mode. Dart out of the fort, knock off a few chiefs, then hightail it back behind the wire to play Xbox and smoke and joke until the next mission. Rangers at the FOB occupied our own little corner of the base and rarely interacted with other units. The 82nd and the "legs" (non-Airborne personnel) did their thing while our platoons took care of our own business.

The 75th Rangers constituted a small community compared to division-sized outfits. As with any small community, rumors, misinformation, and gossip, as well as a great deal of accurate skinny, spread quickly through the grapevine. For example, within two days after Ranger Corporal Pat Tillman Jr. was killed in Afghanistan in 2004, the news had spread throughout the regiment, both stateside and in the war zone. Rangers knew the real story of how he died by "friendly fire" rather than hostile action long before it became public. Tillman was our most famous Ranger, having given up a brilliant professional football career in order to enlist in the army in the aftermath of 9/11.

It has often been noted that the common dogface soldier rarely sees the Big Picture when it comes to war. Although spec ops people were better equipped and better trained to see more than just what went on directly in our own area of operations, Rangers were nonetheless so focused on defeating the insurgency in Mosul that it took the death of a Ranger to make us refocus on a broader field. News about the KIA reached Marez through the grapevine within hours after it occurred.

While 1st and 2nd platoons were concentrating on Mosul, Islamic extremists a few miles north of us were taking over the dense urban terrain of Tal Afar. Only 40 miles from the Syrian border, Tal Afar lay at the center of a vast border-region gateway for foreign fighters. The enemy kingpin there was an al Qaeda operative named Abu Musab al-Zarqawi, reported to be Osama bin Laden's second in command.

Born in Jordan, Zarqawi was a common alcoholic street thug until he found his calling in Afghanistan running a paramilitary training camp in the late 1990s that specialized in poisons and explosives. After creating al-Tawhid wal-Jihad, an organization dedicated to destroying Israel and to establishing a new caliphate, he met Osama bin Laden in 2004 and pledged allegiance to bin Laden and al Qaeda. He became the prime suspect in dozens of international acts of terror, including an attempt to blow up the Radisson Hotel in Amman and the assassination of Laurence Foley, a senior U.S. diplomat working for the U.S. Agency for International Development in Jordan.

As bin Laden's representative in Iraq, Zarqawi ran a "terrorist haven" in Kurdish northern Iraq, the Tal Afar region, and set up "sleeper cells" in Baghdad and other cities before the 2003 invasion, such cells to be activated upon U.S. occupation. In May 2004, a video appeared on al Qaeda Web sites and on Al-Jazeera TV showing five masked men beheading American civilian Nicholas Berg, who had been abducted and taken hostage in Iraq weeks earlier. The video opened with the title SHEIKH ABU MUSAB AL-ZARQAWI SLAUGHTERS AN AMERICAN INFIDEL WITH HIS OWN HANDS.

In September 2004, Zarqawi was reported to have personally

beheaded another American civilian, Owen Eugene Armstrong. He was also implicated in thousands of other killings in Iraq, mostly from bombings. In January 2005, he appeared in an Internet recording condemning democracy as "the big American lie . . . We have declared a bitter war against democracy and all those who seek to enact it . . . Democracy is also based on the right to choose your religion [and that is] against the rule of Allah."

Now, in 2005, Zarqawi held a tight grip on Tal Afar and its schools, mosques, and businesses, which he established as a staging base for terrorist training, a safe passage route into Iraq, and a sanctuary for the ideological indoctrination of uneducated and unemployed teenagers. "Collaborators" were intimidated and publicly executed.

After the fall of Fallujah, Tal Afar took its place as a propaganda tool for the resistance. Tal Afar was about to become Iraq's next hot spot.

Only a single infantry battalion of the 3rd ACR (Armored Cavalry Regiment), a few Rangers, and an unspecified number of other spec ops people were committed to pacifying an area twice the size of my home state of Connecticut. Two platoons of one battalion of the 3rd ACR lost a third of their soldiers killed or wounded in less than four months. Abrams tanks and Bradley Fighting Vehicles hit by IEDs burned in the streets, some of them later found inscribed with the logo of al Qaeda in Iraq on their sides.

On August 25, 2005, Corporal Timothy Shea, a 3rd Batt Ranger with Bravo Company, who had fought the battle for Haditha Dam, died in the Tal Afar district of an IED explosion. Ranger attention all over the country homed in on Tal Afar.

A week later, on September 1, Colonel H. R. McMaster, commander of the 3rd ACR, declared that it was time to take back Tal Afar. Two and a half years after the invasion of Iraq, thousands of U.S. and Iraqi soldiers and hundreds of Bradleys, Strykers, battle tanks, artillery, AC-130 Spectre gunships, F-16 fighter jets, and attack helicopters of Operation Restoring Rights converged on Tal Afar for what would be the biggest battle since Fallujah. About seven thousand Coalition troops, including infantry companies of the Kurdish Peshmerga, Rangers, and U.S. Special Forces teams, waited for H-hour in the predawn on the outskirts of the city, prepared to, as soldiers put it, "clear the pond."

The brunt of the fighting occurred in the notorious Sarai quarters, a labyrinth of medieval-looking alleyways where bands of foreign zealots from all over the Arab world dug in with tough local fighters. Blistering firefights raged at such close quarters that opponents could have hurled rocks instead of bullets at each other. U.S. F-16 fighter jets roared overhead delivering Hellfire missiles, while artillery barrages blasted enemy concentrations. Most of the civilian population fled the city, carrying their possessions on their backs and waving sad little white flags.

The heaviest fighting was mostly over within seventy-two hours. An estimated two hundred jihadists were slain. Four U.S. soldiers died, while a number were wounded, including several from the Ranger platoons. Captain Christopher Molino, ex-platoon leader of my 1st Platoon Alpha Company, now assigned to 3rd Batt as a Ground Force Joint Task Force commander, earned a Silver Star for conspicuous gallantry, in part for saving the lives of wounded Rangers.

It sounded like a good fight, but not one particularly suited for Rangers, who trained to conduct direct-action raids, ambushes, rescues, and other specialty operations. Get in, take care of business, get out again. That was our creed. Alpha Company Rangers at Mosul were not involved directly in the fighting at Tal Afar, although we had previously made raids in the city in futile attempts to run Zarqawi into a Saddam Hussein–type hole where we could capture him. The operation took a lot of pressure off FOB Marez for a couple of weeks as hundreds of our hardened local fighters sneaked out of Mosul and headed north to join Zarqawi. In the best of all worlds, at least some of these turds were statistics now in paradise practicing Sharia law on their virgins.

Intelligence obtained in the operation benefited us at Marez in that it later led to the apprehension of Abu Fatima, al Qaeda's military emir in Mosul. The CIA—"Big Brother"—took care of him.

Just as Colonel McMaster was about to mop up the surviving jihadists, politicians inserted their timid heads and ordered a "tactical pause." The same thing had happened during the First Battle of Fallujah, forcing U.S. Marines to withdraw, only to have to return later for a "Second Battle" against an enemy even more firmly entrenched. One angry Green Beret declared, "This is turning into a goatfuck."

During the "tactical pause," insurgents slipped out of Sarai by mingling with displaced, fleeing civilians. Some of them donned women's clothing and veils. Others forced children to hold their hands and pretend that they were family. Many others hid under produce in donkey carts or in the backs of old Toyotas. One burrowed into a pile of camel and donkey dung. Most of the insurgents were gone by the time Coalition forces received the green light to take over the city. Weapons caches and safe houses were found abandoned. Not a single hostile shot was fired. The insurgents had even taken their dead and wounded with them. The only enemy soldier found was a blackened, rotted corpse left in an alley.

Abu Musab al-Zarqawi had disappeared.

Two days later, he retaliated for his defeat with eleven suicide bombings in Baghdad that killed more than 150 people, most of them civilians, the deadliest series of attacks in the capital since the start of the war. Later, in an issue of *Time,* I read a quote from a man described as a high-ranking U.S. officer.

"We have not broken the back of the insurgency," he said. "The insurgency is like a cell phone system. You shut down one node, another somewhere else comes online to replace it."

37

The fight at Tal Afar had ended a month ago. It wasn't particularly apparent yet in Mosul whether our locals who went north to fight with Zarqawi were practicing Sharia law in any great numbers in paradise because of the battle. Business was back to normal, if by "normal" you meant a daily rash of suicide bombings, car bombs, RPG ambushes, and general all-around mischief and mayhem that included a nightly toll of assassinations, tortures, and beheadings. So, all in all, October 3, 2005, seemed like your average day in Iraq. At least that was how it began.

In broad, heated daylight, six Stryker vehicles resembling creatures of steel from some future Jurassic period prowled the bridge that spanned the Tigris River to link Old Town to Jonah's old stomping grounds. The bridge was a reasonably modern structure that rose in sharp contrast to the dark, twisted streets and alleys below and at either end, a twentieth-century structure juxtaposed upon seventh-century communities. Mosul, at least in this section of the city, was tan and brown because of sand constantly blowing in from the desert to scour off the color on buildings. Most of the color that remained was along the river—the emerald growth of palms and eucalyptus and irrigated vegetable gardens standing out against the otherwise drab monochrome of their surroundings.

Underneath the bridge, the Tigris churned an angry chocolate color as if pissed that still another war was being fought on its banks. Cloverleafs swept below and over the main reach of the bridge at either end. Exit curves dropped down to streets that ran alongside the river and underneath the bridge. Traffic was heavy this time of day, creating a jammed cacophony of blaring horns and rude shouts of road rage. Iraqi drivers were some of the rudest and most aggressive in the world.

I wasn't accustomed to working during the day, which produced an entirely different scenario from the night shift. I felt as exposed in the sun as the man in that old tale who let his wife drive their pickup camper while he took a nap in the back. When he woke up, the vehicle was stopped. He cracked the back door of the camper to take a look outside to see what was going on. He always slept in the nude since it was summer and hot in the camper. Just as he peeped out, the vehicle lurched forward and dumped him naked in the middle of Manhattan. Or was it in the middle of Dallas?

That was how I felt—naked in the middle of Mosul.

The six Strykers traveled in a patrolling pattern of three two-vehicle groups in overwatch, at intervals of a half-block or so to avoid the entire element's getting caught in an ambush kill zone. Typically, insurgents singled out one vehicle to blast, generally the last in the pack, and tried to do as much damage to it as they could before they got the hell out of Dodge ahead of an expected response from the other vehicles. Today we were searching for an HVT code-named Tarzan. Instead of swinging through the jungle, Tarzan drove a white Opel that supposedly crossed the bridge every day about this time. So far, it seemed every other vehicle was a VW Passat, a Chevy Malibu, or a dilapidated hajji clown car racing across the bridge into the collages of rusted abandoned cars and donkey carts on either end.

Vehicles from the 82nd Airborne regularly patrolled the bridge, which meant we weren't out of place or unusual enough to make our Tarzan guy hinky. Insurgents usually didn't fuck with "hard" targets such as Strykers; they concentrated instead on "soft" targets where they could get the most bang for their buck. It was more their style to drive a van full of dynamite into a street market of Shiites or Sunnis—according to your particular prejudices—and set it off in the middle of a bunch of women and kids, then call Al-Jazeera to claim credit for striking a blow against imperialism.

Platoon leader Captain Chad Fleming rode with my squad in the belly of the trail vehicle. Although autumn had descended upon the Cradle of Civilization, the days were still blazing hot, especially to those of us accustomed to working in the cool of desert nights. We hunkered jammed together inside on vehicle benches running down either side and sweated like a bunch of pigs in a tin barn. Smelled like a bunch of pigs, too. There were no windows and nothing to look at except each other and the various steel knobs, corners, and plates of the Stryker's womb.

The driver and tank commander at the controls of the vehicle sat up front at a higher level peering outside through small slitted windows. From the back, all we could see of them was their legs. We communicated back and forth either via the intercom or through our little handheld PRC-148 radios.

The Stryker driver, Cantrell, I think, hailed from somewhere in the Southwest. A cool kid. For some reason—and I think there have been studies on it—most spec ops people came from flyover country in the South, Midwest, and Southwest. Although I knew a few big-city Rangers, the majority of us were small-town or good ol' country boys raised on hot dogs, the Fourth of July, and the American flag. Cantrell broke the monotony and made us laugh with his running commentary, greatly exaggerated, on community life in Mosul since we were unable to see it for ourselves.

"I see blue Opels, green Opels, and a black one with seventeen circus clowns and seventy-two virgins in it, but I don't see no white Opels . . ."

That sort of amusing patter.

"Hey, take a look at this *gahob*. I wouldn't mind a little feaky-feaky with her. She's carrying a mattress on her back. I bet she's smoking hot if you took the bedsheets off her . . ."

"Cantrell, close your yap and keep your mind on business," Captain Fleming finally admonished, but good-naturedly.

"Sorry, sir. It's just that I'm so damned horny—"

"He's got calluses on his jackoff hand, sir."

Disgusting, but you had to love 'em. How many people had I known before the Rangers who would actually give their lives for you?

It was dark inside the Stryker even during the day unless the interior lights were burning. The PL opened the man hatch above our heads to let in a little light and fresh air and allow us to pop up periodically to take a look. We were both standing on the bench with our heads out the hatch above as our patrol convoy swept down off the bridge toward the street that ran alongside the river. In retrospect, opening the hatch and standing in it at that particular time may not have been the best of all moves.

The Stryker executed a long, tight turn coming down the cloverleaf exit from the bridge. The smooth pavement of the cloverleaf turned potholed and rough as the vehicle patrol reached street level to pass underneath the viaduct next to the river. None of us in any of the six vehicles had any warning that, above us on the bridge, insurgents were piling out of vehicles with assault rifles, machine guns, and grenades.

Everything turned chaotic all at once. Jihadists leaning over the banisters of the overpass above our heads opened fire in a skillfully executed ambush. While we were looking for Tarzan, Tarzan's apes had apparently been sneaking up on us, waiting for just this opportunity. Grenades began exploding, automatic weapons chattering in loud waves, all this superimposed on the honking of horns and the screeching of tires as horrified motorists attempted to flee the bridge. Bullets pinged off the Stryker's armored top and sides.

I glimpsed the grenade when it slammed through the open hatch between Fleming and me before we had time to duck inside and slam the hatch. What were the odds that some asshole could have made a major league pitch like that? There was no time to respond. Horrified, I looked directly at the spewing little hand bomb while it detonated in a blinding flash on the floor at my feet, all the fury and fragmentation of the blast contained inside the troop compartment.

I felt sharp sudden pain all along my right side, from my foot to my shoulder, like shards of molten glass ripping into my flesh. The concussive effect of the exploding grenade made my head go numb and crazy. My ears and eyes felt like they were bursting. The sledgehammerlike blow knocked me off my feet and onto the steel floor. Captain Fleming, Joe Edwards, and Private Garrett McTear were all jammed down on top of me and me on them, all of us wounded. I smelled blood and raw, seared flesh and cordite and sweat and . . . God! I heard a yelp of sheer agony and realized it was me.

First Platoon's luck had finally run out. For an instant, that first instant, I thought I was dying. Through the bloodred pain and confusion appeared the image of Kimberly at the company building in Georgia when we said good-bye.

Kim is really going to be pissed off!

38

It was at the same time both harder and easier than you might think to kill a man. I had seen wounded jihadists riddled all to hell with gunfire—and they *lived*. On the other hand, some guy with a little bitty hole in his abdomen or in his arm or leg looked up at you, rolled his eyes, and died. Maybe it had something to do with your *will* to live, that spark inside that you refused to let go.

I saw right away that I was bleeding out from my right arm and leg, but, other than that first terrifying instant when I thought I might be dead, I refused to entertain the consideration that I might not make it. For a Ranger to succumb to failures of mind or body was to admit weakness. I ordered myself to shake it off and get on with business. There was no crying in baseball.

The grenade explosion had set off the fire extinguisher, which filled the bay with a vicious hissing cloud of carbon dioxide. It sucked out all the air. I lay on the deck between the seats and legs of other Rangers, all in a mangled, bloody, struggling heap with Fleming, Edwards, and McTear, the four of us gasping to catch our breath and regain equilibrium after the concussive effects of the grenade. I heard screaming, shouting, and cursing as from a long distance away because of the ringing in my ears. In my befogged state of mind, I took all the clamor to mean that some of us were pretty fucked up.

I smelled the coppery-sour odor of blood in the air, mixed with carbon dioxide from the spewing fire extinguisher. I knew how blood smelled. It wasn't something new. I had never smelled my own blood before, though, not in such large quantities. The deck was slippery with it.

Later, I learned the grenade had hit the steel benches at our feet between Captain Fleming and me, bounced, and detonated between my right leg and Fleming's left leg. The two of us absorbed most of the jolt and shrapnel, preventing greater injuries to the rest of the passengers. Other than Fleming, Edwards, McTear, and me, none of the other five Rangers in the Stryker were injured, almost a miracle considering that a frag exploding inside such a crowded, confined space could have killed us all.

Bullets from the overpass above were still pinging a deadly rhythm against the Stryker's thick skin, the shooters attempting to pump bullets through the open hatch so they could bounce around inside among us like deadly steel balls in a pinball machine. I fumbled for the little PRC-148 attached to my load-bearing harness.

"Get the hell outta here!" I shouted into it.

The Stryker lurched into a tire-squealing takeoff against traffic and ducked in underneath the bridge out of the line of fire. Ben Hunter kept his cool in spite of the turmoil. As soon as our driver braked the Stryker beneath the protective cover of the bridge, he began throwing guys toward the open hatch to get them out and into a security perimeter. Matt Sanders ripped open his first aid cravat and tried to stanch the flow of blood from my arm. I waved him off. I hadn't assessed my wounds yet, but, although groggy and disoriented, I was never in danger of losing consciousness. I took that to mean I wasn't critically injured. I still had fight left.

Barking into the radio, I warned the rest of the patrol: *"Contact! Contact! We're under the bridge. We are fucked up!"*

"Roger, One-One. Calm down and tell us what's going on. Over."

Sgt. Joseph Kapacziewski and Charles W. Sasser

I thought I was calm. *"One-Six Actual is hit, two or three others—get us the fuck out of here."*

Firing from outside ceased as abruptly as it began. That was the way these things went. The hajjis knew we'd be arriving in force like gangbusters after something like this. They jumped back into their Malibus, Toyotas, and clown cars, whatever, and shagged.

Captain Fleming and Edwards appeared to be in worse shape than I, both of them barely coherent. I needed to summon medical attention ASAP. Neither my right arm nor leg seemed to function. Dragging my useless limbs through blood and gore, I managed to reach the back troop ramp, which I unlatched and attempted to drop. Someone had further secured it with plastic tie strips.

I cut the plastic strips using my sheath knife and my left hand. The door dropped against the pavement with a *clang,* releasing smoke and carbon dioxide from the compartment and letting daylight in. I lay on the ramp half in and half out of the vehicle, panting for air like I had just run a marathon, weakly lifting my good hand and my head toward other Strykers now forming a perimeter around mine as they secured the bridge, holding traffic back with weapons ready.

A crowd of locals was already gathering. As usual, the first signs of excitement drew every hajji within hearing distance. They rushed to the sound of gunfire like it was some kind of spectator sport. Rangers eyed them suspiciously and kept their weapons pointed. You never knew if there might not be a prospective martyr in the crowd.

After the initial shock began to wear off, sharp, searing pain ripped through my body. My right leg looked twisted into a bloody, grotesque spiral fracture from knee to foot. The boot pointed about one-eighty in the wrong direction. I tried to straighten it and felt bone ends shifting and grating. I screamed in agony.

Sanders hovered over me. "I'm gonna patch your arm, Kap," he offered.

My right arm looked shattered. Bright arterial blood pumped from it and trickled down the ramp and into the third world filth and shit of the street. That was when I realized this was one injury I couldn't shake off. I attempted to retrieve my med pack with my good hand.

"Gotta stop the bleeding," Sanders muttered.

He looked pale and frightened, but he applied a thick pressure bandage to the wound and held it in place. Blood squeezed through his compressed fingers.

"Captain Fleming . . . ? Edwards . . . ?" I managed.

"McTear, too," Sanders said. "Kap . . . Kap. Be still. It's okay. They're being taken care of."

My ankle and foot flopped back and forth when Sergeant Van Aalst and Specialist Justin Slusher came to drag me the rest of the way out of the Stryker and farther up underneath the bridge to wait for a MEV, a medical evacuation vehicle.

"Sar'ent, drag me on my other side," I pleaded. My left side was still good to go.

Medics loaded Captain Fleming and me on gurneys into the back of the MEV when it arrived. I assumed Edwards and McTear were carted off in a second vehicle. The physician's assistant pumped me fentanyl lollipops on the way to the forward location. Fentanyl is more powerful than morphine. I felt pretty good, floating, by the time we arrived. Sergeant Major Walker and Company First Sergeant Eddie Noland pushed my gurney into the OR.

"Sergeant Major," I asked, my voice slurred, "you think when I get better and all healed up you might send me to HALO parachute school?"

He looked at me and shook his head in amazement. That was the last thing I remembered before going into surgery.

39

GEORGIA 2005

Kimberly:

Joe was coming home. I was overjoyed. How I found out was through another Ranger's wife, Jill Baker, who received a phone call from Ranger Battalion informing her that her husband, Dustin, had left Iraq and would be landing in Georgia in twelve hours. Joe and Dustin were in 3rd Battalion, but Dustin was coming home early to go to school.

Jill sometimes accompanied me while I worked with horses. I enjoyed her company, and going with me gave her a chance to "get out of the house," as she put it. The two of us were on our way to Atlanta pulling a trailer behind the truck to pick up a horse, both of us laughing and chatting up a storm, when her cell phone buzzed.

"Hello?" Jill was a pretty girl, a brunette with big brown eyes.

She almost dropped her Dr Pepper in her lap. She shrieked. I glanced over and was astounded to see her laughing and giggling like she might have gone unexpectedly mad. Tears of joy gushed from her eyes. She tossed the phone on the dash.

"He's on the first plane. He'll be here tonight."

Her eyes popped wide. Delight turned to panic. "Oh, my God! I'm a mess and I haven't cleaned house. I don't want him to come home to that."

They had been married about a year. The horse in Atlanta had to be picked up today. I couldn't turn around and go back.

"We'll get you home in time," I promised. "Did he say anything about Joe?"

"Don't worry, Kim. They'll call when he's on his way."

This was my first experience as an army wife about how these things worked. Wives were told almost nothing about what was going on. Eight to twelve hours was the normal advance notification we received on major movements like rotations overseas or redeployments to Fort Benning. *Don't call us, we'll call you if there's anything you need to know.* Joe explained it had to be that way because stressed-out wives would otherwise be constantly ringing base telephones off their desks.

I put the pedal to the metal and we fairly flew to Atlanta and back. Any traffic cop who pulled me over for speeding would surely have understood. Jill rode the edge of her seat all the way, she was so excited. The sun was going down by the time I got her home. My cell phone still hadn't rung.

I helped Jill clean house and finished a washer load of dishes in the kitchen while she grabbed a shower. Then she hugged me and rushed off to meet her husband.

Feeling a little blue, carrying my cell in my hand in case the call came, I walked outside to where I had parked the truck and trailer at the curb in front of the Bakers' cute little apartment. I paused before I got behind the wheel to drive back to Midland. Purple twilight shadows tethered to Georgia pines and live oaks lining the street stretched down the block. A couple of kids riding bicycles waved. There was an autumn's chill in the air of these last days of September.

I shivered. It wasn't that cold outside. I looked around as though I half expected to see Joe swaggering down the street toward me. I checked the window of my cell phone to make sure I hadn't missed a call. I wondered what he was doing on that violent other side of the world that separated us.

• • •

I waited. That was what army wives did. We waited for our husbands to come home. We waited for phone calls, even those dreaded ones that almost stopped your heart from beating, that cold, impersonal telephone call that "regretfully" informed you that Sergeant So-and-So or Private So-and-So had been wounded or injured in the line of duty in a country far, far away. Even so, that kind of call was preferable to looking out your window and seeing a staff car drive up—*Please, please don't stop here, keep going!* You wouldn't actually accept that it had parked in front of your house until somber officers looking like they were on their way to a funeral got out and walked up to your door. You squeezed your eyes closed. Maybe the officers wouldn't be there when you opened them again.

Nonetheless, knowing this scenario had played out with the wives of other Rangers, I was not the sort of woman who sat around day after day worrying myself to death like so many of the other wives did. Shortly after Joe and I "paperworked," we drove out into the country to target shoot. He set up a target so far away that I could barely see it. He hit it dead center every shot with his rifle.

"You don't have to worry about me, Kim," he said.

Jill Baker and the other wives sometimes asked, "Kimberly, how are you so strong? We're miserable."

Easy enough. I kept busy with school and working at the farm. Joe wouldn't have wanted me miserable. He probably wouldn't have "paperworked" me if I had been the weeping willow type.

Still, I was ready for Joe to come home. Things reminded me of him as I waited through the days for one of those "twelve-hour" phone calls. I passed by the Denny's where we had gone the night we met; I turned around and took our old table. We were still on our honeymoon, almost, when Joe deployed. The jeans and button-up shirt he wore when we married still hung in the closet next to my wedding skirt and blouse. On post, soldiers were fond of macho bumper stickers whose philosophy mirrored Joe's. They made me smile.

A special tone on my cell phone played only if the call came from Joe's number in Iraq. It was a musical refrain—"Take My Breath Away" from the movie *Top Gun*. Joe and I watched it together on TV one night. I know, it was ridiculous and sappy, but if it ever played I knew it had to be Joe. I inspected my phone constantly to make sure it was working and the battery was charged.

Jill Baker and I hadn't seen each other since Dustin got home. I didn't blame her. They had a lot of catching up to do. However, we talked on the phone a minute or so every day. I also spoke with Melanie and Suzanna. Everyone kept asking if I had heard from Joe, and every day I asked Jill if Dustin knew anything about my husband's platoon. All he knew was that when he flew out of Iraq, Joe's platoon was still running missions in Mosul.

A long week like that passed. Finally, alone one morning at Midland Farms, I was feeding the horses in their stalls and sweeping out the aisle through the barn when "Take My Breath Away" took my breath away. It seemed I couldn't get the phone tucked in my jeans out fast enough. Joe was coming home!

"Hey, babe!" I greeted cheerily.

It was really quiet on the other end. I felt an inexplicable chill.

"Joe?"

I didn't recognize the voice that replied. "Mrs. Kap . . . Mrs. Kap, I'm sorry . . ."

I didn't understand. I squeezed my eyes shut. Why was he sorry?

40

In terms of American war dead, the Civil War with 623,026 dead on both sides of the conflict was the most costly in U.S. history. Compare that to the additional 626,000 over the next hundred years, including two world wars. The Civil War, as the Union Army surgeon general complained, was fought "at the end of the medical Middle Ages."

One witness, a soldier from Virginia, described a typical surgeon's tent, "Tables about breast high had been erected upon which the screaming victims were having legs and arms cut off. The surgeons and their assistants, stripped to the waist and bespattered with blood, stood around, some holding the poor fellows while others armed with long, bloody knives and saws [thus the term for doctors, 'sawbones'] cut and sawed away with frightful rapidity, throwing the mangled limbs on a pile nearby as soon as removed."

Although firepower has increased dramatically since the Civil War, lethality has decreased, primarily due to more definitive medical care nearer the battlefield. During World War II, 30 percent of all Americans wounded or injured in combat died. That statistic dropped to 24 percent in Vietnam and down to 10 percent or less in Afghanistan and Iraq.

Somewhere between an average of thirty and fifty general surgeons and ten to fifteen orthopedic surgeons served in Iraq at any one time in either a forward surgical team (FST) or a Combat Support Hospital (CSH, pronounced "cash"). FSTs consisted of a small mobile team of twenty or so medical personnel who provided initial care for the wounded. Their aim was damage control, not definitive treatment. They were not equipped for more than six hours of intensive care.

The CSH was the next step up. Two CSHs with four different sites existed in Iraq, each with a 248-bed hospital capacity and six operating tables. A patient had three days here before, if he was injured critically enough, he continued his medical cycle to the next step—a Level IV hospital in either Kuwait; Rota, Spain; or Landstuhl, Germany. If he required treatment of thirty days or more, he transferred back to the United States for treatment at either Walter Reed Army Medical Center in Washington, D.C., or Brooke Army Medical Center in San Antonio, Texas. It took a wounded soldier an average time of four days to go from the battlefield to a U.S. facility, compared to forty-five days for a wounded soldier during the Vietnam War.

One airman with devastating injuries all over his body reached Walter Reed within thirty-six hours. He survived injuries that would have been unsurvivable in previous wars, losing one leg above the knee, the other leg at the hip, his right hand, and part of his face.

As of November 2004, U.S. casualties in Afghanistan and Iraq numbered 10,726, of which 1,361 died, 1,004 of them killed in action. Another 5,174 were so seriously injured they were unable to return to duty. The remainder, 4,191, returned to their units within seventy-two hours.

Some days were quiet in theater, others not so much so, depending on what was going on. During the Marine and 101st Airmobile fight for Nasiriyah, ten critically wounded servicemen ended up at the FST in one day. The patients included one with shrapnel displayed in his right lower leg; one with a gunshot wound to the stomach, intestines, and liver; one with a gunshot through the liver, gallbladder, and transverse colon; one with a gunshot wound through the rectum; two with extremity (arm or leg) gunshots; and the last with shrapnel from an IED in his neck, back, and chest.

All of them went from FST to CSH to Level IV to Walter Reed within a matter of days; all of them survived.

Early in 2003 when the war began in Iraq, war planners expected Kevlar body armor to provide dramatic protection against torso injuries. However, surgeons soon discovered that IEDs, RPGs, and grenades were causing blast injuries that extended upward underneath the armor and inward through axillary vents. Blast injuries produced an unprecedented number of what orthopedists termed "mangled extremities"—arms and legs with bone, soft-tissue, and vascular damage. Such injuries were potentially mortal. Because they were often extreme and combined with mutilations to other organs, attempts to salvage limbs frequently failed, with the risk of life-threatening blood loss, ischemia (restricted blood supply), and sepsis (blood poisoning).

Every two weeks, surgeons at Walter Reed and in Baghdad reviewed casualties being sent to the hospital in D.C. A typical case list in 2005 provided a clear picture of injuries. They included one gunshot, one anti-tank mine injury, three injuries from RPGs, four from mortar fire, eight from IEDs, seven unspecified, and one as a result of a grenade explosion.

Surgeons partially amputated one hand, one leg from the knee down, and one leg from the hip. They performed one open pelvic debridement, a left nephrectomy and colostomy, an axillary artery and vein reconstruction, a splenectomy, and repaired a scalp laceration and a through-and-through tongue laceration.

None of the soldiers was more than twenty-five-years old.

41

Pain medications kept me in some kind of gray netherworld for days after the grenade dropped through the hatch. People, things, events, *life,* seemed to float in and out in wispy fragments of reality. I hardly knew where I was at any particular moment in time. For all I knew I might be muttering to the IV stand rather than to the nurse.

During fleeting moments of lucidity, I tried to remember the details of what happened under the bridge. *Under the bridge.* That was how I would always think of those few short minutes that threatened to change and disrupt forever my planned career in the army and therefore my life. Most of my squad had been in the belly of the Stryker when the world turned red under the bridge. Under the bridge, Captain Fleming had been wounded also, and badly. I remembered chaos and pain under the bridge, confusion and some thought of death. I remembered fear for my soldiers, concern . . .

I mumbled questions to whoever bothered to listen to my drug-induced ravings. Somehow, although I'm not sure by whom, they were answered in a manner that crept into my consciousness so that I knew the answers but didn't understand how I knew.

"Joe Edwards . . . ?"

He had taken some shrapnel, but would return to duty after treatment.

"Garrett McTear . . . ?"

How was that for luck? One year out of high school, on his first combat deployment, and he already had a Purple Heart. His wounds were less severe than Edwards's.

"Ben . . . Ben Hunter . . . ?"

Oh, God, no! He was under the bridge. He and I had been together almost from the beginning. *He's okay. Can you hear me, Sergeant? He's okay.*

"Private Sanders . . . ?"

Not a scratch.

"Justin Slusher . . . ?"

He must be okay. He helped drag me out of the Stryker.

"Captain Fleming . . . ?"

I remembered seeing him, hearing him, smelling him, under the bridge. He and I absorbed most of the grenade's energy when it exploded between my right leg and his left. He and I were the most fucked up. I remembered in my stupor of pain and drugs hearing the term "amputation." Were they talking about Captain Fleming, about me, about both of us?

"No!" I screamed in abject terror. "Don't take my leg!"

At other times I thought of Kim, kept seeing her face as through a soaped window, like in one of those half-awake, half-sleeping stages of hallucinations when you were so ragged-out on a mission that you hardly knew where you were.

"Don't tell Kim," I pleaded. "Don't tell Kim."

I didn't want her to know what happened, not yet. I didn't want her to see me like this . . .

Kimberly:

It was all a blur. A horrid blur.

"Ma'am," said the voice on the phone, eventually identified as belonging to the Ranger Battalion commander. "Ma'am, I'm sorry . . ."

"Sorry! Sorry about what?"

"Ma'am . . ."

Fear and rage and terror all at the same time. "What's happened to Joe?" It was an accusation.

He wasn't dead or they would have come to the house in a staff car. The colonel on the other end of the telephone remained calm, steady.

"Mrs. Kap, I'm sorry to have to inform you that your husband has been injured."

I gripped my cell phone, as though if I let it go I would drown. Slowly, it all came out in that stranger's voice on the other end of the line. My impression was that Joe had wounds to both legs and to his right arm.

"Is he . . . ?"

My voice trailed off. Is he—*What?* Is he going to make it? Is he okay? How could he be okay if a grenade blew him up?

"He's VSI at this time—very seriously injured. We don't know all the details. He's still in Iraq, but we may have to evacuate him to Germany. We'll contact you later on to let you know."

"Are the Hunter brothers hurt? Ben and Ian?" I demanded with surprising calm. "I'm calling their wives. I need to tell them."

The Hunter brothers and their wives were close friends to Joe and me. The Hunters were also in Iraq. Ben was in Joe's squad.

"They're fine," the battalion commander assured me. "We'll keep you updated."

Updated? My new husband might be dying and they were going to keep me *updated?*

He hung up. Nerves jangling, I called Ben's and Ian's wives, Lori and Abby. They had received no phone calls from the army, but they still sounded troubled. I suspected frightened wives would be ringing the battalion commander's office silly for the next few days.

I drove myself home after the phone call came. I was in perfect control, however. I was often described as being "stoic" and "in control."

I was still living with Mom in Columbus, but two weeks before Joe deployed we had bought a house on a wooded acreage in the country near the community of Upatoi. We had minimal furniture in it so far, but I chose to go there anyhow, to Joe's and my future home. Melanie and my mom both came out to Upatoi to check on me, but I just wanted to be left alone. That was where I stayed, alone, without a TV and the only furniture a sofa and a chair. I continued to work and go to school to keep occupied and not dwell on what might be happening. I had to be strong for Joe; it was my job.

Joe and I had been wed about three months. Our big secret would have to come out now. I put it off as long as I could. Then, dreading it, I dialed Grandma Churchill's number. She was a robust woman with a temper to match anyone, not the easiest person to get along with.

"Why did the army call you instead of me?" she demanded. "We're his next of kin."

"Joe and I are married," I blurted out.

That made the news a double blow for her. That we hadn't informed her of the wedding, I suspected, would remain a black mark against me from now on.

Joe's sister, Erin, and his brother, Randy, offered to drive to Georgia right away, but I let them off. They were still strangers. All that could be done now was to wait for further reports on Joe's condition. Frantic with worry and waiting, I would never have made it without Melanie, my mom, and my sister, Melissa, to help me keep pulled together. The man I loved was thousands of miles away and there was nothing I could do to help him. I didn't even know how badly he was injured, or if—God forbid!—he might be dying.

I didn't sleep much. I crashed in the living room on the sofa or in the chair and waited for the phone to ring with more news. I began to think that maybe the battalion commander was hesitant about telling me over the phone how serious Joe really was. I drove to Ranger Battalion in hopes someone would be honest and let me know what was really going on.

"Don't worry, Mrs. Kap," the duty officer consoled me. "He's just a little banged up."

Banged up was falling off a bicycle, not hit by a grenade.

I threatened to go directly to the Department of Defense. That was how much I knew about the army and how it worked.

"Mrs. Kap, you'll only cause problems for everyone. The Department of Defense doesn't know what's going on since Rangers are in special operations. Go home, Mrs. Kap. We'll let you know everything as soon as we know it here. Mrs. Kap, we're sorry . . ."

Everyone was sorry. Sorry wasn't enough.

Two days later I was still fretting, waiting to hear something, when "Take My Breath Away" brought immediate tears to my eyes. I snatched up the cell phone. A female voice on the other end identified herself as a nurse at the American hospital in Mosul. She sounded as far away as Mars.

"Kimberly? Joe wants to talk to you. He's under sedation. I don't know how much he'll be able to say . . ."

"Just put him on. Please?"

Joe was always so tough and confident. The voice I heard could not be Joe's. The man on the other end of the call was hesitant, shaky, almost like the ghost of the man I knew. No, not a ghost, the *husk* of a ghost. There was not really a conversation between us. How much could you say when one of you was scared to death and the other wasn't really all in it? Joe's side of the exchange was limited mainly to "uh-huh" and "huh-uh."

"Are you all right, Joe?"

"Uh-huh."

"Do you know when you'll be home?"

"Huh-uh."

When we got ready to hang up, Joe's horrible new quaking voice closed with "Kim? Kim, I love you."

That was when I knew how seriously Joe was wounded. We never said "I love you" to one another unless there was a real need for it. I closed my phone and suddenly felt the weight of all that was happening.

Afterward, I barely recalled talking to Kim. Most of the time during those first weeks of repeated surgeries in Iraq and at the Level IV casualty hospital in Germany, I seemed to hang on to this world by a single slender, drugged thread that I feared might snap at any moment. I could never understand how people could get addicted to drugs and *want* to exist in some kind of shadowy dreamland that was neither quite real nor unreal.

I kept hearing foggy conversations that included the whispered word "amputation." Whoever "they" were, they were talking about removing my leg. I went to Iraq on my own two legs; I was going to come back the same way. How could I be a U.S. Army Airborne Ranger without a leg?

I became convinced during one pre-op that if I entered the OR I would come out half a man. I fought to get off the OR table before anes-theologists could get to me. Maybe they strapped me down to restrain me. I remembered raving fiercely.

"No! No! You can't do this to me. Understand? I can't go home like that. I'm a Ranger. I . . . I . . ."

When I came to, hours later, the first thing I did was look for my leg. It was encased in an external fixator, like a big cage spiked with pins going through flesh and bone to hold my leg together. It was gross looking, but I still had it.

I still had my leg.

I was still a full man.

42

GEORGIA 2005

Kimberly:

They lost Joe. I mean, they actually lost him. It started with Ranger Battalion telling me he was in Germany.

"He's not in Germany," I tried to explain. "He's still in Iraq. I know because he called me from Mosul."

It was a tough period of time. I still worked at Midland Farms and attended college at the same time. Fortunately, Suzanna at the farm and my professors at CSU remained understanding of the circumstances and the stress I was under. I e-mailed my principal professor an excuse for not attending class regularly. It happened to be on the same date Joe transferred from Mosul to Level IV in Landstuhl, Germany. By this time, Joe and I were talking by telephone nearly every day. I explained it all in my e-mail to Dr. Gibson:

Hey, Dr. Gibson,

I am writing to keep you posted on our current status. First and foremost . . . the military could really benefit from your communications classes. I have learned that they really struggle in this department . . .

I had great intentions of coming to class today, but Joe

called . . . I am so happy that I got to hear his voice and know that he is going to be okay. He told me a few things that I was unaware of. He did tell me that his right biceps is gone and the doctors are talking about "taking his right foot." I was told that all the surgeries that he has had have been on an arterial tear in that arm—but he told me that he has had surgery all over his body. He told me that he has pins all over his legs, sticking out of bandages.

Now that Joe is stable the next step is to get him to Germany. He is scheduled to head out tonight (our time) . . . Joe told me that he would love to meet me in Germany, but told me that I am not ready to see him. He hopes that he can heal up a bit before I see him.

The Department of Defense—I had telephoned them anyhow—called to tell me Joe was at the military hospital in Germany.

"He can't be. He's still in Iraq. I've talked to him."

Someone switched me to Germany. I still didn't believe Joe was there.

"Ma'am, he's here. I'll have the nurse switch you to his room."

I was stunned. I had spoken to Joe in Iraqs only last night, his time. Could he have been transferred so quickly? I asked the nurse to stay on the line with me when she passed me on to what was supposedly my husband's room.

"Joe . . . ?"

Silence for a long moment. "No . . ."

It wasn't Joe. Whoever he was had come from Iraq with Joe's medical records. As far as Germany knew, the wounded soldier in Room 20B, or whichever room it was, was Joe Kapacziewski.

"Records say he's Joe Kapa . . . Kapa . . ." the nurse insisted.

"Kapacziewski. I don't care what the records say. I should know my own husband."

Ranger Battalion always preached of taking care of its people, of being family-oriented. Here, they didn't even know where Joe was. They had lost him.

They soon found him, however. I might have had an even tougher time keeping track of Joe's travels if it hadn't been for a urology doctor friend of mine. Dr. Ray Petrowski was on active duty assigned to the military hospital in Germany. He let me know when Joe arrived and also went by Joe's room every day to check on him.

43

WALTER REED ARMY MEDICAL CENTER 2005–2006

Kimberly:

Looking back, it seemed that entire period of my life passed in darkness and night. My flight to Washington, D.C., arrived in late afternoon. A liaison from SOCOM picked up Chad Fleming's wife, Kristin, and me at the airport in a staff car and drove us to a hotel near Walter Reed, where both Chad and Joe had been transferred for treatment. I sat in the backseat staring out without seeing, so wrung out from worry and lack of sleep that my mind seemed to blank out on me for long stretches of time.

The soldier driver looked young enough to still be in high school. He glanced worriedly up at Kristin and me through his rearview mirror as he drove.

"Ladies," he asked, "how yeh doin'?"

"We're fine."

That was a lie. City lights passed by in a blur, if I saw them at all. I wanted to see Joe in the worst possible way, but at the same time, I *didn't*. That kind of conflict made little sense to me. It was just that I didn't know what to expect. Joe was still listed as VSI—very seriously injured. I knew him as that shy but macho, supremely confident guy whose life was all wrapped up in being a Ranger soldier.

"Kim, you'll always be first to Kap," Ben Hunter said to me once, "but the Rangers won't be far behind."

How had his being wounded changed him? So far, from what I gathered in our brief talks, he existed in a state of denial in which he expected to heal and return to the Rangers as a squad leader. "They" were talking about amputating Joe's leg—he might even lose his arm—but Joe was having no part of that. He wouldn't even discuss it.

I telephoned the hospital from my hotel room. When I finally got through to his floor, someone told me I wouldn't be able to see him tonight and it would be best if I came in the morning. I didn't argue, but I hadn't come all this way to sit in a hotel room. I took a quick shower, put on a little makeup, and changed into my good jeans for the occasion. The young liaison driver took Kristin and me to the hospital.

It was traffic rush hour, stop and go. We filled the lulls on the drive with conversation. I was more loquacious than Joe. Kids when I was in school sometimes called me "Chatty Kathy." I liked people.

The driver said he had served one deployment in Iraq before his assignment to SOCOM. "Sometimes ah think ah'd rathah be in Baghdad than heah," he said in his clipped New England Oyster House accent.

I rode in the front passenger's seat. I looked at him.

"Evah day," he went on, "ah drive mothahs and wives an' girlfriends to the hospital to see theah wounded soldiers. Evah day. I feel so bad foah them, but theah is nothing ah can do."

"There are many wounded?"

"Yes, ma'am. Theah's a lot, a whole lot. Moah keep comin' evah day on white school buses. They line up out in the hallway on theah littahs an' wait to see the doctahs."

Kristin was ushered directly to Chad at the hospital. The nursing station attendant told me Joe was in surgery. He would have more than forty operations before it was over. I sat on a bench in the hallway outside his room for over an hour by myself, waiting, still wondering what Joe would be like now. Still afraid of seeing him for the first time after what happened.

An older nurse, crusty and formal, came down the hallway, heels clicking on the tile.

"Mrs. Kapa—?"

The name was always a tongue twister.

"Kimberly," I said.

"Yes. Will you please go to the waiting room? Your husband doesn't want you to see him suffering the way he is. We'll come for you once we get him situated in bed."

She came for me two hours later. I heard sharp cries of pain as we approached the door to Joe's room. Gooseflesh rippled up my spine. I hesitated. The nurse placed a comforting hand on my shoulder and looked me in the eyes.

"No one is ever prepared for the first time you see them," she said. "Compose yourself, honey. Don't let him see that look on your face."

I felt my stomach turning over with dread, apprehension, fear, and everything else when I walked into that sterile, antiseptic-smelling room and saw that wreck of a human being that I loved helplessly covered underneath sheets with catheters, IVs, and monitor lines running out from every part of his body. A cast confined his right arm from shoulder to hand. He had an external fixator on his right leg. I saw wide-open gaps of exposed purple flesh. His face appeared gaunt and gray and scabbed from shrapnel wounds.

He was just coming out from under anesthesia and could hardly seem to keep his eyes open. I stood for a long minute inside the doorway, staring at him in shock. Tears formed, but I would never cry in front of him. He slowly turned his head and looked at me. The nurse touched my arm to remind me of her admonition. Joe's lips trembled, moved slowly. No sound came from them, but I understood.

"Hey, babe . . ."

Until Walter Reed, I never realized people could suffer so. I was a southern country girl. I had had my knocks, what with my parents divorcing and everything. Still, I realized later, Mom had always tried to shelter Melissa and me from the harsher aspects of life. Sitting in the hallway outside Joe's room when I had to leave it to allow doctors and nurses to perform some procedure or other on him, I heard people crying and screaming from behind closed doors all along the hallway. I sat weeping and talking to Mom on my cell phone, trying to block it all out and escape into some normality from this hell of pain and suffering.

It turned out Joe had an unusually high tolerance for pain medications. It required unbelievable amounts of painkiller to ease his torture. A pump by his bedside had a button that he could push every three or four minutes to push more anesthetics into his bloodstream. Mostly it was Dilaudid. He hurt so badly that he would have held the button down continuously, except it was on a timer set to provide limited dosages. He awoke screaming in agony if he fell asleep and failed to push the button on time. He became afraid to sleep because it took so much time and drugs to ease the pain again and get him back under control.

I took over the button. Day and night, I perched at his bedside, watching the timer clock while I pushed the button for him every few minutes. We rarely spoke to each other. Joe existed in a fog of suffering and drugs through which we could not seem to reach each other. He knew I was with him. That was enough for now.

That was how it went for much of the next six months. Waiting, either alone in a hotel room, in the waiting room at Walter Reed, or at Joe's bedside while he suffered excruciating pain, more than any human should have to endure. If he hadn't been Joe, I sometimes thought he would never have made it. Soldiers with wounds like his would have died in previous wars that did not have the miracles of modern medicine.

An entire set of holidays would pass like that. Thanksgiving, Joe's birthday, my birthday, Christmas, New Year's, Easter . . . Darkness and pain. That was our lives, Joe's and mine, although we tried to make the best of things.

One night when things seemed stable and Joe was awake and aware, I left for a few minutes to take a shower and change clothes. When I returned, I heard him from all the way down at the other end of the hallway. He was screaming and crying. "Help, it hurts bad, help."

He had dozed off and fallen behind the pain curve. Doctors and nurses on the anesthesia team were running in and out of his room. They had the crash cart out. There were so many people in the room that there was no room for me and I had to stay outside in the hallway.

All that suffering and there was nothing I could do for him. I paced back and forth outside his door. Angry and hurting for Joe, I started yelling at nurses and administrators. "Why can't you do something?" The problem was that Joe, bad as he was, was not the most serious medical case at the hospital. There were many more patients in worse shape, who also required care. Understaffed doctors and nurses were simply overwhelmed by it all.

A nurse ran out of the room. Her face looked pale, and she was crying.

"You've got to make them stop or they'll kill him," she sobbed. "Anyone else given that much Dilaudid would be dead by now."

She cupped her face in her hands. Her shoulders shook.

"I can't watch it anymore," she wailed, "because he's going to die."

She fled down the hallway without looking back.

I didn't know what to do. Having no one else near enough to turn to, I cell-phoned Sergeant Major Dan Thompson, the SOCOM hospital liaison. He had been kind to Joe and me and taken a personal interest in our case. It was midnight when I called. Joe was screaming in the background.

"What is that?" Sergeant Major Thompson asked.

"I need you here," I exclaimed in a burst of tears. "I . . . I . . ."

"I'm on my way," he said and hung up.

I huddled on the floor outside Joe's door and waited for it to be over. That was where Sergeant Major Thompson found me. I had never seen him out of uniform. He came running up in his PT army grays along with the commander of the hospital. The sergeant major offered a shoulder to lean on, and the hospital commander rushed to Joe's bedside.

Gradually, Joe's screaming subsided. The hospital commander came out.

"Everything's under control. He's all right."

I silently vowed never to leave Joe alone again. Ever.

44

Kimberly:

My life revolved around Joe's medical care. What time I wasn't "pushing Joe's button"—something we laughed about later—I was immersed in our finances and in keeping up on everything that was going on. When you were married, what happened to one partner happened to the other. This was my first experience with hospitals. Ironic that it had to come three months, about *ninety days,* after I married a soldier. Here I was overwhelmed by the army, its medical protocols, procedures, and red tape, and trying to keep the remnants of our life back in Georgia on track. Doctors kept assuring me that Joe and I would be returning to our old lives sooner or later, maybe in six months. I doubted our "old lives" would ever be the same again, especially if Joe lost his leg—and maybe even his arm.

I really hadn't counted on this so soon after our "paperwork." I was sure Joe hadn't either, albeit he had kept warning me what I might expect if we got married. When you were young like we were, you never really thought anything bad could happen to you. It always happened to somebody else.

Well, Joe and I were that "somebody else."

Specialist Garrett McTear visited Joe; he was wounded that same day in Mosul, "under the bridge," as they put it. Joe Edwards also showed up; he had likewise been under the bridge. Captain Chad Fleming was at Walter Reed, in another room undergoing the same kind of intensive care as Joe, only it was Chad's left leg compared to Joe's right side. They would soon become hospital roommates and closer friends than before; they had a lot in common.

Oddly enough, because of the hospital, my sister and I became closer than ever. We had never really known each other before, what with Mom's divorce and Melissa getting married while I was still just a child. I talked to her and Mom every day on the telephone and e-mailed them constant details of Joe's condition. I think I did it for my benefit rather than theirs. It helped me sort out in my own mind what was happening as I attempted to put it all in perspective. Mom received from me such enlightening and informative missives as:

> Joe goes back in the OR in the morning. Another washout and his arm will get some work. He will get his arm washed out and a vac will be put on it. Tuesday's surgery will consist of a skin graft and the army should be finished for the time being.
>
> If there are going to be repairs to the foot, it will be done at the end of next week. Unfortunately, he got an infection in his hip today. The anesthesiologist had to remove one of his epidurals because the site became inflamed and swollen today. The epidural that was removed numbed his hip and inside of his leg. The scary thing is that his BIG epidural to the outside of that leg is located on the top of his butt cheek. If the infection spreads . . . BIG BIG BIG trouble!
>
> He stood up again today for six minutes.

This hospital was very, very old. I learned a lot about its history while I was there. I discovered that the plot of land at the confluence of the Anacostia River and the Potomac River that the Walter Reed Army Medical Center now occupied was originally set aside by George Washington. Called first the "Washington Arsenal" and later "Washington Barracks," and dating back to 1791, it was the third-oldest U.S. Army installation in continuous use in the nation, following West Point and Carlisle Barracks.

The larger area was renamed Fort Lesley J. McNair after Lieutenant General McNair, who was killed at Normandy in 1944 by "friendly fire." In 1909 the hospital became Walter Reed General Hospital, the army's flagship medical center.

The hospital was named after Major Walter Reed, an army physician who led the team that discovered yellow fever was transmitted by mosquitoes rather than direct contact. He died here of emergency surgery for appendicitis in 1902.

Congressional legislation authorized construction of Walter Reed General Hospital, now known as "Building 1," in time for the first ten patients to be admitted on May 1, 1909. The decades since then saw its continuous growth until what began as a hospital with a bed capacity of 80 patients became Walter Reed Army Medical Center with about 5,500 rooms covering a floor space of twenty-eight acres that serve more than 150,000 active and retired service personnel from all branches of the military. Medical services for wounded soldiers had been provided at the post almost continuously from the War of 1812 through the American Civil War, the Indian Wars, the Spanish-American War, World War I, World War II, Korea, Vietnam, Panama, Grenada, Desert Storm—and now another generation of warriors was coming in without arms and legs and faces and . . .

Old places were haunted by ghosts, stories, legends, and rumors. No one really talked about it, not openly, but there were whispers among the staff and patients and their family members. As time went on, I overheard talk about mice and rats in the morgue, rat pellets in the ORs, mold and rot due to physical deterioration of the facilities, bureaucratic nightmares, and patient neglect. All this would eventually explode into a big scandal that warranted congressional committee hearings and government investigations. A hospital commander was fired, and the secretary of the army was forced to resign.

In 2005 and 2006, however, there were only rumors, whispers, and complaints like the one I e-mailed to Ian Hunter's wife, Abby:

Life here is non-stop. Every time I think I have a few free minutes, Joe's pain kicks back up and I spend hours putting cold rags on his head and telling him to "breathe deep." He's really tired of hearing that, but that's what the docs told me to say.

Today has been bad because Joe accidentally pulled out one of his nerve blocks at 4:00 A.M. this morning. It took five-and-a-half hours for an anesthesiologist to get up here, and he told us that there isn't a single qualified doctor on staff today to replace the block. NICE! If his pain doesn't subside by this evening, a doctor is coming in to do the surgery. It blows that Joe has to wait twelve hours before anyone will make their way up here.

The good thing was, I never saw any rats.

45

I hadn't wanted Kim to see me the way I was, especially at the beginning when it was bad and I was out of my head with pain. This wreckage wasn't the man she married.

"I don't think she's ready yet," I pleaded. "Tell her to go home. Please?"

You couldn't have kept Kim away with an Abrams tank. I opened my eyes for a lucid moment now and then and there she was. Every time. Even in the middle of the night when pain yanked me screaming out of troubled sleep. Always there to push the button for me, looking tired and sleepy but still awake and beautiful, vigilant. You needn't worry about that girl going to sleep on watch. I had never felt love so deeply and completely for any other human being.

Gradually, I began to get better but not necessarily to heal. Physicians attempted to discuss options with me. *Their* options weren't *my* options.

"Probabilities that you will ever walk again are slim," they told me in that easy bedside manner of theirs, like they might be weighing which of two restaurants to dine at that evening. It wasn't *their* leg they were talking about or they might have had a different tone.

"Your arm has massive nerve damage," they said with that same demeanor. "We can try to repair it, but we don't know how successfully."

I refused to listen. In my imagination I saw myself as Captain Ahab with his wooden peg leg or Captain Hook out of *Peter Pan*. For a while, it didn't seem like an *or* between Captain Ahab and Captain Hook. It seemed like an *and*. Captain Ahab *and* Captain Hook together in one.

"Prosthetics have come a long way since then," I was assured. "They function almost as well as the original."

"Almost? Will I be able to stay in the Rangers as a double amputee?"

That was the question that always turned things quiet.

One morning, nurses pushed Captain Chad Fleming into my room. He looked pale and even more lanky than before in blue hospital attire. His left arm seemed all but healed, but his left leg was cast and bandaged and sticking out at angles from his wheelchair. He grinned ruefully, noticing my *right* leg under the same constraints.

"One of us has spare parts for the other," he noted. "Got an extra bunk for your old commander?"

Chad moved in with me. Kim and Chad's wife, Kristin, got along great; in each other they had someone to pal around with. Chad improved rapidly, as he hadn't been injured as badly as I. Kristin pushed him all over the hospital grounds in his wheelchair. I wasn't much of a roommate. What with medications and my constant pain, I was incoherent much of the time. Even on good days, the farthest I could get from my room was the hallway in a cardiac chair to which I was attached by IVs and epidural poles. It rained much of the time, a cold, drizzling autumn rain that wept against the hospital windows, my only view of the outside world.

"Kim, it's been hard on you . . ."

I wasn't much with words. Unlike Kim, who was a college girl, I had only completed high school before enlisting in the army. Displays of emotion proved especially difficult for me. Taciturn, I think it's called. The old New Englanders were like that. Flinty, self-sufficient, direct-action types of few words and with their emotions in check. Kim knew it was part of my nature. What I couldn't bull out of my way, I ignored. I blocked my mind from considering anything contrary to what I wanted;

I concealed unwanted intrusions beneath forced nonchalance and expected them to go away. I remembered Dad talking about how stubborn I could be when I wanted something badly enough. "Hardheaded" was the term he used.

"Kim, as soon as I can walk again, we'll be on our way back to Fort Benning and Ranger Battalion," I promised. "We'll have our lives back."

Kim got this stricken look on her face. "Joe . . . ?"

I knew the doctors had been talking to her, trying to prepare her.

"Kim . . . ?"

"We have to discuss it."

"There's nothing to discuss."

"Are you sure you don't want to talk about our options?" she persisted.

"I don't need Oprah or Dr. Phil," I responded sarcastically.

Everything was going to be all right, I kept telling myself. Back the way it had been before the bridge.

Chad and I went to the post exchange to shop for new civilian shoes. We bought one pair and shared. We both wore size ten.

"This'll work out," Chad joked. "I'll take the right shoe and you take the left. It's cheaper, too. We each only pay for half a pair."

We looked at each other. Was this what it had come down to? That it took two of us together to make a whole man? I laughed with Chad to cover the little grain of uncertainty sprouting in my chest.

"Maybe we'd better buy two pairs," I suggested. "We'll need them when we get well."

Kim watched us from across the room, the expression on her face saying she knew something I didn't. She was still listening to the doctors.

Rarely had Chad and I talked about what occurred underneath the bridge that day in Mosul. The ambush had gone down so suddenly, with the grenade dropping through the Stryker's open hatch, that each of us recalled only snatches of what happened. Mostly what we remembered was flash and smoke, pain, and the after-fog of sedatives. Our injuries were reminders enough. The two of us would be forever linked because of them and because of that day underneath the bridge.

One day, Kim and Kristin went to freshen up or something and left Chad and me in our room, a couple of war invalids who couldn't walk or run or shoot or fight or . . . So far, Chad's leg was doing fine and amputation was not an option. In my case, amputation remained a persistent dark shadow lurking in the recesses of my mind.

Suddenly, out of nowhere and very quietly, Chad said, "They want to take off your leg?"

He gazed off in the direction of where the Potomac River converged with the Anacostia. I did likewise. We didn't look at each other.

"Are you going to let them?" he asked.

"Out of the question."

We looked some more together off in the direction of the Potomac. I changed the subject because it was too uncomfortable.

"I'll race you to the park and back as soon as we're on crutches," I challenged.

I could tell Kim thought I was refusing to deal with reality, but I was *not* going to be another amputee selling pencils on sidewalks or whatever old disabled soldiers did. At Walter Reed, counselors and psychologists met regularly with the afflicted to help us deal with our wounds and accept the . . . *reality* of our condition. PTSD—post-traumatic stress disorder—was the buzz phrase bandied about constantly as part of the so-called Battlemind program developed by the Walter Reed Army Institute of Research to aid PTSD sufferers. Refusing to accept *reality* was a symptom of PTSD.

I dreaded every session. I had no need for a shrink. I didn't hate my father; he was dead. I had no problems with transference or Oedipus or suppression or nightmares. I sometimes drifted asleep "on the couch," so to speak. My head didn't need shrinking. What I *needed* was to keep my leg and arm and return to duty. Curious, I conducted a little research on my own into PTSD.

Herodotus, the Greek historian, described the first case of PTSD in 490 B.C. in the startling case of an Athenian soldier who, while sustaining no injury of his own, went permanently blind after he witnessed the death of a friend in battle. In the United States, military medical doctors from the American Civil War up through World War II and Korea began diagnosing combat veterans as suffering from "exhaustion," "battle fatigue," or "shell shock." Soldiers who were expected to be tough and without fear on the battlefield were shutting down mentally as part of their body's natural shock reaction. Some faded away mentally and emotionally, their minds escaping into catatonia while they left their bodies behind. Others became exceptionally violent to themselves and those around them, whether friend or foe, a condition that frequently carried over into civilian life when they returned from war. A number of vets, plagued by nightmares, guilt, and a sense of futility, committed suicide.

PTSD, the modern understanding, entered the public consciousness largely because of the Vietnam War. Awareness of the condition and the willingness of the military to accept it as something other than "cowardice," as General Patton termed it, helped delineate certain symptoms that marked its onslaught. Some of these symptoms included flashbacks or nightmares, unexplained anger, hypervigilance, difficulty falling asleep or staying asleep, hyperactivity, irrational fears—and, sometimes, avoiding reality associated with the trauma.

"What are you going to do when you're released from the hospital?" shrinks asked me.

"It's my intention to return to Ranger Battalion as a squad leader."

The learned shrinks looked at each other and shook their heads. *Tsk tsk*. Reality avoidance, a definite sign of PTSD. I dug in. Rangers were tough. We didn't get PTSD—and if I said I was going back to Ranger Battalion then, by God, that was exactly what I was going to do.

46

I strived to keep doubt buried somewhere in a dark closet of my mind or concealed beneath quiet bluster. I could tell Kim had misgivings about my ever being able to return to full active military duty. *Full* duty, not riding a desk somewhere like a FAG—a Former Action Guy.

I held on to hope, and on to my leg, in spite of almost constant pain. Doctors warned me that the pain might never subside due to irreparable nerve damage. Grin and bear it. That was my motto.

The fingers of my right hand refused to move for the first couple of months. They stuck out the end of my full-arm cast-bandage like pork sausages. They were almost the same color as sausages, too. Doctors likewise warned me about the nerve damage to my arm, cautiously signaling that they might not be able to salvage it either. They were considering removing nerves from my good leg and transplanting them to my arm. They didn't know if that would work or not, but it was worth a try. They had only held off so far in hopes that I might regain some use of my arm without radical surgery.

I developed a staph bladder infection, which meant it was dangerous for my roommate, especially one like Chad who was also weak and in recovery. It was an unhappy day when I had to move out of the double room we shared. It wasn't long after that before he was released from the hospital and sent home to complete his recuperation.

Just when things seemed the bleakest, when I needed a shot of hope more than I needed water or food, a miracle occurred. Kim and I were watching *The Sopranos* or something on TV in my room. She was lounged out as best she could in one of the plain hospital chairs at my bedside when, suddenly, she shot up straight and stared at my hand.

"What?" I asked.

"It moved!"

I didn't know what she was talking about.

"You moved your fingers!"

The urban drama of *Sopranos* had nothing on this unfolding real-life drama.

"Do it again," Kim implored.

I blinked. "I didn't do it. It must have done it by itself."

"All right. Now *you* do it. Concentrate."

We stared at my hand together, daring it to just rest there and do nothing. I started to laugh at how foolish we might have appeared to an observer. So did Kim.

My fingertips twitched. The sausages *moved*. Laughter froze in our throats.

"You did it!" Kim all but shouted.

Overjoyed, we were laughing again. Kim threw herself on my bed and hugged me like I had just won a marathon or discovered the cure to cancer. Little triumphs were the children of victory.

"What do I get when I can *walk*?" I teased.

47

My heart pounded against the floor. The sun rose in a red burst of fire to illuminate a stretch of flat desert backed by low brown hills, a scene that reminded me of the terrain around H-1 Airfield in Iraq. Enemy troopers in mass attack formation charged across the desert directly at me, firing semiautomatic weapons and machine guns, hurling grenades that exploded in bursts of black smoke. Bullets zipped past my head.

Aiming my M-4, I began picking off enemy soldiers, feeling the satisfying recoil of the weapon's butt against my shoulder, dropping bad guys as fast as I could shoot to stop their attack—and run up a good score.

Barry Yancosek paced the boardwalk behind the firing line, giving encouragement, squatting next to a soldier to offer advice or assistance on how to cradle a rifle or change magazines with a plastic prosthetic hand or arm. More than three hundred military service members had lost limbs to the wars in Iraq and Afghanistan, about a third of those in the upper extremities. Of the five of us on the line fighting off the attack, I was the only nonamputee.

Feeling and about 30 percent range of motion had gradually returned to my hand and arm following the dramatic performance I put on for Kim by twitching my fingers. However, since my shooting finger remained out of commission, Yancosek thought it good therapy to requalify on the

Firearms Training System (FATS) located in a small, dark, garagelike room at Walter Reed. Yancosek was the civilian contractor hired by the Walter Reed Telemedicine Directorate to run the program. I was learning to fire weapons with the middle finger of my right hand instead of my so-far useless trigger finger.

While some version of FATS was utilized throughout the military for firearms training, Walter Reed was the only place that targeted war wounded as part of the medical center's occupational therapy and rehabilitation program. The virtual weapons simulator was like a giant computer with a screen about as big as that at a movie theater. The weapons—M-16 and M-4 rifles and 9 mm pistols—were modified into the system's main computer with cables. Computer-triggered CO_2 provided lifelike kick with each shot fired. Theater speakers echoed the sounds of the firefight from both "friendlies" and opposing forces. Electronic impulses replaced bullets. "Bad guys" on the screen reacted to hits and near misses, almost like in real life. Essentially, it was like an elaborate virtual reality video game. The big difference between it and real life was that the enemy didn't return fire with live ammo.

The goal of the shooting therapy program, Yancosek explained to new participants, was to rehabilitate wounded soldiers to their original marksmanship levels.

"If a guy wants to stay in the service and requalify, to prove to his outfit that he's ready to go back to work, that's why I'm here," he said when I met him. "But if you just want to shoot, that's okay, too. Guys are poked and prodded, they're sick and tired and hurting, so if you want to come down for ten minutes or so, come on down. I just want to make you happy." Once guys were mobile enough, Barry would take them out to the Chesapeake Bay to practice shooting on waterfowl.

One of the other guys was a sergeant from Texas who shot a 9 mm pistol with his left hand, because the only thing remaining of his right arm was a 6-inch stub. Another sergeant, an artilleryman with the South Carolina National Guard, lost his left arm in March 2005 near Baghdad

Sgt. Joseph Kapacziewski and Charles W. Sasser

to a roadside bomb. He shot with his right hand while holding the front end of the rifle with a hook on the end of a plastic forearm.

I became quite skillful shooting with my middle finger and won many FATS wars during my time at Walter Reed.

One afternoon during my slow recovery, a man appeared in my hospital room like he belonged there. He introduced himself as Harvey Naranjo, with a long and impressive title: "sports and activities coordinator in Walter Reed's Occupational Therapy Amputee Section."

Amputee? I was *not* an amputee.

That didn't faze Harvey. He was dark-skinned, Hispanic, I assumed, with short black hair, thick through the chest, and warm brown eyes that said "I like you" to almost everyone he met. He pulled up a chair next to my bedside and started chatting like we were old friends. He had a sense of humor that left laugh lines at the corners of his eyes.

"Humor is a good thing," Harvey averred. "Rehab is definitely a mentality thing. It's 90 percent psych"—tapping his forehead with a finger—"and 10 percent rehab, because it has to be up to the mentality and the goal of the patient."

I learned something important about Harvey right away. Everyone else shook their heads and looked distraught when I talked about returning to Ranger Battalion. Not Harvey. He was the first, I think, to really believe in me, to channel my energies, push me.

"Whatever you want to do, we'll do it," he promised. "You want to ride horses, skateboard, snow ski, jump out of perfectly good airplanes?" He shrugged like it was no big deal. "We'll do it."

You're crazy, I thought. "Harvey, I can hardly move."

"You can lie there in bed or sit in that wheelchair and not move," he said bluntly, "or you can stir your lazy butt and we'll get started. You can either do what you want, make lemonade out of lemons, or you can feel sorry for yourself and end up handicapped for the rest of your life. It's your choice."

This man was hardcore. My kind of man. He made good on his word, too. The world suddenly began to make more sense.

I saw the Florida Keys for the first time from the seat of a bicycle. Through the Wounded Warrior Project Soldier Ride, Harvey arranged for me and a few other soldiers with malfunctioning legs to hook up in the Miami–to–Key West bicycle ride, about 120 miles down Highway 1. It was an opportunity for the wounded to get together and see what we were capable of if we put our minds to it.

My bike was actually a tricycle made for handicapped athletes. It had a small wheel up front and a low-rider seat between two large wheels by which you propelled it with your arms. Harvey and Kim helped me cushion my leg in its ex-fix so it wouldn't bounce around. By then, my arm was mending and I no longer had to be worried about losing it. However, the strength was not all there, so I was strapped to the handle.

"It's game on," Harvey said with a grin that said it was time for me to either fish or cut bait.

You could feel the excitement in South Miami as bicyclists gathered for the start of the run, the wounded warriors like myself on trikes, tandems, and every other wheeled configuration. I was among a dozen or so trikers who bunched together in the warm March breezes off the ocean to wait for the start of the ride. Harvey and Kim on their bicycles would make the run with me. Kim was all grins and as talkative with excitement as the wild parakeets of Florida.

The run began with a rush and a cacophony of shouts and the hiss of rubber on pavement. Most of us trike riders ended up left among the rearmost. I was determined not to remain there.

It was RIP all over again, the *feeling* of it, I mean. All the long runs and rucksack marches, the sweat and the competition, the camaraderie and pure masculine macho of it. I loved it.

Kim, Harvey, and I hammered away at our vehicles hour after hour. Down two-lane Highway 1 between the salt marshes and across the bridged cuts from key to key, past the tourist strip malls and seafood restaurants and conch houses . . . I worked up a good honest sweat. My right arm ached after having been out of commission for so long. I grinned. There was no quitting in real life.

Sea wind against my skin kept me cooled. I smelled the salt air, felt the sun on my bare arms and my good leg. God, it was exhilarating!

I began to overtake the leaders around Marathon, with Kim and Harvey encouraging me all the way. Some of the riders were sitting by the side of the road huffing and fanning themselves, drinking Cokes. I waved jauntily and kept going. You wouldn't find Rangers sitting by the side of the road.

I finished the ride among the top 50 percent. Harvey looked pleased, but all he did was shrug and remark casually, "Now, let's see what's our next goal to accomplish."

I would have gone stir-crazy if it hadn't been for Harvey Naranjo, Yancosek, Kim, and a retired army general named Bill Leszczynski, who was a friend of the Flemings and visited wounded Rangers at the hospital every single week. General Leszczynski took Kim and me to his home on a weekend pass, a nice reprieve from the hospital, especially for Kim. Although she never complained, I knew she must likewise be verging on stir-crazy.

In April, six months after the bridge, Naranjo sprang another little surprise. He was always coming up with something new in his role as "sports and activities coordinator." This time, therapy for his group of Walter Reed amputees meant a week's vacation snow skiing in Vail. He didn't call it a vacation, but that was what it was.

"Just because it's therapy doesn't mean you can't enjoy it," he reasoned.

Everyone on the bus except me was an amputee. One of them joked about how it had cost him an arm and a leg for a vacation like this. Harvey cast me a knowing look: He had mentioned nothing all this time about my giving up a leg, for the ski trip or anything else. I knew, however, that he was working on me, preparing me in that good-humored way of his for that eventuality.

Cheryl Jenson, who ran the Vail Veterans Outdoor Program in conjunction with Harvey's therapy activities at Walter Reed, assigned me to a trim ski instructor named Ruth. Ruth took a casual look at my ex-fix with the eighteen pins going through my leg below the knee to keep everything in place.

"How am I going to ski with *that*?" I asked, pointing in disgust at my useless limb.

Ruth padded it down, put me on a bi-ski, tied a line between her waist and mine, and away we went to the top of the . . . bunny slope.

We started out slow. The two of us must have cut quite a sight, what with Ruth leading/pulling me downslope on my odd-looking ski contraption, my padded, caged leg sticking out to one side. By the end of the week, however, I was going to the top of the runs and skiing with Cheryl, Ruth, and Harvey all the way down the mountain.

"See?" Harvey gloated. "Nothing is impossible with attitude."

Kim laughed. "Attitude he has."

I was on my way back. Nothing was going to stop me.

48

The months seemed to run together. I was still having terrific, almost constant pain. There were nights of such severe torment that I couldn't sleep and Kim sat up with me. Army doctors didn't know what to do—except amputate.

I refused to entertain the thought. "I'm not going to be an amputee. They'll bust me out of Ranger Battalion."

At first I had to use a wheelchair at Walter Reed because of my arm being bandaged and in a cast. As soon as the cast came off and I regained use of my right arm, I abandoned the wheelchair in favor of crutches and refused to use the chair anymore. It lurked empty in a corner of the room as though mocking everything I stood for as a Ranger.

Chad had been gone for weeks by this time. I had hated to see him go, but it was probably best that we separated. Being in the same boat, so to speak, we tended to use each other as crutches. I almost dreaded going out into the real world again—and it would be much worse if I had to go out as an amputee. People staring, maybe even pitying me.

"Friends outside may not react to things as well as people here at Walter Reed," Harvey Naranjo cautioned us. "Other people may be a bit more standoffish."

Nurses and counselors thought it a good idea that I meet Army

Specialist Nick Beintema, whose room was down the hall from mine at Walter Reed. Beintema had been with Colonel H. R. McMaster's 3rd Armored Cavalry Regiment trying to keep a lid on Tal Afar in the months preceding Operation Restoring Rights, during that period when two platoons of the 3rd ACR lost one-third of their men KIA or WIA. Beintema was one of those soldiers wounded.

"I have a real bad feeling this time," Beintema had told his parents before deploying for his second combat tour to Iraq.

Beintema, twenty-two, the same age as I, was one of six soldiers aboard a Stryker on a recon when a roadside IED ripped into his vehicle. Four other soldiers were killed in the blast, including the guy sitting next to him and the guy across from him. Beintema suffered shrapnel wounds to his face and chest, a broken jaw, and a concussion, and both legs were shattered. Surgeons tried to salvage his legs, but they ended up amputating his right leg at the knee.

He wheeled himself into my room. A nurse introduced us and stood back out of the line of fire. I nodded cautiously. I understood why he was here—to persuade me that amputating my leg wasn't the end of life. My eyes shifted to the stub of his right leg sticking straight out like some obscene protrusion. I was always running into amputees at the FATS range or through Harvey Naranjo, but for some reason Beintema's leg was the ugliest, most revolting thing I had ever seen. Probably I thought so because I suspected the nature of his mission.

He was a slender, earnest-looking kid from California and, I was told, an avid outdoorsman like me who loved to hunt and fish. We looked each other over for a few minutes. He spoke first, getting immediately to the purpose of our meeting with foul-mouthed bluntness.

"What are you still doing with that fucking thing?" he demanded, indicating my leg. "Why don't you let them cut that piece of shit off so you can get on with business?"

He was one gross, loudmouthed little sonofabitch, I thought, but he did it with a grin from ear to ear that even endeared him to the nurses whose asses he patted at every opportunity.

"What, you think you're the only poor bastard that's ever lost a leg?" he went on as cheerfully as though he might be talking about losing a favorite pair of jeans or something. "You can get a new, better leg and still do everything the same as before."

I glared, angry not so much at him as at the Walter Reed staff for presenting me with what might well be an image of my future self.

"Is that why they brought you here?" I challenged, unable to curb my anger as well as I normally controlled other emotions. "They want you to convince me to let them cut on me so I can become a one-legged man like you?"

That was unfair. I knew it was unfair, but I felt like a fight. Wouldn't that be a sight? Two one-legged soldiers brawling.

"Fuck you." Nick yielded. "I'm trying to help. I thought you needed to know."

"I don't want any part of it."

I turned my head and glowered at the nurse. My heart pounded against my chest wall. "Take him out of here," I rasped. "Get him out. Don't do this to me again."

I turned my back to him, leaning on my crutches. I heard the hiss of his wheels as he left the room, trailed by the crisp clip of the nurse's heels. I was sitting on the side of my bed, still seething, when Kim returned from the snack bar. She sensed something was wrong.

"Joe, what's up?"

"I'm not doing it," I snapped. "Never."

After that, Nick and I kept running into each other around the hospital and, later, during therapy at Brooke Army Medical Center in San Antonio. He would greet me by glaring at my useless right leg and snapping, "You still carrying around that worthless piece of shit?"

He was obscene, forward, and entirely irreverent, but gradually we got to talking and soon enough became best friends. He might joke about cutting off my leg, but he was serious that it should be done.

It was different, however, with Green Beret Chris Self, now a master sergeant and still a member of the 5th Special Forces Group out of Fort Campbell, Kentucky—and he only had one leg. I had heard through the spec ops grapevine that Chris was hit, but I didn't know the details until later in 2006 when Sergeant Major Dan Thompson, the Walter Reed liaison, introduced me to Chris's wife, Dana. Chris and I hadn't seen each other since we were Ranger buddies during Ranger School in 2003, which seemed a lifetime ago, so much had happened since then. Our separate duties had carried us in different directions.

By this time, I had been more or less released from the hospital, which meant I spent time at home with Kim in Georgia while traveling frequently back and forth to Walter Reed for continuing therapy. I happened to be at Reed for therapy at the same time Chris and Dana were there. By this time, I was at least thinking about letting surgeons have my leg. Pain often yanked me awake in the middle of the night. I would lie in bed glaring resentfully into the darkness. It was not going to be an easy decision, although it was beginning to appear my other options might be running out.

"Does your husband like to ride bicycles?" I asked Dana to confirm she really was my old friend's wife.

"How did you know that? He has five or six of them."

"Did he go to Ranger School?"

Dana's face lit up. "You're Kap!" she exclaimed. "Chris talks about you a lot."

On December 28, 2005, about three months after I was wounded under the bridge, Chris and his Special Forces team foiled a sixteen-man Iraqi prisoner escape. He was shot through both legs in the firefight, evacuated to Germany, and subsequently ended up at Walter Reed.

It was old home week for him and me. After the usual manly

embraces, pounding each other on the back, exchanges of "Batt Boy" and "Green Weenie," and catching up on the times and old acquaintances, there was an awkward pause while we surveyed each other's fucked-up right legs. He wouldn't have his amputated until July 2006.

"Damn!" he said.

"Damn!" I agreed.

Chris and Nick Beintema were to become part of my counseling group in the difficult months ahead while I weighed my medical options. Chris's amputation when he had it done was elective. He put it off for over six months.

"It was the pain that finally convinced me," he explained after his amputation. "Part of the time I was hurting so bad I almost lost my mind. The rest of the time I thought I had lost my mind because of all the pain pills."

Chris's story later appeared in an issue of *Professional Soldier,* published by SOCOM.

"When I was in Walter Reed, doctors were optimistic about my nerves healing," he related in the interview, "but over the next seven months my leg never improved. After six Electromyograms (muscle [and] nerve function tests) and three different neurologists, the conclusion was I would never run or be athletic again. The only option that would allow me to continue to do the things I love was to have the leg amputated below the knee."

"There's nothing you can't do on a prosthetic leg," Chris insisted. "You can walk without pain, run, ride a mountain bike . . ."

"Are they letting you stay in Special Forces?" I asked.

That got to the core of it. I thought I had him there. Of the more than three hundred amputees generated by the wars in Afghanistan and Iraq, a number remained on active duty, but none, as far as I knew, had been allowed to stay in special operations units like the Green Berets, Navy SEALs, or Army Rangers as door-kickers.

Six months after Chris's amputation, he exited a C-130 over Fort

Campell, Kentucky, deployed his parachute, and executed a near-perfect PLF (parachute landing fall) with his new bionic leg.

"We have all known soldiers that can contribute to Airborne units that can no longer jump," Chris told the *Professional Soldiers* interviewer. "But jumping is a part of being Special Forces. I have always loved to jump and knew that if I was going to stay in I would have to be able to jump again . . . I have always intended on staying in the army until I no longer enjoyed what I was doing. I had just extended to stay until twenty-five years, and I felt it was my responsibility to try to stick to that commitment. I felt like I can still contribute to the army and Special Forces."

In the article, Chris explained that he had several prosthetic versions—one for everyday use, one for SCUBA diving, one for riding a bicycle, and a running leg that he intended to use in several upcoming marathons.

Less than a year after his amputation, he would deploy downrange into a combat zone with the 5th Special Forces Group as first sergeant for Headquarters Support Company. He would be *supporting* the combat operational detachments.

Okay, I was wrong. There *were* some spec ops amputees who remained in special operations. Only they were in support positions. Certainly no amputee in spec ops, or anywhere else in the military for that matter, had returned to full combat status that I knew of.

"I didn't choose what happened to me, so I would not say that I am tough and all," Chris told his interviewer. "I have simply tried to improve on what I have. I think that is what makes our Special Forces so good; we constantly focus on improvement instead of looking at the negative side of a situation."

I tended to look upon Chris as my mentor; I had been in spec ops about five years to Chris's over twenty years. I admired and respected him tremendously. What he said about amputation made sense, but I wasn't ready for it yet. If prosthetic limbs were as good as everyone kept telling me they were, why shouldn't an amputee be allowed to return to duty as a complete soldier?

49

FORT BENNING 2006

General Doug Brown, commander of SOCOM, a kindly-looking former army aviator, always stopped by Walter Reed to visit spec ops patients whenever he happened to be in D.C. He was heading back to Tampa on the afternoon he came by my room. When he discovered I was being discharged as a permanent patient, the responsibility for my further therapy having been transferred to Martin Army Hospital at Fort Benning, he offered to fly out of his way to return Kim and me to Fort Benning. I hesitated. On a *general's* private airplane! I was only a buck sergeant. Kim, however, thought it an incredibly generous gesture and accepted for us.

All the while I was in the hospital, people were always passing through to visit wounded soldiers—celebrities, military brass, politicians . . . I always felt uncomfortable around them. The visitors I truly wanted to see, old friends I had grown up with in Connecticut, were the ones who made my day. Kelly Franklin, Kevin Martin, Bob Germain, my old wrestling coach, Ryan Forcier—they kept me, well, connected to Connecticut and my roots. Of course, Kim's mom or her sister and brother-in-law were there, along with my grandparents, other Rangers like Jermaine Wilson, who was now a civilian, the Hunter brothers . . .

Platoon Sergeant Jared Van Aalst rarely missed telephoning me at least once a week. Mostly it was a bullshit session, joking around as

Rangers will, catching up on the latest goings-on in the platoon, who was in, who was out, who was being promoted or getting married or divorced or whatever. During the last few weeks, however, our conversation took on a different tone, as if he had something to tell me but wasn't sure how to go about it.

"What's going on, Kap?"

"I'm getting there, Sar'ent."

"We're training up for the next deployment."

"Don't leave without me."

That was when it started getting sticky. He had this thing in his voice.

"Kap, we'll have to talk about it."

"Sar'ent, I'll be there."

"Kap . . . it'll be good to have you back."

He didn't sound like he meant it.

Nonetheless, arriving on a general's plane or not, it was good to be back at Fort Benning with Ranger Battalion where I belonged, away from the daily pain and grind of hospital life. I had been away so long that it almost seemed Walter Reed was my permanent duty station and Naranjo and Yancosek and the others in D.C., my permanent fire team. It had been almost a year ago, in July 2005, that Alpha Company rotated to Mosul. I was wounded in October. Since then, I had spent most of my time at Walter Reed undergoing therapy and over forty surgeries as doctors attempted to save my leg and I continued to hold out for nothing less.

"When you coming back to the platoon, bud?" my buddies asked optimistically, while glancing doubtfully at my leg in its steel-framed support.

"Soon as I get this damned thing removed."

"You were a good Ranger, Kap."

"I *am* a good Ranger," I corrected.

I believed Harvey when he said I could do anything I wanted to do. I believed in myself.

Other combat spec ops soldiers were struggling to overcome the same obstacles I confronted in attempting to get back into the fight. An article in *The Wall Street Journal* detailed the struggle of Army Special Forces Staff Sergeant Andy McCaffrey, who lost his right arm below the elbow to a grenade accident in Afghanistan in 2003. He retaught himself how to shoot, do pull-ups and push-ups, and parachute with his fake limb. He worked himself into the best physical shape of his life.

"A lot of people see this hand when they first meet me and nothing else," he said. "There is a thick line between people who have lost a body part and those who haven't. As an amputee you always have to prove and re-prove yourself."

So far, none of what he accomplished, meeting all Special Forces standards, was enough. His company commanders, one of them said, hoped "that Andy would accept that he does have his limitations. I understand he is looking for answers. But that doesn't change the fact that the limits are there."

In July 2005, McCaffrey received a waiver from his medical board and deployed to Afghanistan with his Special Forces unit. His job: scheduling aircraft in and out of the Special Forces base camp and serving as the battalion retention manager, helping soldiers reenlist. A *support* position.

"They offered me a job I can basically do with no hands," he complained.

Finally, my ex-fix went, replaced by a full-leg hard plaster cast that produced intolerable itching. I used Kim's mom's knitting needles to stick down inside the cast and scratch until blood appeared. Fort Benning's Dr. John Bojescul, a friend of Kim's, replaced the cast for me once a week so my leg could get some relief.

Even I had to admit I wasn't healing as fast as I thought I should. Finally, Sergeant Van Aalst sent word he needed to see me. A formal on-the-books meeting. I had a bad feeling that morning. I sat at the table of our dining room in the country outside Upatoi and stared out the window while the sun rose through the summer greenery of the live oaks and

pines out back. Kim knew not to try to talk to me when such moods over-
came me. She walked up from behind, put her arms around my shoulders,
and kissed me on the cheek.

"Joe, it'll be all right. I married you, I didn't marry a Ranger."

Didn't she understand? Man and Ranger were the same thing.
Ranger was my identity, had been since I was eighteen years old and Officer
Mark Bernier of the Bristol PD drove me to the army recruiter in Spring-
field, Massachusetts.

I sighed deeply, got up from the table, and pulled on a crisp "sand lot"
uniform. The right leg of the trousers had to be split up the seam to ac-
commodate my cast. Kim drove me to the post; I couldn't even drive a
freaking car. I felt like a kid being summoned to the principal's office. I
knocked on Sergeant Van Aalst's door and walked into his cubbyhole office at the Alpha Company 1st Platoon Tactical Operations Center. He
looked up from working on the morning report. The expression on his
face said it all.

"Sit down, Kap."

"I'll stand for it, Sergeant. If you don't mind."

He sighed deeply. He was only doing his job. You didn't have to like
it to do it. I might have done the same thing in his position. At least he
didn't say "I'm sorry" like everyone else seemed to do.

"Kap, you're not going to be able to stay in the company," he announced bluntly.

I felt the ground fall out from underneath my feet.

"I talked to our new first sergeant for you, Kap. I have to agree with
him. There's not room for you in the company anymore. You're holding
up a slot that we have to fill for the next rotation."

Just like with McCaffrey: We had to accept our limitations.

The platoon sergeant glanced at the cast on my leg. He glanced
away. Then he looked at me straight. I refused to allow him to see that
this was the most devastating day of my life, that a grown-ass man was

standing there in front of his desk trying not to break down and bawl like a baby.

"Sar'ent," I said, struggling to keep the quiver out of my voice, "do you recall what you told us about never giving up before we started RIP?"

He blinked.

I turned and hobbled out on my crutches with as much dignity as I could muster.

50

Kimberly:

We brought Joe's wheelchair home with us. It lurked in a corner, and I dusted around it during housecleaning.

I went out to dinner with my friend Melanie the evening of the morning Joe met with Sergeant Van Aalst. He wouldn't talk about what happened. He sat at the table in our house and stared out the window. I fixed his dinner, but he insisted I go out with Melanie instead of eating with him. I knew he wanted to be alone to mull over whatever had transpired that day.

The house was completely dark when I returned. Puzzled, since it was still early, I went in and turned on the lights. Joe was sitting in the dark. I ran to his chair and dropped to my knees.

"Babe?"

He swiped away tears with the back of his hand and turned his head, ashamed that I had caught him crying.

"Are you hurting?"

He sat there as unresponsive as a stone statue in a park, refusing to open up and discuss whatever plagued him. He remained awake most of the night. The silence was more unbearable than his crying. That night marked a low point in his rehabilitation.

The next day, he explained how Sergeant Van Aalst had informed him that he had to leave Alpha Company. To make matters worse, a friend at battalion headquarters gave him a further heads-up, "You're going to be transferred out of 3rd Ranger Battalion." Bitterness crept into Joe's voice and attitude for the first time ever.

"They want you when you can fight," he commented in his harsher tone, "but once you get damaged they're ready to throw you on the trash heap."

We never expected this to happen. Before, everyone kept assuring Joe that there would always be a place for him in the Rangers. Apparently, that wasn't true when push came to shove. Joe's fears had been well founded all along. There was no room in the 3rd Batt for cripples.

After Alpha Company redeployed to Fort Benning from Mosul, Company First Sergeant Eddie Noland, who had rushed to the bridge that day, transferred over to Ranger Operations Company as its first sergeant. Knowing I was about to be booted out of 3rd Batt, perhaps even out of the army on a disability pension, I went to see him about a job. He kept his promise to take care of me and put me to work in his arms room. It wasn't much of a job, but I was still undergoing therapy, and any job was a port in the storm. A temporary port, to be sure, since anything I did was likely to merely delay the inevitable unless some kind of miracle came along.

Through her work with horses, Kim became acquainted with a civilian surgeon in Columbus, Dr. Leland McCluskey, who specialized in ankle replacements and offered at least a ray of hope. Kim showed him my X-rays. I was not a candidate for replacement, he said, but there was some possibility that he could fuse my ankle with plates and screws and restore most of its function. By this time I was desperate. Army doctors had given up on everything except amputation. I was willing to try anything to stay active.

"It's never going to be as good as new," Dr. McCluskey cautioned.

"But I can walk? I can keep my leg?"

"There are no miracle cures, son. We'll do the best we can."

The leg became a little better after Dr. McCluskey bolted me back together, but I was never able to get beyond that strange, slow, uncomfortable gait. The pain remained, day by day slowly draining away what little hope I retained.

51

Kimberly:

Joe danced at our *real* wedding, he *danced*! On his new plated-down, screwed-in ankle courtesy of Dr. McCluskey. No crutches, no wheelchair. I never saw such a grin on Joe's face. So he limped, okay? So he wasn't the most graceful Fred Astaire (I liked old movies, too) on the floor. When it came to dancing, Joe was not Mr. Twinkle Toes anyhow. Fact is, I begged him before the *real* wedding to take a couple of dancing lessons from a local dance school. I didn't think he had ever been to even a high school dance, and if he had I was sure that shy man I married—twice—stood off to himself and watched, like he had that night we met at Coach's Corner. A girl had to look behind the wallflower to see the truly remarkable man Joe Kap was.

It wasn't a true wedding, as Joe and I had already had our paperwork from the courthouse. We held the ceremony at Oakhurst, an elegant-looking events center on groomed grounds next to a lake at West Point, Georgia. We couldn't have chosen a better site for Yankee Joe to get hitched to Southern Belle Kim than in a genuine southern mansion—well, a replica thereof. It was held outdoors in the summer sunshine with the reception afterward inside the hall.

"It's so country I hope I don't step in a cow patty," Ben Hunter joked.

Joe and his brother, Randy, his best man, stood up front while my Uncle

Sherrod walked me down "the aisle." You didn't realize anything was wrong with Joe's leg at all so long as he didn't move around. He looked handsome in an ivory suit, one of the few times I had seen him dressed up other than when he wore army dress greens. Tears of joy flooded my eyes as I acknowledged my mother and Melissa, who served as matron of honor, along with dear friends in the assembly—my best friend, Melanie, of course, and Suzanna Lampton from Midland Farms, both of whom had gone through my and Joe's unusual courtship with me, as well as the ordeal of his being wounded in battle only weeks later; Sue Beth Bunn; Rachael Peek and her children, Guy, Jack, and Lillie, whom I had babysat for many years. The ceremony was full of my people as well as soldier friends of Joe's from Ranger Battalion and his family friends from Connecticut, like Ryan Forcier and Kevin Martin. Joe's mother, Lori Briglia, and his grandparents were there. I was afraid Grandma Churchill still might not have forgiven me for "sneaking off" with Joe to get married at the courthouse a year ago.

We didn't have a preacher, since technically we were already married. Instead, Melissa's husband, Jim, my brother-in-law, performed the ceremony.

Joe was such a trouper, and he was ready for the traditional first dance after the exchange of nuptials. He proved a bit awkward on his ankle. While he didn't exactly sweep me onto the dance floor, what he lacked in finesse he made up for in enthusiasm. It was a grand day.

As the reception wore on, however, I noticed he seemed to be in a great deal of pain. He began sitting as much as possible. Sweat appeared on his forehead. By the time we went home, he couldn't walk from the car to the door. Surely the neighbors must have thought the groom had imbibed too much wedding punch as they peeped out their windows to watch the bride half carry, half drag him over the threshold. He literally *crawled* across the kitchen floor to the bedroom; he had stood on his ankle for so long that it had locked up in pain.

Joe went straight to bed. I sat on the kitchen floor with Joe's mother to open our wedding gifts and relive the day.

• • •

Joe's leg appeared to improve some over the next weeks. He continued to work in the arms room on post, but I noticed by his deepening melancholia that his hopes of returning to Battalion were diminishing. His latest surgery turned out not to be the miracle he counted on. He remained in constant pain, his gait slow and shambling, no matter that he tried to conceal it from me and everyone at Fort Benning. The turning point came one day near the end of September when Midland Farms hosted its annual point-to-point race.

One of the events was a lead-line race in which children rode ponies in a slow heat for about 50 meters across the grass. Two adults assisted each tiny jockey, one leading the pony while the other made sure the little jockey stayed in the saddle and didn't get hurt. Joe insisted on partnering with me, although I was apprehensive about his running on his bad leg.

"Hey, babe, we have to take it for a test run sometime," he argued.

Our pony was a sweet little shaggy black named Bella. Henry, our jockey in the saddle, was about three years old and could barely contain his excitement. He bounced up and down and flapped his chubby arms while Joe and I laughed and Joe steadied him in the saddle. I took a short lead on the pony's halter and moved us up to the starting line.

About a dozen ponies and their riders and grooms exploded—in slow motion—from the starting line when the whistle blew. Most of the ponies refused to go faster than a walk, while the others managed a bone-jarring trot. Apparently, the ponies were refusing to concede they were even in a race.

"And they're off!" Joe called out in a stentorian voice through his laughter.

We were having a great time. Joe was good with kids.

Our team pulled out ahead to lead the field. Little Henry was still babbling and bouncing in excitement while I dragged the pony and Joe trotted alongside the miniature animal to hold Henry in place. The finish line lay just ahead; we were winning this thing. I saw Henry's parents jumping around to cheer us on.

Suddenly, from behind, I heard what sounded like a dead tree limb breaking. Alarmed, I whipped around in time to see Joe stumble. He held on to the little boy, however, long enough to cross the finish line.

Both screws in Joe's ankle had snapped. The pain must have been excruciating, although Joe tried to ignore it. He walked around for the rest of the day, but at a much slower pace, with a more pronounced limp, and in obvious agony. I saw by the look of horror on his face that he thought he had taken his last shot at keeping his leg. We had tried everything to save it. What else was left?

52

By now, early spring of the year 2007 was rapidly approaching and I had been out of action since October 2005. Snapping the pins in my ankle was, I suppose, the point of no return. I had no intention of riding a desk or working in the arms room for the rest of my military career. I seriously began to consider amputation; it was obvious to everyone—*had* been obvious to everyone except me for quite some time—that I was not returning to Ranger Battalion with a leg as fucked up as mine. Beintema and I talked about it again; I cornered Chris Self and Chad Fleming, consulted Harry Naranjo and Barry Yancosek . . . The idea slowly took root.

I discovered I wouldn't be the first warrior in history to lose a limb. Biomechatronics, the science of replacing body parts with artificial limbs, had been around for centuries. Other soldiers had lost arms or legs and returned to battle.

Egyptians were among the first pioneers in the science; archaeologists recovered a mummy's body from the era of the New Kingdom who had been fitted with a wooden toe. Herodotus the historian passed down the story of a Persian soldier named Hegistratus who sawed off his own foot to escape the chains of his captors and later replaced it with one carved from wood. Pliny the Elder told of how a Roman general replaced an arm lost in combat with one made of iron designed to grasp a shield when he returned to battle. Knights during the Age of Chivalry were fitted with similar prosthetics that allowed them to carry their shields.

The Renaissance produced prosthetics constructed of copper, iron, and steel as well as of wood. The first functional ones that served more than as mere cosmetics or as props or braces began appearing early in the 1500s when German mercenary Götz von Berlichingen developed a formidable iron hand that moved by using springs and releases, allowing him to grasp a sword, dagger, or shield in order to pursue his trade in warfare.

Wooden "peg legs" and "hand hooks" were almost as old as recorded history. It took World War II with its surplus of maimed warriors to launch a rich era in the development of practical artificial limbs. Captain Ahab's wooden leg was on its way out, replaced by modern revolutionary devices like the "Sabolich Socket" and the C-Leg prosthesis that used lithium-ion batteries to make knee joints work for above-the-knee amputations.

Lester Sabolich of Oklahoma City helped pioneer the field of biomechatronics back when replacement limbs were still made of wood and aluminum. His son John invented the Contoured Adducted Trochanteric-Controlled Alignment Method (CAT-CAM) socket, whose later evolution, the Sabolich Socket, lashed into place on a stub to distribute the weight evenly over the existing limb. That was one of the first huge improvements toward the modern artificial leg that attached to a stump by vacuum and padded cuff to permit near-full functioning of the surrogate limb. John's son Scott still built legs in Oklahoma City in a practice so respected that it was known as the "Mayo Clinic" or the "Silicon Valley" of prosthetics.

The modern mechanical leg was a miracle of modern science. Prosthetics for athletes, which I would require, possessed a number of features whose elements I pondered over and over as the pain in my leg and foot persisted and doctors repeatedly told me that bone fusing was simply not going to work. No one prosthetic by itself would serve my purposes. As an amputee known as a transtibial or BK (below the knee), I would need several spare legs—one for ordinary walking, one for running or use in irregular terrain, and others for such activities as swimming or riding bicycles.

The newest model of "energy-storing prosthetic foot" allowed the user, as Chris Self asserted, to do anything an ordinary two-legged man could do. Its heel compressed during initial ground contact and then released to spring the body forward. The leg was energy absorbing to minimize the effect of high impact on the musculoskeletal system and was ground compliant to provide stability on all types of terrain. The leg and foot even rotated like a real limb.

Double amputee Oscar Pistorius and his new energy-storing feet and legs were already creating controversy as he vied for a spot on next year's 2008 Summer Olympics. He would be briefly ruled ineligible for competition due to his alleged mechanical advantage over runners with real flesh, blood, and bone ankles.

"They're as good as new," Chris Self said but added ruefully, "Well, almost . . ."

Captain Chad Fleming and I sometimes met at Walter Reed where we both underwent therapy. At this point, he was not considering amputation of his own leg, but he supported my decision if that was what I chose to do.

He would eventually give in to amputating his leg as an elective procedure since his limb would never return to full function, but he held out a lot longer than I did.

As for my leg, it was becoming increasingly clear that I had to do something radical if I intended to stay in Ranger Battalion.

53

Kimberly:

Ranger Mike Hack and his wife, Alicia, lived on the other side of our road from Joe and me. Soldiers and their wives generally socialized with other soldiers and their wives. One night the four of us went out to dinner and stopped off at Coach's Corner on the way home to have a beer and see who was hanging around the soldiers' bar. I wasn't much for drinking, but everyone seemed to be having a good time chatting and laughing. Then somebody played "God Bless the USA" on the box.

Joe got that look and I saw tears in his eyes. A hush fell over the table. It was an awkward moment, even though Mike and Alicia understood the struggle Joe was going through.

I jumped up. "I think it's time to go home," I exclaimed.

I witnessed more tears from Joe that first year or so than I would ever see again. It was disconcerting, no matter that I understood the emotional ride he was on. To him, it must have seemed a whole part of his life was being stolen. I actually thought I hated the army sometimes for what it was doing to him.

I led him outside, and we sat on the curb by the car. Darkness settled around us. The air felt cool with approaching autumn.

"Kim, you don't have to stay with me," he offered after a long pause during which we sat holding hands and looking off toward Fort Benning.

"People won't see me if I lose my leg. What they'll see is an amputee, a one-legged man, and they'll feel sorry for me. And for you. You deserve better."

"I have the best," I reassured him. "Joe, we're a team. I can show you the paperwork. Right there in black and white it says, 'For better or worse, in sickness and in health, till death do us part . . .'"

"It doesn't say anything about one-legged."

"We won't be one-legged. We'll be three-legged."

That got a little chuckle from him.

"Joe Kap, I never want to hear that kind of talk again, do you understand? Or I'm going to chew off your other leg."

We were silent. Some Rangers and their wives or girlfriends came by from the parking lot. Joe put on that macho front of his. The Rangers bumped fists with him.

"Hey, Kap, when you getting off your sorry ass and coming back to work?"

When they went on inside, Joe lifted his head and looked at the full moon.

"Kim, I don't know if I'm ready for this," he admitted, "but I know now it has to be. There's a job needs doing overseas and I have to do it."

The next day he flew to Portsmouth Naval Hospital to pre-op for amputation of his right leg. He chose the navy hospital because of his research into two of the leading proponents in the United States of the Ertl method of amputation surgery. According to Raymond Francis, the prothesist who would handle Joe's case, Dr. Daniel Unger, who performed the procedure at Portsmouth, was one of the leading surgeons in the field.

From what Joe and I learned in our research, the Ertl method had been developed by Janos von Ertl in Hungary for treating World War I casualties and others involved in reconstructive plastic surgery. His sons and grandsons had carried on the tradition in a method of surgery that had proven to enable amputees to have more function and a higher quality of life than traditional surgical methods. Neither Joe nor I fully understood the technical aspects of it, but if Joe was going to have it done he should have it done by the best. His goal was still to return to full combat Ranger duty, whether with one leg or both.

54

Kimberly:

Some Navy SEALs at Portsmouth Naval Hospital became buddies with Joe while he underwent pre-op and waited for surgery. Two or three at a time were always dropping in on us to bring coffee and books or to just hang out and "scuttlebutt," as they called it. Joe and the army called it "bullshitting." SEALs were of the same caliber as Rangers; they had that same supermacho self-confidence and presence that seemed to be standard issue among special operations forces. Also, like Joe, like all the other Rangers I knew, they were always full of hijinks and practical jokes. I never met a spec ops guy who took himself too seriously. His job, now, he was serious about that, but not about himself. I sometimes suspected they used buffoonery as a way to protect their inner cores, to cover up emotion and vulnerability. Of course, that was just a woman's point of view.

I should have guessed the SEALs wouldn't let a little thing like Joe's losing a leg pass with any solemnity.

On the day of Joe's surgery, Joe's brother, Randy, several of the SEALs, and I held down the waiting room outside the OR. The OR people came for Joe before the sun rose. Joe and I, we were both ready for it. We had this kind of "let's do this and get it over with" attitude by now. Joe and the SEALs were laughing and cutting up about it.

"Wonder if they'll give me my big toe to keep in a pickle jar?" Joe cracked.

I was told it would be hours before I could see him again. I should have become accustomed to waiting outside ORs by now, considering all the surgeries Joe had undergone, but this time seemed different. This time *was* different.

Rather than sit for hours waiting anxiously, Randy and I went out with Ranger Regimental Chaplain Paul Lasley for chicken wings. It helped keep my mind busy while we waited, since there was nothing else we could do anyhow.

I dreaded what it might do to Joe when he came out of anesthesia and looked down to discover the reality of at long last having actually lost a part of himself. He probably wouldn't say much. I understood that, I understood him. He wouldn't let his feelings show. What I worried about was what would happen deep down inside when he realized that, having given up his leg, he might also have to give up his expectations of returning to the Rangers on full duty.

How often had I heard him say something like "Being part of the regiment means everything to me. I can't imagine doing any other job. It's the guys you work with. I wake up every morning and go to work with six hundred of my best friends."

I had talked to my mom and my sister about it. "It's so tough, because this is all he wants. He's stubborn, God knows he's stubborn—but I think we've done our time, done more than our fair share. I don't want to ever get another one of those phone calls."

I never heard "Take My Breath Away" without thinking of that terrible day I received the phone call notifying me that my husband had been critically wounded in Iraq.

The reality of it finally struck me when OR people wheeled Joe into recovery. I felt blood rush from my head and I had to sit down when I realized his leg had actually been cut off. To lighten up the event, the OR people had rigged underneath the sheets a giant clown's foot to replace Joe's missing foot. When Joe opened his eyes, Randy and those rough warriors from the Navy SEALs were standing around his bedside sniggering to themselves in anticipation of his reaction.

Joe glanced down after a few moments. He gravely inspected the monstrosity of a foot and, without the slightest change of expression, drawled, "Damn!"

That was Joe—cutting up and laughing on the outside while no one but me understood what might actually be happening on the inside.

55

The amputation wasn't as traumatic as I feared. In fact, it was almost a relief, what with living with indecision and the constant pain all these months. It wasn't over yet, though, not the pain. Infection followed infection. I was in and out of hospitals for the first few months, enduring not only the brutal torment from the amputation but also the agony of phantom pain. I had been warned, but until I experienced it I would not have believed it possible for a leg that wasn't there anymore to hurt so fiercely. At times, I could have sworn some hajji from hell was poking the sole of my nonexistent foot with an ice pick. I automatically reached to massage or rub or scratch my foot and was always surprised to find it missing.

Since I possessed some kind of natural immunity to pain meds—doctors had to knock me nearly unconscious to obtain results—I mostly endured as stoically as I could in order to spare Kim. She was a good scout about it, patient and loving as she pushed me around once again in my wheelchair until I could get fitted for a prosthesis. She watched helplessly as I mastered crutches all over again with one leg missing.

It was one ugly thing, that stump. I recalled my reaction to Beintema when he appeared with his stub of a leg—and now I had one almost identical to his.

The regimental surgeon at Fort Benning, Colonel Russ Kotwal, set me up for amputation rehab therapy at the Center for the Intrepid at Fort Sam Houston, Texas, one of the Brooke facilities. The chief physical therapist, Major Campbell, was an old Special Forces soldier. He listened patiently while I explained that my goal was to return to Ranger Battalion as a squad leader and eventually a platoon sergeant. My objective had not changed from day one underneath the bridge. Losing the leg had changed nothing.

Major Campbell nodded. "Staff Sergeant Kap," he promised, "we'll get you back where you want to go. I'm assigning you the meanest son of a bitch we have on the staff as your therapist."

In walked Justin Laferrier, a former marine who had left the Corps following Desert Storm, the first war in the Gulf, to become a civilian physical therapist working with military amputees. We looked each other over. By appearance alone, Laferrier was enough to make men quake in their boots. Stacked on a mere 5'6" frame stood over 200 pounds of pure muscle, to the top end of which was fixed bright red hair in a crew cut supplemented by an equally bright mustache and goatee. He stuck out a hand the size of a ham with fingers like thick sausages. Another sausage served as his nose.

"Huh!" he snorted. "So you only got one leg." Not cutting any slack and not the least embarrassed by his unsympathetic approach. "Are you going to whimper about it or are we going to get to work?"

I felt like I was on my way back the day I received my new mechanical leg and had it fitted. The prosthestist, Joseph Sedowski, advised me to use a universal one, the Pathfinder II, that allowed me to run, skip, and jump out of airplanes. Just getting out of bed in the morning and into that Frankenstein of metal, wire, plastic, and rubber proved an elaborate process. First, a thick neoprene liner covered the residual limb; it was hot and sweaty and prone to cause abrasions and sores if left on too long. The artificial leg followed, cuffed by vacuum to the stump. A long elastic sleeve from the top end of the artificial leg extended past my knee and up the thigh. Fortunately for my ambitions, my knee was natural and in good shape.

Walking on the leg proved to be its own awkward process. It was like trying to balance half my weight on a stilt. At first, since I couldn't feel the ground with my foot, I had to concentrate to take one tottering step at a time. Kim watched me stumbling about like an eighty-year-old man with an inner-ear issue, but she was smiling because I was finally walking again.

"Hey, girl. It just takes some getting used to. I'll be chasing you around the bedroom in no time—and catching you."

That made her giggle.

Justin Laferrier was loud and obnoxious and aggressive. We got along fine. For six months he crushed me on a daily basis, made me do things I thought I couldn't do. He poked fun at me, beat me up with exercises, smoked my ass—and made me love it. I owed him and guys like Harvey Naranjo and Barry Yancosek a lot. They believed in me almost as much as I believed in myself.

I healed fast, but I kept pushing. I walked short distances, then expanded my range. Finally, I was jogging all over Fort Sam Houston. I ignored pitying looks from soldiers attending troop medic or Special Forces medic specialist training. I could almost hear them saying to each other, "Poor guy lost his leg in Iraq."

Don't poor-guy me. I'll be smoking your asses in no time.

First Sergeant Eddie Noland came frequently to Brooke to check on me; he and I did my first rucksack march together.

Sometimes I pushed so hard that the incision on my stump split open. Or I busted out of the socket and lost my leg, sprawling on the ground like a bug whose legs some dirty-faced kid had pinched off. I glared away any soldiers who thought to rush over to help.

"I'm not a cripple."

Less than five months after surgery, I was running again. *Running,* not jogging. In October 2007, the Center for the Intrepid discharged me. I returned to Fort Benning, where First Sergeant Eddie Noland assigned me as cadre to help out with holdovers awaiting the next RIP training cycle. About six years ago—had it been so long ago?—I was on the other end of the Ranger Indoctrination Program as a candidate instead of as cadre.

"What are you going to do now?" Laferrier had asked me as we shook hands on the day I was discharged.

"Go back to Ranger Battalion as a squad leader."

He nodded thoughtfully. "Make me proud," he said, "or I'll come down and whip your butt again."

It should have been obvious to everyone that RIP wasn't enough for me, no more than First Sergeant Noland's arms room was enough. No one at Battalion ever said no to me, at least not to my face. I repeatedly assured everyone from the battalion commander down the chain of command to Platoon Sergeant Jared Van Aalst that I was ready to go back to work. They all seemed to come up with an excuse. No Ranger in my condition had ever qualified to return to direct combat operations.

"What if your Stryker was hit again? Could you scramble out of a burning vehicle as fast as a soldier with two good legs? Could you pull a fellow soldier to safety?"

" Staff Sergeant Kap, a leader's job is to mitigate risks in battle. With your prosthesis, you could be increasing risks for other soldiers."

"What if you lost your leg on a mission?"

"What ifs" drove me crazy.

"If someone gets shot in the leg," I reasoned, "he has to redeploy for medical treatment. I carry a spare leg with me. Look," I pleaded, "just give me a standard and I'll meet it."

Very few enlisted soldiers ever attempted to return to the front lines after losing a limb. Most soldiers simply gave up. I didn't intend to give up.

Word came down from Regimental Command Sergeant Major Doug Pallister that I "had to be able to physically perform to the same standards as other Ranger leaders—no waivers, no special considerations. No matter what position or grade, every Ranger needs to meet the Ranger standard."

That was all I asked for. Sooner or later, the three-man Physical Evaluation Board would have to give me a "med board" to declare whether I was fit or unfit for duty. I made a list of all the soldier tasks I needed to perform in order to return to my job and set about amassing a record that would give the board no choice but to clear me.

Can you jump?

Guys in the Ranger Regiment were training up for the Best Ranger competition. Joe Edwards, Ben Hunter, and some of the old guys were still around. They were parachuting out of UH-60 Black Hawk helicopters. I rigged up a 'chute, joined a stick, and jumped at 1,200 feet. It was my first jump since being wounded. I worried that wind shear might pull off my false leg.

Master Sergeant O'Conner, the drop zone safety NCO, came running over after we landed. I nonchalantly rolled up my 'chute and stuffed it into my bag.

"Piece of cake," I said.

O'Conner asked me if I wanted to do it again. I made a second jump.

"Okay," the chain of command challenged, "what about a combat night jump with equipment?"

"No sweat." It wasn't, either.

I constantly trained. Hunter said I was like Sylvester Stallone in *Rocky*. All I needed was the museum steps in Philadelphia to complete the picture. I rucksack marched for miles. I ran so much that I became a familiar figure everywhere on post, hammering along on my one strong leg and my carbon fiber one. Guys paused when I pounded by to thrust fists in the air and shout encouragement.

"Go, Sergeant Kap!"

I completed the Basic Noncommissioned Officers Course. I requalified in every physical requirement from RIP—and made sure each was duly noted for my medical evaluation board. Within ten months from amputation, I completed the full Army PT test, including a 5-mile run in under forty minutes and a 12-mile road march in less than three hours carrying a 40-pound ruck. Humping a load like that on my back threw off my balance, but I did it.

I learned the hard way that I couldn't slow my descent with only one good foot while fast-roping down a 50-foot line carrying 60 pounds of equipment. I hit the ground hard, like a sack of shit, and my gloves were smoking as though they were about to burst into flames. From then on I wore two pairs of gloves so I could grip the rope tighter and control my descent.

It became obvious to anyone paying attention that I was not going to go away. Each week, I strode up to Ranger Special Troops Sergeant Major Chris Hardy—*strode,* not *limped*—and stood crisp in uniform and beret before him to ask him what else I had to do.

"I've done all you've asked of me, Sergeant Major. I've passed everything RIP candidates do to get into regiment."

Sergeant Major Hardy came over to my side. So did Sergeant Van Aalst before he transferred out of Company back to the sniper platoon. Master Sergeant Billy Pouliot became Alpha Company's first sergeant. First Sergeant Pouliot agreed to take me back as a squad leader. For about four hours that morning, I thought I was back in, that everything was finally falling into place. I was packing my gear at the RIP platoon headquarters the next day when the chain of command got together and reneged.

"Staff Sergeant Kap, we can't just throw you back out there as an amputee," I was told. "We want you to do a full-training cycle. We'll consider your request when we get back from rotation."

56

Alpha Company departed for Iraq and left me behind as cadre to smoke RIP holdovers. I was furious. That was the closest I ever came to telling myself it wasn't worth it. I knew what the chain of command was trying to do—pile so much shit on me that I would get discouraged, quit, and save everyone from having to make a decision about me. I could tell Kim thought I was at the end of my patience and endurance. She may even have been a bit relieved that it was almost over.

I moped around for about two days feeling sorry for myself. Then I pulled myself up by my phony leg and got back to work. I was still a Ranger. Rangers led the way. Rangers never gave up.

A new batch of would-be Rangers reported in from Airborne School, all of them feeling like they were the toughest bastards this side of hell. I stalked out onto the PT grinder in the chill predawn of that winter of my discontent, garbed out in a black PT uniform down to my running shoes. As cadre, my job was to both motivate the candidates and disabuse them of the notion that they were badder than bad.

Looking at them, growling at them to make sure they knew who was in charge, I couldn't help seeing the green kids Ben Hunter, Roundy, Lockhart, I, and all the others must have been on a day like this six years ago when the cadre smoked us at PT, running our sorry asses into the

Georgia dirt. Some of the guys I knew then had since been killed in the Global War on Terrorism, while others returned to civilian life or transferred over to other outfits.

To the RIP holdovers that first morning I was just another hard-ass cadre as I broke their ranks into PT formation and led them through the obligatory warm-up squats, bend-and-reaches, thrusts, and, of course, push-ups. Next came the part I anticipated.

"Two minutes to stretch out on your own before we do a little running," I announced.

While forty or so men gyrated and reached and stretched, I sauntered to the front of the formation in full view of everyone and began removing my outer garments in preparation for the run. Off came the PT sweatshirt down to black T-shirt. No one paid any attention.

Next my sweatsuit bottoms down to shorts. I heard eyeballs begin to pop. The entire platoon seemed to let out a collective gasp when they saw the rest of me for the first time. Everyone froze in place for a long moment, staring.

"He's only got one leg!"

I had long since passed through the stage of being self-conscious about it. I displayed it defiantly, like a combat medal. I was still out to prove to the battalion, to the medical board, to other Rangers, and to myself that, one-legged or not, I was as good and as tough as any other Ranger.

There was always a wiseass in every group. I overheard, "He's going to smoke us on *that*?"

I simply looked them over as I took off the prosthesis, cast it aside, and replaced it with my running leg, making sure everyone had a good look. Then I put the hurt on them. Ran their sorry asses into the Georgia dirt. Smoked them. I jogged *backward*. I ran circles around the formation while I humiliated and exhorted the holdovers to greater effort.

"Pick it up, girls, pick up the pace . . . You're slow, you're lazy, your breath stinks, and you don't love Jesus . . . You're never going to make it, ladies."

I was temporarily mad at the world, trying to prove I was good enough to go back to my platoon, prove I could still do it. I picked out the wisesass who foolishly observed what he considered to be my shortcoming. He was sweating and huffing like a freight engine.

"Whassa matter, soldier?" I taunted. "You can't keep up with a one-legged man?"

I sprinted ahead and waited for the formation to catch up, sprinted out again, showing off what I could do on my mechanical leg with its curved foot mechanism.

"He ain't human. The army *built* him. He's the Bionic Man!"

Someone must have been watching old Lee Majors reruns.

The platoon considered it a challenge and a matter of honor to keep up with me. I sometimes saw guys like Hawkins and Davenport out running on their own time. "Sar'ent, we're gonna smoke *your* ass sooner or later," they pledged. I grinned and picked up the pace.

My holdover platoon composed its own running Jody calls. Mornings, we'd pass other PT formations, suck them under with our pace, leaving them behind in a swirl of voices raised in cadence, taunting, mocking, rich in a certain pride that *this* instructor wasn't fully human and, by implication, neither was this platoon.

> *Two old ladies lying in bed.*
> *One looked over to the other and said,*
> *I wanna be an Airborne Ranger,*
> *I wanna live a life of danger . . .*
> *Whatta you say?*
> *One Two Three Four!*
> *Bionic Man, give us some more!*
> *Airborne! Airborne! All the way!*

One morning with still a half mile to go, I looked over and Hawkins and Davenport looked back at me and grinned. I threw down the gauntlet.

"All right, let's see what you got!" I yelled. "Platoon, to the finish line!"

"Let's go, pussies!" Hawkins shouted back over his shoulder to the rest of the formation.

My orderly run turned into a thundering-herd free-for-all with the platoon strung out all along the remaining half mile. Hawkins and I led the pack, with Davenport and several others panting at our heels.

Hawkins was long and lanky, a runner's build, and he was as determined to beat me as I was not to be beaten. My lungs burned from the exertion. Breath whistled through my throat. There was no way I was going to lose this. I would die first. I would pound my mechanical leg into nails and shrapnel and then I'd run on my hands if I had to. I had too much to prove to lose.

Hawkins pulled out ahead by a pace, then two paces. Less than 200 meters away burned the lights around the grinder. Units from the Airborne School and the infantry schools out warming up for their own runs stopped to watch. All activity on the grinder ceased as Hawkins and I led the pack into the wash of light, pounding toward the finish line. We must have cut a strange sight—the tall holdover RIP candidate neck and neck with the cadre on a leg of carbon fiber springs and levers flashing back glints of light.

I put everything I had into that last 100 meters. Although I ran every day to get so physically fit the Rangers couldn't boot me out, this was the first time I had given my leg the supreme test. If it couldn't take this, it couldn't take combat.

My stump went numb from the hammering. Then pain began shooting up through my thigh into my groin and all the way to my brain.

I pulled up even with Hawkins. We flashed across the finish in a dead heat and collapsed side by side on our knees to catch our breath. I was in so much pain that I had to work to keep it from showing. I thought I might have split open my scar—but even if I had no one would ever know about it.

Sgt. Joseph Kapacziewski and Charles W. Sasser

The rest of the platoon surrounded us. They were amazed; this was something they'd be talking about for a long time. Hell, I was a Ranger, wasn't I?

"Sar'ent," Hawkins gasped, "how do I get a leg like that?"

"Made in Iraq," I gasped back.

57

Come right down to it, I should probably have died that day under the bridge. In any other war, I likely *would* have. As many as 30 percent of soldiers seriously wounded in previous wars like World War II, Korea, and Vietnam expired because of the time it required to get them somewhere for definitive treatment. Medevac helicopters in Vietnam reduced casualty rates, while medical treatment within minutes of the front lines in the War on Terror further decreased fatal casualties. All Rangers—not just medics—were trained in a "casualty response system" to immediately take care of blood loss, lung collapse, and airway obstruction. They could apply tourniquets or pressure bandages and open a patent IV.

Matt Sanders, Slusher, and the other ordinary Joes who began working on the wounded after the grenade thudded down through the Stryker's open hatch were the heroes of that day; they likely saved our lives by their quick response to stop blood loss. Because of guys like them and the training they received, only 8 percent of the nearly four hundred casualties the Rangers would suffer in the decade after 2001 would die.

You could take that kind of odds to Las Vegas with you. Still, Kim questioned why I was trying so hard to go back. If I beat the odds once, did it not stand to reason that the odds doubled the next time? If you lost one leg already, did that mean your chances were doubled of losing another? It was her fear that you only tempted fate so far. She wanted what I wanted, I understood that, but I couldn't blame her if she secretly prayed that the Rangers turned down my efforts to return to combat.

Why would you *want* to keep returning to war?

You had to be in the Rangers, to experience spec ops, in order to understand. It was something visceral, even primitive. It went beyond rational understanding. I was a simple soldier. Maybe army shrinks might answer questions like that. All I knew was that getting out was not an option. I served because my nation was at war. Did that sound naive? Okay, I was naive.

We had all made a commitment. I started right after 9/11, had been through it from the beginning, and wanted to finish it with my buddies, my friends. Rangers since their inception, since back to Rogers's Rangers and the Swamp Fox and Colonel Darby and all the others throughout American history, had paid the ultimate sacrifice for our freedom. I couldn't have looked myself in the mirror if I weren't out there on the front lines living the Ranger Creed.

During my time at RIP while my guys were overseas, I drove myself relentlessly to become more tactically and technically proficient. It had taken months to get this far. I still had farther to go, what with all the army red tape to untangle and the army's institutional resistance to putting guys like me back in harness.

I was still fighting the medical board for a decision when Alpha Company returned from deployment in March 2008. I had completed every task required of any soldier, but still the med board dawdled. I think it was because so few amputees wanted to return to actual combat, and no one in higher-higher wanted to be responsible for allowing the first. I had to do something, as it was apparent the med board wouldn't.

My medical packet contained Enlisted Evaluation Reports that documented my recovery and established my fitness for duty. After all, I had 100 percent accomplished every task required of any Ranger. I simply pilfered one of those documents, circumvented the med board, and took my "Fit for Duty" letter from the medical board directly to Sergeant Major Chris Hardy at Regiment. I figured the med board members would be so relieved to have the decisions taken out of their hands that they wouldn't question it if regiment made the call. I counted on other Rangers taking care of their own.

"Let's do it, Kap," Sergeant Major Hardy said.

I had known the sergeant major since I returned from Walter Reed and worked in the arms room. He was a straight shooter. Someone later disclosed the gist of his argument when Hardy approached the colonel.

"Joe Kap continues to fight when he's faced with adversity. Sir, if I could create every soldier in his image, we'd have a damned good outfit."

Twenty-four hours later, the sergeant major summoned me to his office. I had hardly slept the night before, I was so anxious. Hardy stood up from his desk when I walked in. My heart pounded. There was nowhere else for me to go if he turned me down.

Suddenly, that tough old Ranger grinned and thrust out his hand.

"Job well done, Sergeant Kap. Report to Alpha Company. First sergeant has a squad waiting for you."

Almost a year and a half after amputation, I was back on the line as a squad leader in Alpha Company, 3rd Battalion. The first amputee to return to full combat duty in the Ranger Regiment.

58

Kimberly:

He finally did it. He was back in the fight. Our son Wyatt, born in May 2009, was less than a week old when Joe deployed to Afghanistan for his sixth rotation into a combat zone, his second deployment since losing his leg. I had yet to come to terms with his leg. I didn't like it, and I didn't care if I was being fair or not. I saw how hard it was for him to master its use to get back where he was before his injuries. I also had misgivings about his returning to war with a disadvantage—and the leg *was* a disadvantage—that could get me another "Take My Breath Away" phone call.

Joe was ready to go. He got excited packing his bags to leave.

"Babe, it's what I do."

"You're a father now, too."

"I never want my son to say one day that his old man used an excuse not to do his duty."

How far did duty go? Joe's was a simple answer: I will shoulder more than my share of the task, whatever it may be, 600 percent and then some.

Joe's duffel bag and his old 75th Ranger aviator's kit bag stuffed with gear waited on the stoop inside the front door. If you didn't know about Joe's leg, you would never have noticed it beneath his desert battles and tan boots. His hair was trimmed Ranger short, his jaw locked and loaded, his cap pulled cocky-low over his eye. He was driving himself in for the Ranger muster since we didn't want to take Wyatt out in the cool predawn air.

Joe grinned and winked at me.

"Babe, it's me, okay. It'll be all right."

We were accustomed to saying good-bye. After all, we had had enough practice at it. We usually kept our farewells brief and unemotional. I never wanted to be one of those army wives who clung, who went all to pieces every time her husband got ready to leave. You saw them at the company area every time, wailing and gnashing their teeth and scaring holy crap out of the kids. It was embarrassing.

Joe strode into the nursery, where Wyatt was sleeping in his crib. I hardly noticed the slight irregularity in his gait anymore. From the doorway I watched him stand above his infant son, looking down for a long moment. He reached and traced a finger gently across the infant's forehead. He bent and kissed Wyatt on the cheek.

"Take care of your mommy," he whispered. He didn't know I was watching.

He straightened, looked at me, and smiled.

"I have to go."

He didn't *have* to go, he *wanted* to go.

We kissed. I held him a bit longer than necessary before he shouldered his duffel, picked up his parachute bag, and strode out across the darkened yard toward his pickup truck. A 5-inch tree stump stuck up on the front lawn. Joe either didn't see it in the dark or he wasn't paying attention.

He caught the boot of his mechanical leg on it, stumbled, and fell hard, bags flying. Seeing him on the ground like that, scrambling to regain his feet, I flashed an image of him in Afghanistan trapped and hurt and unable to get up or get going. I had to hold back my tears.

This was such a bad idea. I mean, were the mountains of Afghanistan the best idea we could come up with?

59

AFGHANISTAN 2009

This 2009 deployment to Afghanistan was actually my second deployment as an amputee. I deployed the first time with my mechanical leg in 2008, to Bagram Airfield, where I had first landed in country in 2002. It turned out to be nothing more than a shakedown cruise for my leg, and not much of a test working in a TOC. The Talibs must have gone to Miami Beach for the winter or something. There were more than the usual number of Taliban hijackings of NATO convoys on the other side of the border in Pakistan, which pissed off the Americans and created tension between Pakistan and the United States. Otherwise, the biggest thing for me was that I reenlisted for another five years.

By the time Alpha Company Rangers returned to Afghanistan in the spring of 2009, however, the "Taliban heartland" in the remote and sparsely populated regions of southeastern Afghanistan was beginning to burble a little over the flames as the Talibs prepared for the summer fighting season. NATO intelligence indicated that Taliban strength was growing to around twenty-five thousand fighters, almost as many as before 9/11 and more than in 2005. More foreign fighters were showing up than ever before—from Pakistan, Uzbekistan, Chechnya, Syria, Iran, Jordan, Turkey, Saudi Arabia, even western China.

In January 2009, three thousand soldiers from the 10th Mountain

Division arrived in country, the first wave of the expected surge of rein-forcements ordered by President George W. Bush and now honored by President Barack Obama. General David McKiernan, U.S. commander in Afghanistan, was calling for as many as thirty thousand additional soldiers. It was being reported that a successful counterinsurgency strat-egy would require half a million troops and five more years of fighting.

High-profile terrorist groups like the Hezb-e-Islami Gulbuddin (HIG), the Haqqani Network, and Mullah Omar's Quetta Shura, whose core members had been together in some instances for nearly thirty years, were causing major problems. HIG first fought the Soviets, then focused on fellow Afghans in a brutal internecine struggle. There were no Rules of Engagement for these groups; they ruled by sheer terror. Well equipped, they blended into the population and didn't care who they killed. They knew the land, every ridgeline, every stream, every mountain, every cave—and their full attention had now turned toward the hated "infi-dels" of the Coalition forces.

The 2009 deployment promised to be an interesting year. Rangers began beating the Hindu Kush Mountains for enemy training camps and HVTs. That was how my platoon, the 1st, ended on one of the darkest nights of the year, up high in the Khost-Gardez Pass, "the Death Pass," where we had been ambushed by an unknown-sized force of Talibs. As I ran my squad on a flanking maneuver along the ridgeline, trying to cut off "squirters," loose shale had given way beneath my boots.

There I went, ass on the ground, blasting in a miniavalanche right down on top of an insurgent crouched next to a tree on the slope below. It was so dark we failed to see each other until we might have reached out and lit each other's cigarette. He was slower on the uptake than I—bad on him—and I pumped his sorry ass full of lead.

Nearby, farther down, his buddy started screaming, *"Allahu Akbar! Allahu Akbar!"*

Crazy bastards!

From up top, my squad opened up with a machine gun, shooting at sound. The exchange was one-sided in our favor, with lead flying over my head as I lunged back up the ridge slope toward cover.

That was when I lost my leg.

Before that happened, I thought I was going to make it back to the ridgeline and safety. I was scrambling uphill on my boot toes and my one free hand, the other hand full of an M-4 rifle. A rock loosened as I reached for it as leverage. It bounced once. I felt it thump the boot on my prosthetic hard and twist it.

Next thing I knew, my carbon fiber leg had slipped out of its cuff and dumped me facedown ignominiously and as helpless as a bug impaled on a pin. I heard my artificial leg bouncing off rock as it slid downhill in the dark toward the enemy machine gunner.

For maybe a second, I called myself every kind of a fucking one-legged fool. I was pissed, too. My only thought was that I had to retrieve my leg; I had left its replacement back at the FOB.

I yelled something at my guys on the ridge, something like "prep a frag. I gotta get my leg!"

Now one-legged, I slid back downhill on my butt in a landslide of dirt, dust, rock, and shale. Sliding fast and so out of control that there was no way I could defend myself. I had to depend on my buddies at the crest of the ridge to take care of the bad guy before I ended up snuggled in his lap—and trust them not to shoot me instead of him in the darkness. They were bringing some shit down on him like he had probably never seen in these mountains before.

Like he would never see again, either.

I slid right down on top of him. There my leg was, caught among rock debris next to where his PPK machine gun lay silent in the dust. I shouted for Smitty and the others to cease fire. The guy was out of action, dead, riddled all to hell with bullets.

He stank, too. I noticed it as I quickly reattached my runaway leg to its rightful place. Did these guys never take a bath?

I climbed to the military crest to rejoin my squad members.

"What happened, Kap?" Housner asked.

I shrugged. "Nothing."

Like I always said, one of my guys lost a leg, we lost *him*. I lost a leg, I just put it back on—and I was back in the fight.

EPILOGUE

BY CHARLES W. SASSER

The U.S. Army 75th Ranger Regiment is the only fighting force in the U.S. military to see continuous combat since the War on Terror began after 9/11/2001. The end of the year 2012 marked over four thousand consecutive days of regimental combat. Now promoted to sergeant first class (E-7) and platoon sergeant with 3rd Battalion at Fort Benning, Joe Kapacziewski has been in the fight almost from the beginning.

He made his first combat deployment, to Afghanistan, in the summer of 2002. Wounded on his fifth deployment, to Iraq, in October 2005, he has, as of April 2012, rotated into combat five times since the loss of his leg, the only Army Ranger serving in direct combat operations with a prosthetic limb.

On April 19, 2010, during his eighth combat deployment, Kapacziewski's patrol ran into an ambush outside a village in eastern Afghanistan. After a fellow Ranger fell to withering enemy fire, shot through the belly, Sergeant Kap and another soldier dragged him 75 yards to safety and administered first aid that saved his life while heavy machine guns tried to kill them. His actions earned him an Army Commendation Medal with "V" for Valor. He had previously earned a Bronze Star for Valor—and a total of three Purple Hearts for combat wounds.

"He doesn't know the meaning of the word 'quit,'" fellow Rangers say of the man most simply know as "Kap."

Since losing his leg, Kap has also completed three triathlons and finished the New York Marathon twice on behalf of the Lead the Way Fund, a nonprofit organization established to raise money in support of disabled U.S. Army Rangers and the families of Rangers who have died, been injured, or are currently in harm's way around the world. He has also run in every Operation One Voice's annual 600-mile relay race since 2007 and clocked a 7:10 pace during the 2008 Army Ten-Miler.

"Races and triathlons have helped to keep me motivated to get in shape," he told an interviewer. "I never really participated in those types of events before, but I was given different opportunities after losing my leg. I enjoy competing and each race is a new challenge. They keep me motivated."

When not deployed to war zones, he often visits wounded soldiers at Walter Reed Army Medical Center and Brooke.

"I want them to know it's not over just because they've been hurt. They face the most difficult challenge in their lives, but I let them know they're not alone. They can still make a huge impact not only on other soldiers but also the army in general. Whether it's limb salvage or amputation, we talk about their different options. A lot of them have valuable experience they can pass on. It's hard to find guys who have lost limbs who have gone back on the line, but I let them know it's possible. When you put your mind to something, you can accomplish it. A lot of it is giving them time to do the rehab so they can go back to doing what they want to do."

Kap's dream was to be a good soldier. After his amputation, he was afraid other soldiers would look upon him as an amputee rather than the good Ranger he was.

"The first few months walking around, a lot of people would do double takes. I had a lot of pressure on my shoulders, wanting to prove I could do anything everyone else could. Over the years, nobody gives it a second thought anymore."

"He had that light at the end of the tunnel," Sergeant Major Eddie Noland said, "and he wasn't going to stop until he got there."

Kap gives his wife, Kim, and the Ranger chain of command much of the credit for his postamputation success. Now a platoon sergeant, he feels he has the best job in the army. "I will lead my fellow Rangers by setting the example in all we do and by being relentless in the pursuit of the nation's enemies."

On May 24, 2011, he became the first enlisted soldier ever to receive the No Greater Sacrifice Freedom Award in Washington, D.C. This annual Freedom Award is given to individuals who epitomize selfless service to the nation. Past recipients include Army General David Petraeus, commander of troops in Afghanistan, and General James Conway, former commandant of the Marine Corps.

Honored in 2011 with Kap was Army Chief of Staff General Ray Odierno, the commander of U.S. Joint Forces Command and former commander of U.S. troops in Iraq. Typically humble and unassuming, Kap said he was a little embarrassed about being singled out for the honor. "Everyone here in the regiment is a team player, so being recognized as an individual is a little awkward."

Kap and Kimberly are the parents of two sons: Wyatt, born in May 2009; and Cody Jared, born in September 2010 and named after Master Sergeant Jared Van Aalst, who was killed in action in Afghanistan in August 2010. Now twenty-nine years old and a soldier since he was eighteen, Sergeant First Class Joe Kapacziewski continues to live his dream of remaining in the fight as a United States Army Ranger, "leading the way." If an enemy grenade could not stop him, other Rangers say, it is unlikely anything else will. He may be the world's first truly bionic man.